Euphemania

ALSO BY RALPH KEYES

I Love It When You Talk Retro

The Quote Verifier

The Courage to Write

The Writer's Book of Hope

Is There Life After High School?

"Nice Guys Finish Seventh"

The Height of Your Life

Chancing It

The Post-Truth Era

Sons on Fathers

The Innovation Paradox

We, the Lonely People

Timelock

The Wit and Wisdom of Harry Truman

The Wit and Wisdom of Oscar Wilde

Euphemania

OUR LOVE AFFAIR
WITH EUPHEMISMS

RALPH KEYES

LITTLE, BROWN AND COMPANY
NEW YORK · BOSTON · LONDON

Little, Brown and Company
Hachette Book Group
237 Park Avenue, New York, NY 10017
www.hachettebookgroup.com

First Edition: December 2010

Little, Brown and Company is a division of Hachette Book
Group, Inc. The Little, Brown name and logo are trademarks of
Hachette Book Group, Inc.

The publisher is not responsible for websites (or their content)
that are not owned by the publisher.

Library of Congress Cataloging-in-Publication Data
Keyes, Ralph.
    Euphemania : our love affair with euphemisms / Ralph Keyes.
      p. cm.
    ISBN 978-0-316-05656-4
    1. English language — Euphemism.   I. Title.
    PE1585.K49 2010
    423'.1 — dc22   2010025983

10 9 8 7 6 5 4 3 2 1

RRD-IN

Printed in the United States of America

For Colleen Mohyde, my friend and agent,
who's been an unwavering source of support and
good counsel for as long as I've known her

Contents

Euphemania

1

Mincing Words

I<small>N KENT HARUF</small>'s novel *Plainsong,* two elderly bachelor brothers agree to take in a pregnant high-school student. When she arrives, they show her around their old farmhouse. At the threshold of a small room, one says, "Here's where you step out." The girl looks puzzled.

"You know," explains the man. "The commode. The indoor outhouse. Well, what do you call it?"

"That'll do fine," says a teacher accompanying the girl.

"That's what she always called it," continues the man, referring to his mother. "I'm just trying to be proper. I'm just trying to get us started off on the right chalk."

Aren't we all? This man was struggling with the age-old challenge of finding respectable euphemisms for dubious terms. Any word or phrase that gives us pause is a candidate for euphemizing. What gives us pause varies from place to place, however, and from era to era. Is it God? Better we should say *gosh.* Does talk of breasts make us queasy? Try *bust.* How about shit? *Shoot* will suffice. Lying sounds harsh, but *spinning* not so much.

We all rely on euphemisms to tiptoe around what makes us uneasy, and have done so for most of recorded history. Euphemisms are a function of their times. Sexually unresponsive women were once considered *frigid*. Then they were simply called *inorgasmic* or given the more hopeful designation *pre-orgasmic*. Today, *female sexual dysfunction* has become a euphemism for this condition. As for men, what once was called *impotence* has given way to *erectile dysfunction*. Neutralizing such uncomfortable terms doesn't just make it easier to talk about frigid women and flaccid men; it also allows drug companies to openly hawk their wares.

An excellent way to determine what we find embarrassing is to examine our verbal evasions. They indicate what's on our minds. What's bugging us. What makes us uneasy. What topics we consider taboo.

During a dinner party in Virginia before World War II, Winston Churchill asked the butler for some breast of chicken. According to Churchill family lore, a woman sitting next to him reprimanded the British guest for using this vulgar term. And what should he have asked for? "White meat," Churchill was told. The next day, Churchill sent the woman a corsage with the message, "Pin this on your white meat."

Using euphemisms is the verbal equivalent of draping nude statues. Doing so substitutes unthreatening words for ones that make us fidget. For this to work, the substitute words and what they allude to must be familiar. Would a recent immigrant from Kathmandu get the sexual subtext of "Your place or mine?" Unlikely. A euphemism can only do its job if most people recognize what's actually being discussed. Renaming "piss" *poss* would only confuse matters. Metaphorically calling it *lemonade* isn't much better. On the other hand, referring to *number one* is likely to elicit a nod of recognition. When an environmental activist said she'd stopped using "TP for number one," no further explanation was needed.

During the run-up to Barack Obama's inauguration, an FBI agent said they were preparing to help people get out of Washington "in case of an event" (presumably a terrorist attack or an assassination attempt). That same euphemism—*event*—has also been applied to nuclear power-plant accidents. To say that Obama's inauguration or a nuclear power plant could be subject to *a wahoo* or *an occasion* would technically involve a euphemism but one without any traction.

Of course, some euphemisms can be awfully subtle. This is especially true when talk turns to marginalized members of society. Before the term "gay" came to the rescue, heterosexuals commonly referred to homosexuals as having unspecified *tendencies, predilections,* or *preferences.* They were *like that. That way. Theatrical.* In news stories, "flamboyant," "confirmed bachelor," and "never married" could, and can, allude to gays.

Press accounts are a treasure trove of euphemisms. When journalists report that a public figure was "exuberant" or "flushed," they may be trying to tell us he was drunk. A reporter who wants to signal that a man is pompous without using that word can say he has *gravitas.* An obnoxiously loud-mouthed individual may be called *colorful.* We all use circumlocutions this way. Someone with a bad temper is *mercurial* or *moody.* A dysfunctional family whose members alternate yelling at one another with pouting can be called *complicated.* That word is also applied to couples who nearly have their hands on each other's throats on a regular basis. ("They have a complicated relationship.") As marriage counselors say, such couples have *unfinished business.*

Euphemisms represent a flight to comfort, a way to reduce tension when conversing. They are comfort words. Euphemistic discourse softens the harsh, smoothes the rough, makes what's negative sound positive. It is akin to diplomatic language in which "We had a frank exchange of views" might mean, "We hurled insults at each other for a full hour."

Euphemisms add nuance and vagueness to conversation that's often welcome. Could anyone get through a day without heeding a *call of nature* or speculating about whether Jason and Amy may be *sleeping together?* Civilized discourse would be impossible without recourse to indirection. Euphemisms give us tools to discuss touchy topics without having to spell out what it is we're discussing. In her novel *The Land of Green Plums,* Nobel laureate Herta Müller portrayed a Romanian seamstress measuring the legs of a school headmaster for a pair of trousers she plans to make him. "At the crotch," wrote Müller (who uses no quotation marks), "she took a deep breath and asked: And where do you keep the key to the cellar, Mr. Headmaster, on the left or the right? Always on the right, he said. And for the cellar door, she asked, would you rather have buttons or a zipper?"

Particularly when it comes to topics such as sex, the body, and body wastes, euphemisms can be a blessing. These terms don't just scrub conversations clean, they keep us from having to acknowledge that we even know the words being euphemized, let alone what they mean. Or that such matters are on our mind. Referencing something like sex by saying "They were intimate" lets us allude to this topic without having to admit, "Yes, I think about naked bodies heaving in passionate embrace. Okay?"

Via the double entendre, euphemistic talk can be both discreet and bawdy, especially in mixed company. Even the most upstanding members of a church choir may enjoy an occasional veiled allusion, so long as they don't have to acknowledge what's actually being discussed. When men are present, a respectable spinster is unlikely to say, "I wish I could find a stud." But when stud finders came up during a discussion of home renovation in one such group, a proper middle-aged divorcée felt perfectly comfortable saying, "I could use one of those."

Euphemania

Eupheme was the nurse of ancient Greece's Muses. Her name literally means "good speaking" (*eu* = "good," *pheme* = "speaking"). Related Greek words mean to "speak fair" and to "use an auspicious word for an inauspicious one." They are the root of today's "euphemism." That term usually refers to polite words but not always. Although I began this project with the assumption that a clear distinction could be made between genteel euphemisms and other types of substitute words such as slang, jargon, and double entendres, the further I got, the more apparent it became that this distinction was too sharp. I came to see a broader matrix of substitute words that are euphemistic but not necessarily genteel. When, with a group of couples whose men were about to go hunting, a woman pinched her husband's ear and announced, "We have to unload daddy's gun before he can go anywhere," was she using slang, a double entendre, or a euphemism? Or all three?

This is why my definition of euphemism is broad: words

or phrases substituted for ones that make us uneasy. Even slang terms can give us a hip way to avoid saying the unsayable. When a soldier reports that he *offed* an enemy, *greased,* or *whacked* him, on the one hand that's slang; on the other, such substitute words keep him from having to use the word "killed." Similarly, although it's hardly genteel for a woman to say that she and a man *partied* or *got it on* or *did some horizontal dancing,* this does keep uglier words out of the conversation.

Technically, euphemisms are a form of synonym. But they have far heavier freight to carry. That freight is what *Euphemania* is all about. It is not meant to be a compilation of euphemisms (many such books exist already). Rather, it's a consideration of the ways euphemisms enter our conversations and how they reflect their time and place. Euphemizing most often results from an excess of politeness and prudery, but it can also demonstrate creativity and high good humor. Shakespeare was not polite and was hardly prudish, but his plays brim with euphemistic wordplay.

As we'll see throughout this book, euphemisms are created in a wide variety of ways and for a multitude of reasons. This usually involves reducing the temperature of overheated terms. The hotter the topic, the cooler the words we rely on to discuss them. "They're upstairs in my bedroom getting to know each other better." "We rendered several hundred enemy soldiers inoperative." "The detainee was subjected to in-depth interrogation." "Eric engaged in inappropriate behavior. He was acting out."

Therapists, self-helpers, and recovery groups have given us a bonanza of mild euphemistic terms to take the place of spicier ones. Under their tutelage, we've replaced "problems" with *issues* and *challenges.* As the economy collapsed late in his presidency, George W. Bush said, "Our financial markets continue to deal with some serious challenges." Bush continually referred to global warming as an *issue,* not a "problem." He wasn't the only one to fall back on this type of circumlocution. Philanderers, I've recently read, have *zipper-management issues.* In lieu of "What you just said really pisses me off," any one of us can say, "I have issues with what you just said." Those who used to suffer from mental illness now have *mental health issues.* Thanks to the magic of modern psychotherapy, being able to say "she vented" allows us to avoid saying "she screamed in a rage." Liars are *in denial.* Patients who once had "nervous breakdowns" now have *nervous breakthroughs.*

Although it's gained momentum in recent years, the practice of turning negatives into positives has pride of place in the history of euphemism creation. After all, the Cape of Good Hope was once known, more accurately, as the Cape of Storms. What is actually death insurance has long been called *life insurance.* Impoverished countries once considered undeveloped became *underdeveloped,* then *less developed,* then *developing.* Today, they are optimistically called *emerging.* A manufacturer of inexpensive woodstoves calls the residents of such countries *emerging consumers.*

Putting a neutral sheen on negative experiences is a related, long-standing practice. Like their modern counterparts, ancient Greeks and Romans used the phrase *if anything happens to me* instead of "should I die." When they executed a prisoner, Romans said he was *led away to punishment* or simply *led away.* "Execution" itself is a onetime euphemism, evolving from the execution of a death warrant. In medieval times, prisoners condemned to die were *put to execution.*

Their euphemistic history helps explain the significance

of many terms in current use. In the midwestern town where I live, brown paper grocery containers are called "sacks," not "bags." This always puzzled me until, in the course of researching this book, I discovered that *bag* is a euphemism for "scrotum" in some parts of the United States. When it comes to brown paper grocery containers, therefore, another term was needed to avoid that one. Hence, *sack*. (Those who live in settings where "sack" is synonymous with "scrotum" had best stay with "bag.")

To neutralize words that make us uncomfortable, euphemisms routinely convert vivid terms into innocuous ones. Yesterday's "tombstone" is today's *grave marker*. "Dumps" are now *landfills* or *transfer stations*. "Rubbish" became *garbage* then *waste*. What once was a "life jacket" is now a *flotation device*. Our grandparents' "clothesline" has been upgraded to a *wind-energy drying device*.

Euphemisms are nothing if not adaptable. A BBC correspondent just back from covering the conflict in Congo told a radio interviewer that soldiers there were *"self-provisioning."* When asked what this meant, the correspondent conceded that it was a euphemism for "loot and steal." Obviously, language evolves constantly. But in public discourse especially, its evolution has been in a blandly euphemistic direction. Taken to an extreme—as it so often is—such discourse can be deadly. That's because it enlists words in the service of evasion rather than communication. This is euphemania: taking the sting out of frank, clear words by converting them into inoffensive, synonym-like versions that desensitize us to the implications of, say, torture (*applying pressure*) or a stock-market collapse (*equity retreat*).

Euphemism as Tracking Device

Euphemisms are an accurate barometer of changing attitudes. That is the theme of this book. Verbal evasions put a spotlight on what most concerns human beings at any given time.

There is no better illustration of our changing euphemistic climate than the way we refer to children whose parents aren't married. These "bastards" or "children of sin" became *illegitimate children,* which begot *born out of wedlock.* During the late-eighteenth century, *born on the wrong side of the blanket* was a slangy euphemism for those presumably conceived somewhere other than a married couple's bed. In the Midwest, *gone to visit her aunt in Indiana* was once a euphemism for going to a home for unwed mothers. Today, we care so little about the marital status of a child's parents that we seldom even bother with such circumlocutions. At worst, we talk of *love children* or a *love child.* In general, though, the increasingly common fact that a child's parents aren't married is barely considered worth a euphemism.

The terms we use and those we avoid reflect deeper concerns, which change over time. Several centuries ago, when religion reigned, we converted "damn" to *darn* and "hell" to *heck.* Then prudery kicked in, and the gonads became *family jewels,* and the vagina, *down there.* Today, it's death, disability, and discrimination that provide fodder for euphemisms, as we grope for inoffensive terms to designate loved ones who have died, those with physical or intellectual limitations, and members of minority groups.

Although a society in which bumper stickers say SHIT HAPPENS and T-shirts proclaim LIFE IS A BITCH, THEN YOU DIE may have dispensed with many of the genteel euphemisms used in days of yore, it has hardly dispensed with euphemisms altogether. Even topics we discuss more candidly today than before are still subject to euphemizing, though with updated terminology. According to a 2008 press account, for example, a Belmont, Massachusetts, resident reported to police that an "anatomically correct term" had been spray-painted on a local fence.

Much as we might like to think that our modes of expression involve a straight trajectory of opening up, shedding inhibitions, and becoming more candid, that's just not the case. The terms and targets of our euphemizing have simply shifted. An explosion of topics have become eligible for euphemistic discourse: not only the usual suspects of sex, body parts, and bodily secretions, but also money, diseases, and certain foods, to name just a few of the many subjects we euphemize today.

Euphemisms have gone from being a tool of the church to a form of gentility to an instrument of commercial, political, and postmodern doublespeak. Our time is one in which "sweet words dance hand in hand with dreadful facts," writes D. J. Enright in the excellent essay collection *Fair of Speech: The Uses of Euphemism*. Originally meant to avoid blasphemy and be polite, euphemisms are now just as likely to be a tool of cover-up and obfuscation. Businesses that once showed "losses" now have *negative cash flow*. Politicians don't "lie" but do sometimes *misspeak*. Bombardiers no longer "drop bombs"; they unleash *vertically deployed antipersonnel devices*.

Because what makes us uncomfortable changes with the times, there is a constant demand for new euphemisms. And we are up to the task of supplying them. "It is a poor week when I fail to note two or three new euphemisms," observes euphemism compiler R. W. Holder.

The Euphemism Carousel

Euphemisms must step lively to keep pace with changing attitudes. Another era's tacky comment is today's hip remark. Yesterday's polite euphemism is tomorrow's prissy evasion. "Cherry" was once considered more respectable than "hymen." Now, just the opposite is true. The former is thought to be vulgar, the latter decent.

Since language is in constant flux, as are social values, euphemisms can quickly lose their utility. Good words become bad words become good words again, in endless succession. Euphemisms are like a verbal carousel: some words hop on, others jump off, still others stay put for the entire ride and sometimes lose their euphemistic status in the process. Those that do their job capably, with minimal fuss, slip easily into the vernacular and stay there. *Sleep with* has been a euphemism for sex for centuries; *pass away* for dying since the Middle Ages. *Cemetery*—from the Greek word for "sleeping place"—was initially a euphemism for the more ominous "graveyard" but proved so functional that it became our standard term for this setting.

Like "cemetery," a notable number of today's everyday words began as euphemisms. *Penis,* Latin for "tail," in Cicero's time was put to work as a euphemism for the male sex organ. Once this term lost its euphemistic cover, others stepped up to take its place, then shape-shifted. "Dork" was originally a synonym for "penis." Similarly, "jerk" once referred to a man who masturbates (echoes of which can still be heard in today's phrase "jerk off").

In an eye-opening study, linguist Muriel Schulz explored the carousel ride of words that refer to women. A striking number morphed from innocent to dubious to downright derogatory. Early on, "nymphet" referred simply to an attractive young woman. So did "broad." "Hussy" evolved from *huswif* ("housewife") in Old English. But the trajectory of women-specific words Schulz analyzed wasn't always downhill. Some were rehabilitated. Before retrieving its good reputation, *wife* had become a euphemism for "mistress" in the Middle Ages; *niece* for the illegitimate daughter of a priest. *Girl* at one time referred euphemistically to prostitutes. So did *cat*. (Think *cathouse*.)

Like courtesans who become society matrons, tainted euphemisms can regain their respectability over time. It's not at all uncommon for terms once considered vulgar or risqué to lose their stigma. "Poke," a sometime synonym for "fuck," today is a cute term for contacting someone online or for giving a patient an injection ("a little poke"). "Bloody"—once the most offensive of words in Britain—is today a relatively innocuous piece of verbal punctuation. "Blast" was once considered so blasphemous that English schoolchildren were punished for uttering this word. In 1869, a linguist warned that the term "ornery" is "shocking and should never pass the lips of any one." As that onetime synonym for "lewd" began to be used semiaffectionately ("he's an ornery cuss"), it lost its shock value in the same way that "bastard" went from being pure profanity to an occasional term of affection ("You old bastard, you!").

This is typical of the carousel whirl in which words are both soiled and cleansed. Even as some euphemisms go mainstream, others are contaminated by association with the topic they refer to and become just as dubious as the word they replaced.

They're fallen euphemisms. The classic example is *fart*, a medieval euphemism that over time took on the odor of the act it referred to and itself became offensive. Similarly, *retarded* was originally a polite way to describe those more rudely called "idiots," "imbeciles," or "morons." Today, the word "retarded" is considered so insulting that there is a movement to ban its use.

In a related process, respectable terms that are requisitioned as euphemisms can quickly lose their respectability. Cicero complained that when "penis" became a euphemism for the male sex organ, it could no longer be used to refer to animals' tails. During Cicero's time, Roman youth used *deliciae* as a playful euphemism for sex (it essentially means "a diversion" or "pleasure"). After taking on sexual connotations, however, *deliciae* itself became taboo. Some centuries later, when "occupy" became a euphemism for lovemaking during the late Middle Ages, that term could no longer be used in polite conversation. A similar fate befell "intercourse," which originally simply meant "to communicate" before it was commandeered as a polite synonym for copulation (to the chagrin of residents of Intercourse, Pennsylvania). "Hook up" used to mean little more than connecting with someone. Today it can mean so very much more.

This is a constant problem with euphemisms. Using them can be like trying to conceal the naked body of an actress beneath a gossamer gown. Euphemizing represents a forlorn hope that renaming something might change its essence. Negative connotations are not in taboo words themselves, however, but in what they refer to. As a result, euphemisms can only protect our sensibilities for so long.

Consider how we deal verbally with the sensitive topic of

insanity. Here, terms that start out as euphemisms invariably end up as affronts. This leads to a constant verbal turnover. In their definitive books *Euphemism and Dysphemism* and *Forbidden Words,* Australian linguists Keith Allan and Kate Burridge have explored this verbal degeneration in some detail. The term *lunatic* was initially a euphemistic reference to a form of mental illness associated with changing lunar phases. *Touched* originally suggested that a demented person had been touched by God's hand. At one time, *deranged* simply meant "disordered" or "disturbed" before it took on more ominous connotations as a euphemism for "mad." *Crazy* derived from the more benign term "crazed," which meant "flawed" or "cracked." *Cracked* itself is an enduring synonym for "mentally ill," though not one we'd now consider polite. Today, we turn to psychology for neutral descriptors such as *syndrome* and *disorder.* How long such terms will stay respectable is anyone's guess.

In a gruesome illustration of euphemism degradation, *concentration camp*—a term initially used by the British as an innocuous name for internment centers they created during the Boer War—became sinister due to the hideous reality of what took place in Nazi death camps that also used this name. Several decades later, when reporters said tens of thousands of interned Tamils were in concentration camps, Sri Lankan authorities took offense. They insisted that these were actually *welfare camps.*

The Euphemism Cookbook

As we'll see throughout this book, euphemisms are created in a wide variety of ways. The most common way is to simply substitute an acceptable word for one that's considered unacceptable. (*Sugar! Fudge!*) Sometimes these substitute words are invented ones that sound similar to the verboten term. (*Shucks! Fooey!*) In the process, we often assign harmless little words to stand in for charged ones. *Do,* for example, is commonly used as a synonym for "fuck," "kill," "defecate," and other questionable acts.

In some cases, the word substituted comes from another language, carrying scant odor of taboo. When Americans are not sure if it would be a good idea to say "balls" aloud, they can always resort to the Spanish *cojones* and often do. *Soixante-neuf* is a double-duty euphemism, one relying on both French and numbers to refer to mutual cunnilingus and fellatio. (Those willing to forgo the added cover of French simply say "sixty-nine.") "Cunnilingus" and "fellatio" themselves have a Latin root. Latin has done a lot of euphemistic heavy lifting over the millennia. Think "phallus," "pudenda," "areola," "testes," "coitus," and so many more. College students in medieval Europe were advised to use Latin words instead of ones in the vernacular that might be considered profane. Modern sex educators use as many Latin terms as possible to avoid embarrassment when discussing body parts. In an account popular in England some decades ago, a British soldier who had been shot in the buttocks during World War I was asked by a woman visiting his hospital ward where he was wounded. The soldier responded, "I'm sorry, ma'am. I can't say. I never studied Latin."

Professional jargon, much of it Latin based, is another primary source of euphemisms that rely on the "blind them with science" approach. Thus, *prophylactic* for "condom," *localized capacity deficiencies* for "traffic bottlenecks," *seismic activity* for "an earthquake." When it comes to ostentatious, euphemism-loaded speech, many believe the more syllables, the better. The near-meltdown of the nuclear plant at Three Mile Island was initially called an *unscheduled energetic disassembly*. An airline's annual report referred to a crash of one of its planes as an *involuntary conversion*. In the auto industry, a car crash is called *rapid* or *sudden deceleration*. This sometimes results in a *thermal event* (i.e., a fire). "Event" is an invaluably ambiguous word when it comes to euphemizing. What most of us think of as "hand washing," hospital administrators call *a hand hygiene event*.

Other euphemistic discourse goes in the opposite direction. Particularly in the areas of sex, body parts, and bodily functions, small is beautiful: *poo, pee, do, it*. Linguist Robin Lakoff illustrates the difference between these approaches by comparing the words of a doctor who says, "Copulation may also be enhanced by the use of oleaginous materials," with a terser way of saying the same thing, "Selma told me she found Jimmy and Marion doing it with mayonnaise!"

Words such as "it" more than earn their keep when euphemisms are needed, as when sexy Clara Bow was called "the it girl." Other unusually useful euphemistic terms include *certain* ("a woman of a certain age"), *interesting* ("she's in an interesting condition"), and, especially, *special* (special assistant, special needs, Special Forces). As R. W. Holder writes in *How Not to Say What You Mean*, "special" is a word that "makes the ears of a collector of euphemisms prick up."

Requisitioning proper names is a common euphemizing tactic and has been for eons, though the names themselves vary with time and place. When "Jock" was a more common moniker, it got pressed into service as a synonym for "penis" (leaving an echo behind in "jock strap"). After "Jock" developed dubious connotations, another common form of euphemizing was employed: substituting a single letter in an offending word to convert it into one that's inoffensive. Thus, the football fans' cry "Knock their jocks off!" gave way to "Knock their socks off!"

The least imaginative way to create euphemisms is by simply replacing one or more letters in a word with punctuation marks: "g-dd- -n!" "The h-ll you say!" "You c.cks.cker." "F**k you!" Because this approach calls undue attention to the deleted letters, it's rather self-defeating. As a Florida judge once observed in a censorship case, "'f......pigs' is unlikely to be seen as referring to police officers who are 'foolish,' 'fawning,' 'finicky,' 'flaccid,' 'foppish,' 'frantic,' 'fretful,' or 'fascist.'"

The Victorian era was the heyday of typographical euphemisms. During that prudish time, first letters followed by dashes or asterisks replaced many a word deemed suspect. Somerset Maugham called Victorian England a setting in which "asterisks were followed after a certain interval by a baby." Well into the twentieth century, the upright Malcolm Muggeridge referred to members of his generation as "asterisk men." And it wasn't just English authors who self-censored this way. Their American counterparts also felt a need to engage in prudent euphemistic punctuation. In his 1883 novella *In the Carquinez Woods,* even down-to-earth Bret Harte portrayed a priest who confesses, "When I have often wrestled with the spirit I confess I have sometimes said, 'D—n you.' Yes, sir, 'D—n you.'"

Going beyond mere punctuation as a source of all-purpose euphemisms, we've put "bleep" to use in the same way. ("Bleep you!") *Expletive* is another euphemism that often comes in handy. ("Expletive deleted.") Other multipurpose euphemistic words include *blankety-blank, doo-dah, thingama-jig, thingy, whatsit, whatnot,* and *you-know-what.* According to ABC News, disgraced financier Bernard Madoff said he "didn't give a blank" about his sons (who had turned him in to the authorities for running a Ponzi scheme).

Clipping words fore and aft is another euphemistic strategy. "Whipped" is one such word, clipped from the vulgar "pussy-whipped," which is a more vivid way to say "henpecked." "Bull" is a reasonably respectable clip of "bullshit," and "mother" used in a proper tone of voice can pass muster in a way that its root — "motherfucker" — could not. During the brief period when George Wallace's wife, Lurleen, stood in for him as governor of Alabama, bumper stickers appeared that read GOVERNOR WAL-LACE IS A MOTHER. After examining this sticker on the bumper of a car in Detroit, a group of street toughs approached its owner.

"Hey, man," said one.

"Yes?"

Pointing at the bumper, "That's only half a word."

Acronyms and abbreviations are forms of euphemism that have gained popularity over time. The *A* that New England Puritans made adulterous women sew on their clothing and that colonial Pennsylvanians branded on the foreheads of third-time adulterers might be seen as a precursor. Leprosy, which was initially euphemized with the eponym *Hansen's disease* (after Dr. G. H. A. Hansen, who discovered its underly-ing cause), later became simply *HD.* Abbreviations and acro-nyms gained popularity in America's New Deal era, then really took off during World War II and its aftermath. They were ideally suited to the postwar euphemistic sensibility: sterile, vague, easy to create and manipulate. The pharmaceutical ads so common on television today are like a glossary of euphemistic initials: not just ED (erectile dysfunction) and PMS (premenstrual syndrome) but COPD (chronic obstructive pulmonary disease), IBS (irritable bowel syndrome), and GERD (gastroesophageal reflux disease), to name just a few. Your over-the-counter drug is their OTC. Initializing this way is a spreading source of euphemism, one that makes our language pithier but poorer.

THE SCUNTHORPE PROBLEM

Victorian euphemizing strategies are alive and well on the Internet. There, content filters do the work that used to be left to human censors, only with no sense of nuance. "Hello" gets changed to *hecko* online, "class" to *cl****, "wish it" to *wi** ***. A filter that replaces "nigga" with *nubian* revised "niggardly" to read *nubianrdly*.

This is known as the Scunthorpe problem, so called because an early content filter used by AOL prevented residents of Scunthorpe, England, from registering accounts due to the second, third, fourth, and fifth letters of their town's name. Those living in Penistone, Sussex, and Lightwater faced similar problems (in the latter, "twat" being a no-no). For that very reason "saltwater taffy" showed up in one online forum euphemized as "sal*female genitalia*er taffy."

Auto-replace has been problematic when put to work on behalf of particular agendas. In the most celebrated example, a Christian website whose filter automatically converted the word "gay" to "homosexual" ran an Associated Press article about sprinter Tyson Gay. The article began, "Tyson Homosexual was a blur in blue, sprinting 100 meters faster than anyone ever has."

(continued)

In the realm of cyber-Bowdlerizing, miscontruable names are especially vexing to those who have them, as men named Dick sometimes discover when searching their name on the Internet and encountering D*ck. Due to the magic of automatic euphemizing, George W. Bush's vice president is sometimes mentioned online as *thingy Cheney*. In chat rooms that proscribe "shat," the actor William Shatner has been discussed as *William S***ner*.

Spam filters pose particular problems to those whose names trip warning signals. E-mails from anyone named Lipshitz are at constant risk of being blocked, as are ones sent by anyone named Cockburn. (Craig Cockburn of Scotland solved that problem by writing his name with a zero instead of an *o*: C0ckburn.) The word "cock" alone is sometimes changed to **** online. In that regimen, gun hammers are ****ed, human beings **** their heads, and forum participants debate the moral quandary of ****fights.

It's as if we subcontracted the job of euphemizing taboo words to HAL the computer in Stanley Kubrick's film *2001: A Space Odyssey.* (Only HAL was more nuanced.) What is to be done? Users are not without options. To work around ham-handed cyber prudery, when discussing a manuscript, members of one chat room began writing *m****cript*. Other site hosts make a game out of foiling filters, reprogramming their own to translate "bitch" into "gluestick," say, or "shit" into "cheese." The reprogrammed filter of one online forum automatically changes "fuck" to "gently caress" ("Gently caress you!"). Another alters any mention of "hell" to read "New Jersey." A third changes all questionable words to "Melanie Griffith." What have they got against Melanie Griffith?

Roll Your Own

When interviewing lexicographer Jesse Sheidlower on National Public Radio about his book *The F-Word,* Robert Siegel substituted the word "floss" for "fuck" (sparking protest from listeners who asked him to consider the implications of this euphemism for dentists, to say nothing of fastidious flossers). In a similar gambit, the *New Yorker's* Tad Friend replaced every word referring to intimate body parts in an obscenity-filled routine by a Canadian comedian with "Wayne Gretzky" (e.g., pointing to his mother and wife in the audience, saying, "There's the Wayne Gretzky I come from, and there's the Wayne Gretzky I go home to"). Malcolm Muggeridge used the same approach when reviewing *Eros Denied: Sex in Western Society* by Wayland Young. In place of what he called "the verb which occurs on almost every page," Muggeridge substituted Young's first name ("he Waylanded her good and proper"). His review was titled "W**l*nd*ng."

Think of this as roll-your-own euphemisms. Here is where we see the creativity of euphemism invention in its purest form. To give their children euphemistic words for ticklish body parts, some parents create their own. When a young girl asked her father what that thing was dangling between his legs as he got out of the bath, he told her it was his *handy gadget.* Well into adulthood, she used *handy gadget* as a euphemism for "penis." The mother of a friend of mine advised her children that this organ was a *jingle bell.* Another told her sons to call it their *link a link.* "My mother called mine a 'sisser,'" reports a Floridian about her vagina (conceivably because *cicer* was a synonym for "penis" used by Juvenal). "My mom used to call it a 'fuzzy peach,'" says another American woman. "My mum always used to call it your 'nooks and crannies,'" chimes in an Englishwoman.

As for what emerges from such body parts, those who aren't content to fall back on the standard *wee-wee, doo-doo,* and *pass gas* get imaginative. *Tushie music* is what a family in Los Angeles called flatulence. Another dubbed the crackling version *frying eggs.* Every family has its own terms for calls of nature. Some refer to it as *biz* overall. Excrement might be *happy toads,* the act of creating them *a big job* (as opposed to the *little job* of urinating). In one family, defecating was called *big business;* urinating, *wets* (as in "Dad, Dad, pull over! I've gotta go." / "Wets or big business?"). Since *number one* and *number two* are such sterile euphemisms for urine and feces, a mathematician threw in a bit of education by providing his children with *the square root of one* and *the square root of four.*

If the most common reason to euphemize is as a flight to comfort, less appreciated is the fun one can have when doing so. As linguists Keith Allan and Kate Burridge observe, "The importance of language play among human beings has been generally ignored." In *Forbidden Words,* Allan and Burridge call attention to how many substitute words—especially in the area of sex and excretion—"show remarkable inventiveness of either figure or form; and some are indubitably playful."

We will see illustrations of that fact throughout this book. Lavatories, for example, inspire all sorts of elliptical expressions. Among the more imaginative of innumerable euphemisms for this room is *where the Queen goes on foot.* One of the great all-time rejoinders came from the pen of German composer Max Reger a century ago. In response to a critical review of one of his compositions, Reger wrote, "I am sitting in the smallest room of my house. I have your review before me. In a moment it will be behind me." Would this riposte have been as devastating (or amusing) if Reger had written, "I'm sitting on the commode and am about to wipe my behind with your review"? I don't think so.

Event-Based Euphemisms

After an orator in ancient Rome said it was the duty of a freed slave to have sex with her former owner, *duty* became euphemistic for "sex" among young Romans. "You aren't doing your duty by me," they would say, and "He gets a lot of duty."

Duty was an event-based euphemism. In this common form of the genre, well-known episodes provide the basis for euphemistic allusions. In some parts of China, homosexuality was once called the *passion of the cut sleeve.* This referred to an ancient tale about an emperor who cut his sleeve so he could take leave of his male lover, who lay asleep on that sleeve, without disturbing him.

Such euphemisms have meaning only to those familiar with their context. During the 1970s, for example, *discussing Uganda* became a way of describing sexual activity among swinging Londoners. This alluded to a story popular at the time that involved a young couple who made love in an upstairs bedroom during a party in someone else's flat. When asked later what they'd been doing, the young woman said, "Discussing the situation in Uganda." For a time thereafter,

"Would you care to discuss Uganda?" was the hip Londoner's sexual come-on.

Event-based euphemisms typically enjoy the life expectancy of a fruit fly. Most die out with the memory of those around at their inception, if not sooner. Only old-timers know why a fart was once known as *a one-o'clock* in Australia (because before World War II, a cannon was fired at that time of day from Fort Denison in Sydney's harbor, a practice that did not resume for nearly half a century). And who today would refer to bedbugs as *Norfolk-Howards?* At one time, some Britons did just that. Because "bug" was considered a vulgar word in Victorian England (as opposed to "insect"), an unfortunate Londoner named Joshua Bug wearied of the opportunities his last name presented for laughter. In 1861, Bug changed his surname to Norfolk-Howard. After this face-saving gambit was announced in the *Times* of London, he found that his new name had become a euphemism for the old one. ("That mattress was full of Norfolk-Howards.")

More than a century later, when in England as a Rhodes scholar, Bill Clinton had a go at smoking marijuana. While campaigning for the presidency two decades later, Clinton admitted this but said he "didn't inhale." That became an overnight euphemism for getting high on marijuana. ("I used to inhale when I was in college.")

This euphemism survived somewhat longer than most that are event based do and can still be heard on occasion. "The point was to inhale," Barack Obama has said of his own youthful marijuana use. Another event-based euphemism that could prove durable is *wardrobe malfunction.* After Justin Timberlake explained that this was why Janet Jackson's nipple was exposed when he tugged at her bodice during the halftime show of Super Bowl XXXVIII, *wardrobe malfunction* quickly became euphemistic for exposing parts of one's body (especially when singer Britney Spears began doing this on a regular basis). When actress Emma Watson inadvertently displayed some underwear in public, she denied that this was a Britneyesque flash, calling it more of a "wardrobe malfunction."

A few years after Janet Jackson's flash, Senator Larry Craig (R-ID) pled guilty to soliciting sex from an undercover police officer in the adjacent stall of an airport men's room by tapping his toe beneath the stall divider. *Toe tapping* then became a euphemism for gay solicitation. When Craig explained that his foot appeared beneath the next stall's divider because he had a "wide stance" while seated on a toilet, *wide stance* became a euphemism for closeted gay behavior. Two years later, after North Carolina governor Mark Sanford said he was hiking the Appalachian Trail when he was actually canoodling with his mistress in Argentina, *hiking the Appalachian Trail* enjoyed a vogue as a euphemism for "having an affair." ("I think Jason and Amy are hiking the Appalachian Trail.")

To keep track of such euphemisms, one must be au courant newswise. It also helps to be up on contemporary pop-culture references, ones in which *Steely Dan* can refer to either the rock band by that name or an erect penis. An even more esoteric modern euphemism in this area is *sunglasses*, referencing an often-erect sunglass-wearing rock guitarist. ("OMG! Sunglass alert!")

Obviously, euphemisms cover a lot of ground and serve many masters. How did they become such a central part of our discourse? To answer that question, we must go back to the earliest known euphemisms, ones created in the caves, forests, and savannas where our ancestors found some things so frightening that they could only speak about them indirectly.

2

From Bears to Bowdlerism

Bears are scary animals. They are so scary that early northern Europeans referred to them by substitute names for fear that uttering their real name might beckon these ferocious beasts. Instead, they talked of *the honey eater, the licker,* or *the grandfather.* The word "bear" itself evolved from a euphemistic term that meant "the brown one." It is the oldest known euphemism, first recorded a thousand years ago. Because the word that "bear" replaced was never recorded, it remains a mystery.

Animals figure prominently in the history of euphemizing. It was quite common throughout the world to give feared animals euphemistic names. This was something that late-nineteenth-century anthropologists often noted. Because members of the Wajagga tribe near Mount Kilimanjaro in East Africa believed that nearby predators had been sent by the dead to attack them, they only talked of such animals elliptically. Lions were *the lords from the underworld;* elephants, *the chieftains.* Alternatively, in hopes of driving elephants away with ridicule, they would call them *woman's bag* since this huge animal's hide was wrinkled and cracked like market bags used by women. Some Malays called elephants *the tall ones*, tigers *the striped ones*, crocodiles *the gap-toothed thingammy-bobs*. The Oraons of India's Chota Nagpur region warily referred to tigers as *long-tailed things* and to snakes as *ropes*.

Words originally were not considered distinct from what they named. Those who believed this thought that referring to something by name risked summoning that entity. To say "husband" or "wife" presented no problem (for the most part). Saying "tiger," on the other hand, or "Zeus," was another matter. Who wanted to beckon them? This ancient fear is echoed whenever we say, "Speak of the devil, and he'll appear."

Because early humans thought words had the power to alert whatever they named, including predators, enemies, and evil spirits, not using the actual words for such ominous entities seemed prudent. Substitute words provided a safe vehicle for talking about frightening, taboo, or sacred topics. Like modern euphemisms, they were a way to fend off things that gave our ancestors pause by not referring to them directly. When embarking on a long sea voyage, members of the Alfoor tribe near Papua New Guinea thought it wise to fool eaves-dropping spirits about their intentions by using substitute words. In place of "straight ahead," they'd say *bird's beak*. Instead of "starboard" (to the right), *sword*. Rather than "lar-board" (to the left), *shield*.

A capacity to speak indirectly in this way undoubtedly quickly followed our ability to create and use words. The bet-ter our ability to express ourselves, the more need we felt to avoid being direct when doing so might court danger, cause anxiety, or give offense. Hence euphemisms. Euphemisms are a key indicator of increasing complexity of speech. Saying what we mean takes a high order of intelligence. It takes an even higher order to *not* say what we mean, while still conveying our thought.

Euphemisms gestate best in the loam of our most primitive emotions: terror, lust, and revulsion. Imagine early men and women trying to come up with a way to discuss, say, shit. Like us, they most likely had an actual word for feces, but one they found unpleasant to use in everyday conversation because of the image it evoked, to say nothing of the smell. Presumably, therefore, they created a new word, one that didn't portray the topic quite so directly: *brown stuff*, say, or *mushrooms*. ("I almost stepped on some mushrooms over there.") A couple about to copulate might ask, "Shall we go behind that tree and relax?" An interloper who caught them in the act might later report that he'd seen this man and woman *relaxing*.

The need for euphemisms to talk not only about bears and evil spirits but also about each other must have become apparent early in human history. Without oblique language, how could we gossip? Then as now, each group developed its own euphemisms for touchy topics such as sex. The Trobriand islanders whom Bronislaw Malinowski studied early last century used the phrase *sit at* euphemistically for "copulate." "They sit at the garden way" was their way of saying, "They copulate in or near the garden." Members of the Mehinaku tribe of central Brazil call surreptitiously soliciting extramarital sex *alligatoring*. That's because in their tribal mythology, alligators are both highly sexual and unusually canny. Mehinakuans who want to have a dalliance retire to a discreet jungle clearing known as *the alligator place*. "Shall we visit the alligator place?" might sound innocent to an outsider but not to the Mehinaku. To them, this is a question fraught with significance.

Mollifying Spirits

Unlike Christians' belief in God's essential goodness, our early ancestors believed that the deities they worshiped were not always benevolent. Many were closer in spirit to the evil wizard in J. K. Rowling's Harry Potter books, Lord Voldemort, who is generally referred to as "He Who Must Not Be Named" or "You Know Who." As with Voldemort, our ancestors thought that referring to deities by name might provoke their terrible wrath. If such dangerous spirits did not overhear themselves being discussed, they might leave us alone. Or so it was thought.

In time, this belief was integrated into theology. Recall the relationship of our word "euphemism" with the Greek *eupheme* and related words. In ancient Greece, *euphemizein* meant "speak with fair words" and often referred to terms used in place of ones considered sacred. Its opposite was *blasphemein,* the root of "blaspheme," meaning "to speak lightly or amiss of sacred things." Many early euphemisms were a means to avoid being blasphemous.

Among the ancients, this wasn't just a matter of piety. Greek and Roman deities were not always nice. Many were rather cranky, a bit testy, easily provoked. Hoping to curry favor with such mercurial gods, some Greeks called them *the Kindly Ones* or *the Gracious Ones*. In a similar spirit, the Irish later tried to appease nasty fairies by referring to them as *good folk*.

Not using the actual names of spiritual figures was considered a shrewd strategy for keeping those figures from knowing that they were on your mind. It also suggested reverence and awe. This tradition persisted into the Judeo-Christian era. It lives on in the frequent use of Christian terms such as *the Almighty, our Creator,* or *Heavenly Father,* instead of making direct reference to God, and in the Jewish tradition of recording his name as G-d or *Yahweh.*

Until quite recently, those who wished to wreak maximum verbal havoc uttered blasphemous expletives. Even under the most dire provocations—a stubbed toe, say, or a thumb banged with a hammer—our pious ancestors would not have dared take the Lord's name in vain by calling out "Oh, God!" "goddamn!" or even "damn!" In Gilbert and Sullivan's operetta *H.M.S. Pinafore,* Captain Corcoran expresses a common attitude toward the last word in centuries past:

> *Though 'Bother it' I may*
> *Occasionally say,*
> *I never use a big, big D*

Today, we marvel that such a word excited sufficient horror to call for euphemizing, but it did. Consider tinkers and their *damns* or *dams.* These itinerant utensil repairers were not known for having civil tongues. In fact, their constant swearing was so notorious that "not worth a tinker's damn" became a common catchphrase. This saying posed problems for tender ears, however, so an alternative etymology emerged, explaining that "dam" referred to the mound of dough that tinkers built around a flawed utensil segment that they then flooded with solder. Since this dam could be used only once, something of no lasting value might be described as not worth a tinker's dam.

In more reverent times, the penalty for using blasphemous words was far greater than a mouth washed out with soap. Christians particularly dreaded the prospect of an eternity spent with flames burning their ankles and the devil's trident poking their behinds. To those who avoided using a term such as "hell," the fiery depths were very real. Summoning the devil by calling out his name ("The devil!") or that of his headquarters ("Hell!") was serious business. Today "Go to hell!" is among the mildest of epithets. But at a time when the prospect of being consigned to an afterlife of eternal agony was so vivid and feared, it was a dire curse.

As a result, the market was robust for substitute expressions to avoid blasphemous ones. Early on, "God" was euphemized to *gog, gosse, gom,* and *gad,* to name just a few. "Lord" could be *law, lawks, lawzy, lawdy, land,* or *losh.* More obvious euphemisms such as *gosh darn* and *heck* and *Jimminy Christmas* were supplemented by others, such as *zounds* (for "God's wounds") and *gadzooks* (for "God's hooks"). At the other end of the religious spectrum, *deuce* and *dickens* stood in for "devil," and *an uncomfortable place* or *that other place* for "hell."

Nearly a century ago, a University of California linguist collected hundreds of euphemistic American exclamations. Some showed remarkable ingenuity. "Jesus Christ" became *Jeans Rice, grease us twice, cheese and rice,* and various other dairy-based euphemisms, such as *sweet cheesecake* or *cheese and crackers. Gee* itself was a shortening of the name of God's Son. "Christ" alone inspired *cripes* and *crikey.* "Damn" gave way to *darn, dang, ding-bust* ("I'll be ding-busted"), *jim jam* ("I'll be jim-jammed"), and *jim swiggle* ("I'll be jim-swiggled"). "Hell" became *Helen, Halifax,* and *hen.* Or, as Canadians call the devil's abode, *h-e-double-hockey-sticks.*

Innocuous expressions such as *"Dear me!"* and *"Good gracious!"* had the added benefit of giving users a moment to regroup. Saying something like *"Holy mackerel!"* or *"Criminy!"* gave speakers a split second to pivot from blasphemy to acceptability. Medieval Englishmen who started to say "By God!" could shift quickly to *"By Jove!"*; antebellum Americans to *"By gum!"* Best of all was *"By Godfrey!"* Even "I swear!" was routinely replaced by *"I swan!"* after the mid-eighteenth century. Those who were tempted to say "Good God!" could think twice and say *"Good gravy!"* Charlie Brown—a creation of devout Christian Charles Schulz—would never say "Good God!" He would say *"Good grief!"* however, and did—often.

Piety and Profanity

Since our pious ancestors were so restrained when it came to swearing, it's easy to conclude that they were verbally restrained in general. Nothing could be further from the truth. From ancient times on, lewd talk has been at least as common as it is today.

Terms such as "shit," "arse," and "teat" are among the oldest English words in continual use. Chaucer's work was filled with expletives. In *The Reeve's Tale,* Aleyn uses a verb for copulating common at that time when he says, "I have thries [thrice] in this shorte night / Swived the millers doghter bolt upright." In *The Miller's Tale,* Nicholas takes a direct approach to courting Allison: "And prively he caughte hire by the queinte." (The Middle English term *queinte* was later shortened to "cunt.") A few centuries later, playwright Ben Jonson freely used phrases such as "Shit o' your head" and "Turd t' your teeth." A widow in the 1618 play *Amends for Ladies* by Nathaniel Field exclaims, "O man, what art thou when thy cock is up!"

One reason that William Shakespeare is such a pivotal figure in literary history was his ability to combine earthy speech with sly metaphor. "Pistol's cock is up," he wrote in *Henry V*, "And flashing fire will follow." Shakespeare routinely couched bawdy episodes in elliptical terms for the sheer delight of entertaining audiences with his naughty wordplay. Shakespearean scholar Pauline Kiernan has tallied more than 180 synonyms for female genitals in the Bard's plays, 200 for the male version, and 700 verbal variations on sex play. "Even ardent Shakespeare fans," writes Kiernan in *Filthy Shakespeare*, "experience bum-numbing moments during long and apparently tedious exchanges of verbal banter that make little sense to us because we don't realize that the harmless-sounding words are actually exuberant displays of sparkling coded sexual dialogue." The results are classic examples of the mingling of code words, slang, and euphemism. When Angelo in *Measure for Measure* calls his lustful longing for a young nun "a strong and swelling evil," "swelling" refers both to his growing feeling and his rising penis. Hamlet refers to the "country matters" that can be found between "maids' legs." When an elderly shepherd comes upon an abandoned baby in *The Winter's Tale*, the old man surmises that it is the result of "some stair-work, some trunk work, some behind-door-work." Kiernan translates this speculation about the baby's origins into modern vernacular: "a shag behind the back stairs, a furtive fuck inside a trunk or a screw up against a wall."

It's difficult for us to comprehend how many words and expressions we think of as profane were commonly used in Shakespeare's time. This is partly because such terms weren't as taboo back then, partly because common folk in particular weren't all that concerned about proper speech. To them, bad words were ones that offended the Lord, not earthy terms for body parts or body wastes or matters sexual. Before a growing middle class clamped down on speech considered coarse, the King James Version of the Bible (1611) freely incorporated such terms as "piss," "teat," "give suck," and "whorish." Even among devoutly Christian American colonists, talk we might consider lewd did not seem so to them. Puritans in Massachusetts wrote so candidly about sexual activity in their ranks that heavy censorship was required before such writing could be published in modern editions. At the end of the seventeenth century, an English travel writer observed of New Englanders, "notwithstanding their *Sanctity* they are very *Prophane* in their common *Dialect*." A few decades later, an English clergyman wrote from Maryland that visitors like himself were not exempted from the "obscene Conceits and broad Expressions" of its residents. Yet this colony had a statute that provided for boring a hole through the tongue of first-time blasphemers, branding a *B* on the forehead of second offenders, and executing anyone who dared blaspheme a third time.

Cleaning Up Potty Mouths

During his reign from 1603 to 1625, James I, himself no slouch in the swearing department, fined members of his court twelve pence for each curse they uttered there. An Act of Parliament in 1623 made it illegal to swear in general. Subsequent laws that proscribed speech considered blasphemous or seditious accelerated the need for judicious euphemisms. Oliver Cromwell retained the King James approach to swearing when warning his soldiers in 1642 that "Not a man swears but pays his twelve pence." Repeat offenders risked having their tongues pierced with a hot iron. In 1694, Parliament passed an Act for More Effectual Suppressing Profane Cursing and Swearing.

As more people moved into the middle class, social insecurity mounted — about language especially. Upwardly mobile residents of England and its colonies turned to primers for guidance. Books on proper speech were especially popular. In America's first grammar, a William and Mary professor wrote in 1721, "None of good Manners use nasty Expressions, and foul vulgar Terms, which are nauseous, and odious."

In the prelude to the Victorian era, fear of blasphemy gradually gave way to fear of impropriety. Sex, body parts, and bodily functions became subjects of mounting verbal concern. Anxiety about taking the Lord's name in vain was rivaled by apprehension about using inappropriate language. This was especially true among those who regarded themselves as genteel or wished to be seen that way. By using proper verbal evasions — what linguists call "minced oaths" — status-conscious speakers of English distanced themselves from the vulgar mob. In *The Life and Opinions of Tristram Shandy,* Laurence Sterne depicted a mid-eighteenth-century gentleman who when provoked consulted a list of mild oaths that he considered acceptable substitutes for profane ones.

Pioneering dictionary compilers such as Samuel Johnson left out words they considered inappropriate. Although Johnson included "piss," "turd," "arse," and "fart" in his 1755 opus, he omitted other terms such as "shit," "penis," "vagina," "cunt," and "fuck." When a proper London lady congratulated him for keeping such words out of his dictionary, the lexicographer responded, "Then you have been looking for them?"

Beginning in Dr. Johnson's time and throughout the next century, bourgeois Englishwomen in particular grew increasingly prudish. As the Industrial Revolution left more and more women at home with time on their hands, developing good manners became both their occupation and preoccupation. In *Little Dorrit,* Charles Dickens satirized this sensibility with the character Mrs. General, whom the newly affluent Dorrits hire to teach them how to be more refined. A truly refined mind, she tells them, is one that appears to be "ignorant of the existence of anything that is not perfectly proper, placid, and pleasant."

"Refinement" was the word of the hour among the upwardly mobile. Freshly minted members of the middle class were keen to demonstrate how respectably they could speak. Fastidious concern about propriety fueled a constant demand for more euphemisms, especially in the areas of sex, secretions, and anatomy. When it came to the body, it wasn't just talk of reproductive organs that raised eyebrows. Reference to any part at all became questionable. In 1810 novelist Susan Ferrier wrote a letter to a male friend in which she referred to cutting corns off her feet. For this breach of decorum, Ferrier later observed, she was subjected to "the scorn of the virtuous and the detestation of the pure in heart," adding, "I must have had some ingenuity, if I could extract either immorality or indecency from a corn! But so it was. I was reprobated...as one of the abandoned of my sex."

To those who laid the foundations for the Victorian

era, language was seen as something that needed to be purified, cleansed of any terms that might inspire improper thoughts. Mastery of euphemisms became no less a part of womanly arts than the ability to make crumpets and gracefully pour tea. "What did she say?" asks the narrator of Jane Austen's 1816 novel, *Emma*. "Just what she ought, of course. A lady always does." Linguist Kerry Linfoot-Ham has determined that *Emma* is filled with oblique references to erotic activity. They include "a little movement of more than common friendliness" (seductiveness), "*go away* in the evening attended by her pleasant husband" (going off to have sex), and "flutter of pleasure" (sexual excitement itself). One character's pregnancy was referred to simply as "her situation."

Among women of Austen's class, language grew increasingly circumspect. Considered too vulgar for tender ears, "sick" was replaced by *ill*. "Sweat" became *perspiration,* and "spit" was euphemized to *expectorate.* At an extreme, a profanity such as "cunt" was referred to as *the monosyllable.*

One reason for the heavy use of euphemism in literary works at this time was that books were so commonly read aloud within families. This was what motivated a retired English physician named Thomas Bowdler to edit a collection of Shakespeare's plays for tender ears. In *The Family Shakespeare,* "Out damn'd spot" was revised to "Out crimson spot"; Romeo and Juliet were a chaste young couple; and Ophelia's suicide became an accidental drowning. Bowdler was sure that the Bard himself would have approved. In recognition of his efforts, we still call censorship of all kinds "bowdlerization." Dr. Bowdler later had a go at the Bible.

Deleting bad words from the Bible was a practice of long standing, one the American lexicographer Noah Webster took to new heights. Even though the King James Version had been considered appropriately reverent during two centuries of use, Webster concluded that some of its language was unsuited to the more refined discourse of his time. In Ruth 1:11, Naomi's question, "Are there yet any more sons in my womb?" was changed to "Shall I bear more sons?" Biblical mothers would no longer "give sucke" to their babies in Webster's Bible, though they would *nurse their young ones.* The line "they may eat their own dung, and drink their own piss" in Isaiah 36:12 was refined to read "they may devour their vilest excretions." Even seemingly inoffensive phrases such as "the river shall stink" in Exodus 7:18 gave way to "the river shall be offensive in smell."

A combination of religious fervor and upward mobility, with its attendant verbal insecurity, made the early-nineteenth century what H. L. Mencken called a "Golden Age of Euphemism." As language grew more "refined," entire new areas of discourse became candidates for verbal evasion. This trend did not go unnoticed. Nathaniel Ames, who spent years at sea after being expelled from Harvard in 1814, was less dismayed by the guttural talk of his fellow seamen than by the flowery circumlocutions he encountered on shore. There Ames heard squinting referred to as *optical indecision,* indigestion called *dyspepsy,* and a woman who shamelessly flirted with every man in sight described as *very free in her manners.* Ames was also put off by the growing use of euphemistic foreign expressions. "Our mother tongue is fast assuming a dress like that of a state's prison convict," he wrote, "one leg of its inexpressibles being made of Greek, and the other of French, while the waistbands are made of Latin."

"Inexpressibles"? Surely Ames would not use this mealy-mouthed euphemism for "trousers" that was common in his time. Yet he did. Even plain-speaking Nathaniel Ames wasn't willing to flout the nineteenth-century taboo against using this word or "breeches," for fear that doing so might make ladies swoon. In John Baldwin Buckstone's 1835 play "Dream at Sea," one character reprimands another for referring to breeches. "Hush," he is told, "you should say *inexpressibles.* That's the way genteel people talk."

During the first half of the nineteenth century, a wide range of other euphemisms for trousers were auditioned: *irrepressibles, indescribables, ineffables, unutterables, nether garments, continuations, don't name 'ems,* and *mustn't mention 'ems,* to mention just a few. In *Sketches by Boz* (1836), Charles Dickens wrote that one character wore "light inexplicables without a spot." In *The Pickwick Papers* (1836–37), a servant named Trotter "gave four distinct slaps on the pocket of his mulberry indescribable." Six years later, in *American Notes* (1842), Dickens said of a growing boy, "it had been found necessary to make an addition to the legs of his inexpressibles."

If direct reference to trousers was taboo in Dickens's time, mention of stockings was considered downright degenerate. *Hose* was the preferred synonym in antebellum America, though *long socks* would do in a pinch. And what of underwear? Fear was rampant that saying the word "panty" might evoke an image of this portal garment, and who knew where that might lead? Better one should say *undergarment, underthing, unmentionable,* or *smalls* (short for *small clothes*).

When women wore corsets, there was always the troubling prospect that this word might enter men's minds and emerge from their mouths. While visiting Cincinnati in the early 1830s, a German tourist was reprimanded for saying "corset" in mixed company. *Foundation,* he was informed, was the preferred synonym. (In England, it was *stays*.) During her own sojourn in Cincinnati a few years later, Frances Trollope, mother of English novelist Anthony Trollope, found that "many words to which I had never heard an objectionable meaning attached, were totally interdicted, and the strangest paraphrastic sentences substituted."

Like Mrs. Trollope, visitors from abroad often commented on the unusually stilted language Americans used at this time. Alexis de Tocqueville thought the guarded discourse he heard so often when touring the United States might be due to the fact that men and women mingled freely there, forcing both sexes to choose their words carefully. In other words, the very social freedom and egalitarianism that Americans prized made them feel a need to self-censor when in mixed company. The fact that Americans routinely saw themselves as on their way to affluence (if not there already) made them feel it was crucial to use the right words, ones they thought would help them on their journey.

This presented a problem to foreign visitors, even ones who spoke English. Which words needed to be avoided and which ones were appropriate wasn't always clear. Shortly after Tocqueville returned to France, the English naval captain Frederick Marryat got in trouble one summer day in 1837 by innocently asking a young American friend whether she'd hurt her leg after taking a tumble while they visited Niagara Falls. The outraged woman informed Captain Marryat that this word was *not* used in her country. When the aristocratic Englishman begged her pardon and asked what word *was* used for this body part, she responded "limb."

The need to avoid saying "leg" at this time led to remarkable euphemistic creativity. In addition to the pedestrian *limbs*

(a shortening of *nether limbs*), mid-nineteenth-century synonyms for "leg" included *understandings* and *underpinners*. In
his 1849 novella *Kavanaugh,* Henry Wadsworth Longfellow
excerpted this rule from the prospectus of a fashionable girls'
boarding school: "Young ladies are not allowed to cross their
benders in school." A few years later, author Richard Meade
Bache talked with an American woman who stammered
about before averring that women in New England tended to
have well-formed *extremities* (i.e., arms and legs).

In this ticklish verbal climate, even the extremities of
poultry had to be approached with care. At a hotel, Bache
overheard another woman ask a waiter to bring her a chick-
en's *trotter* (leg again). During the same era, an English visitor
to America was puzzled when asked by a woman at a dinner
table if he'd please give her "the first and second joint of a
chicken" (i.e., the leg). As Winston Churchill later discovered,
polite guests at American tables knew that asking a poultry-
serving hostess for *white meat* instead of "breast meat," *dark
meat* instead of "a thigh," and *a drumstick* in place of "a leg,"
saved embarrassment all around. Prior to his tour of the
United States, Captain Marryat witnessed a similar fastidious-
ness in the West Indies, which he parlayed into a passage in his
1834 novel *Peter Simple.* The protagonist of that book is seated
beside a local woman at a dinner in Barbados. "Fate had placed
me opposite to a fine turkey," he reports. "I asked my partner
if I should have the pleasure of helping her to a piece of the
breast. She looked at me indignantly, and said, 'Curse your
impudence, sar. I wonder where you larn manners. Sar, I take
a lilly turkey *bosom,* if you please. Talk of *breast* to a lady, sar; —
really quite *horrid.'*"

Poultry presented all manner of verbal pitfalls at this

time. "Cock" in particular posed serious problems. This word was short for "cockerel," a male chicken. But "cock" was also short for "watercock," the spigot of a barrel, leading it to become slang for "penis." Unfortunately, that tainted term was embedded in many others. In the United States especially, previously innocent terms such as "cockeyed" and "cocksure" could no longer be used when both sexes were present. Under this regimen, "weathercocks" became *weathervanes;* "haycocks," *haystacks;* and "apricocks," *apricots.* Those burdened with last names such as "Hitchcock" and "Leacock" began to feel under siege. In response, an American family named "Alcocke" changed their name to *Alcox.* Fearing that this might not be adequate, before siring a daughter named Louisa May in 1832, Bronson Alcox became Bronson *Alcott.*

In the United States, male chickens became *crowers,* then *roosters.* This was not without controversy. "The word *rooster* is an Americanism," noted Richard Meade Bache, "which, the sooner we forget, the better. Does not the hen of the same species roost also?" One compiler of Americanisms quoted an English critic who defined "rooster" as "a ladyism for cock." An English visitor to the United States professed to have heard a *rooster-and-ox story* (i.e., "a cock-and-bull tale"). A mid-nineteenth-century spoof written by Canadian humorist Thomas Haliburton featured a Massachusetts woman who described her brother as a "rooster swain" in the navy. When a man she knew pressed her for the meaning of that rank, the young woman responded, "a rooster swain, if you must know, you wicked critter you, is a cockswain; a word you know'd well enough warn't fit for a lady to speak."

Along with male chickens, bulls posed problems for

proper speakers. In this case, it was the mental images conjured by this snorting, raging, rapacious animal that aroused concern. Presumably, not referring to bulls directly would censor those images. This led to a wide range of euphemisms, *male cow* being the most popular. Other acceptable synonyms included *cow-critter, cow-brute, cow man, seed ox, toro,* and *roarer.* Also permissible were *he-cow* and *gentleman-cow.* Many of those reciting Longfellow's 1841 poem "Wreck of the Hesperus" sacrificed rhyme for refinement when they revised the last three words of one line—"like the horns of an angry bull"—in this fashion:

> *She struck where the white and fleecy waves*
> *Looked as soft as carded wool;*
> *But the cruel rocks they gored her side,*
> *Like the horns of a gentleman cow.*

Victorians' Secrets

The transition from piety to propriety reached its peak during the Victorian era. Reverence was in decline at this time, prudishness on the rise. Laws banning blasphemy in Britain broadened to proscribe obscenity and "indecency." British judges in such cases focused less on sacrilegious expressions per se than on the words used to express them. To avoid being charged with blasphemy, wrote a British legal scholar in the late-Victorian era, authors were advised to "abstain from ribaldry and licentious approach." In her book *Word Crimes: Blasphemy, Culture and Literature in Nineteenth-Century England,* Joss Marsh makes a compelling case that issues of class lay at the heart of this transition. Terms banned as indecent were ones commonly heard on British streets, if not in its drawing rooms. To Marsh, this illustrated a "fear of words endemic in a culture addicted to euphemisms."

Euphemistic speech became an important means by which the newly affluent distinguished themselves from the vulgar masses. When a proper Victorian lady murmured to her pharmacist that she needed some *curl paper,* he reached beneath the counter and handed her a box containing sheets of what we would call toilet or lavatory paper. Should a sneeze erupt from this woman's nostrils, she might apologize for her *nose spasm.* Instead of reading the King James Bible with all its crude words, she could turn with relief to a new translation that was filled with euphemisms.

Despite the devout Christianity being promoted at this time, it was fastidious concern with proper deportment that really drove evasive speech among Victorians. "The prudery of evasion was more indebted to middle-class gentility than to the Puritan revival," concludes historian Walter Houghton in *The Victorian Frame of Mind.* A euphemism-rich vocabulary developed by Victorians is the sound track of their era. Respectable Englishmen and -women no longer "went to bed"; they *retired.* Wives didn't "get pregnant"; they were *en famille.* What produced their pregnancy was only referred to in the most oblique terms. Victorians' lives may not have been purer than those of their ancestors, observed author-editor William Makepeace Thackeray, but their mouths certainly were. Thackeray himself, who considered his era more "squeamish" than moral, rejected a poem by Elizabeth Barrett Browning because it included the word *harlot.* Yet *harlot* was originally a euphemism for "whore."

In the privacy of his own notes, Thomas Carlyle called a

famous French courtesan "that old wh-re." When his nephew Andrew Carlyle edited these notes for publication in 1858, "wh-re" proved too bold and was changed to "female." Following Nathaniel Hawthorne's death in 1864, his wife, Sophia, combed through her husband's journals to clean them up for public consumption, deleting every mention of "whores" and "pimps." Hawthorne's expression "of that kidney" became "of that class." The author's widow also fastidiously replaced the word "leg" with "limb" wherever it appeared.

This type of bowdlerizing reflected continued concern about referring directly to certain body parts. The articles of clothing that covered them remained problematic too, particularly those closest to the skin. As late as 1908, an English author referred to two young women wearing gowns so short that they displayed "certain heavily-frilled cotton investitures of the lower limbs" (i.e., petticoats). *Linen* was a common euphemism for underwear among Victorians, echoed in today's concern about "washing one's dirty linen in public." "Lingerie" first appeared in the late-nineteenth century, a word borrowed from the French that only gradually became suggestive.

As historians of the era keep reminding us, the Victorians were far lustier than we imagine or they would have had us believe. An underground trade in erotica was robust at that time. Queen Victoria herself enjoyed collecting, and even drawing, pictures of naked men. Some forty-two thousand children were born out of wedlock in England and Wales in 1851 alone. A mid-nineteenth-century doctor estimated that one in twelve unmarried Englishwomen had "strayed from the path of virtue." For the historical record, however, the Victorians' words spoke louder than their actions.

The list of words that proper Victorians thought required euphemisms was especially long when it came to sex. Any term that conveyed even a breath of sexuality was subject to revision or deletion. During English legal proceedings, rape was referred to as "taking improper liberties" or "feloniously ravishing." Other kinds of sexual imposition—including molestation of children—came under the heading of "acting in an indecent manner." "Certain" was an important multi-purpose word in divorce-related testimony and might refer to *a certain organ, a certain unnatural vice, a certain posture,* or *a certain condition* (i.e., pregnancy).

The monumental *Oxford English Dictionary* was published serially during this period, commanding attention not just for the words included but also for those left out. As a contributor to the *Cambridge History of the English Language* later noted of this classic work, "They excluded some infamous four-letter words, moving directly from *fucivorous* to *fuco'd,* for example, although they entered other 'Anglo-Saxonisms', such as those between *shisham* and *shiver,* alleging however that these words are 'not now in decent use', the same judgment made of *fart.*"

AN INTERESTING CONDITION

In his 1864 novel, *Our Mutual Friend,* Charles Dickens portrays a wife dillydallying for several paragraphs before telling her husband "there is a ship upon the ocean......bringing......to you and me......a little baby, John."

Why not just say "I'm pregnant"? Because in Dickens's time,

(continued)

pregnancy was a sensitive subject. It brought to mind events that led to this condition, and the body parts involved. Instead, pregnant women were dubbed *with child, in a family way,* or simply *expecting.* A line in an 1861 book about Mexico illustrates the kind of verbal tap-dancing that this subject evoked: "Whenever a Zapoteque woman is about to add one to the number of their community, the expectant father of the child assembles all his relations in his cabin."

Pregnant Englishwomen who were made to stay abed used to be referred to as *confined.* In one case, a proper Victorian lady read aloud to a group of friends a letter about an unmarried woman named Mary that began: "We are in great trouble. Poor Mary has been confined…" She paused—this being the last word on a page—then fumbled about for the letter's next page, which had fallen to the floor. Only when the woman picked it up and resumed reading did her shocked listeners get to hear the end of this sentence: "to her room for three days with what, we fear, is suppressed scarlet fever." They breathed a sigh of relief.

In an interesting condition was a popular nineteenth-century euphemism for pregnancy, as was *in a delicate condition.* Or just *condition.* ("A woman in your condition.") At the turn of the past century, the phrase "I'm pregnant" in *Anna Karenina* was translated into English as "I am with child." Several years earlier, German translators relied on "I am blessed" for the same phrase, trusting readers would get the message.

Another euphemism—*in a family way*—persisted well into the twentieth century. Francophiles preferred *en famille* or simply *enceinte.* When several episodes of *I Love Lucy* were built around an obviously pregnant Lucille Ball, the first was titled "Lucy Is Enceinte." Within another, Lucy wrote a note saying, "My husband and I are going to have a blessed event!" She later referred to herself as *expectant.*

During World War II, pregnant Women's Army Corps members discharged from service were said to have *back trouble.* Civilians in the same condition were *eating for two. Starting a family* is a more modern euphemism, as are *anticipating* and *carrying.* Colloquialisms range from Shakespeare's *round-wombed* to the subsequent *bow-windowed* and more recent standbys such as *in the pudding club, having a bun in the oven,* and *under construction* (on the chest of maternity T-shirts with an arrow pointing downward). In spoofier contemporary times, an online compilation of euphemisms for pregnancy included "buying sardine and pickle futures," "flipping the bird at the Chinese government," and "another eighteen years down the toilet."

Proper Speech on the Silver Screen

Even though Victorian attitudes waned after World War I, they found refuge among censors of movies. These modern-day Bowdlers accessed a well-stocked pantry of euphemisms for alternatives to the smut they saw creeping into scripts. Pennsylvania's censors demanded that a "loose woman" in D. W. Griffith's 1920 film *Way Down East* be called an "adventuress." A year later, the same censors concluded that having a character exclaim "It's a boy!" in a film suggested too boldly that a baby had just been born. They proposed instead, "The boy is better" (leading one film critic to call this "the first case of pre-natal screen colic" on record).

In 1922 leading moviemakers hired onetime chairman of the Republican National Committee Will Hays to help them toe the verbal line. Even though the advent of talkies complicated his work, this snaggle-toothed Indianan was up to the job. His office made the producers of one movie muffle "damned" in its sound track. According to Gerald Gardner, author of *The Censorship Papers,* because "Oh God!" was considered too blasphemous for moviegoers' ears, "a generation of screenwriters ground their teeth as they typed 'Oh boy!'" Alternatively, they came up with nonsense euphemisms such as "Godfrey Daniels!" for W. C. Fields and "Jumping butterballs!" for the Marx Brothers.

By 1933, Hays reported that his office had required that some twelve hundred changes be made in scripts and story treatments during that year alone. Words banned by the Motion Picture Production Code included not just "hell" and "damn" but also "virgin," "fairy," "goose," "Gawd," "madam," "pansy," "tart," "razzberry," "S.O.B," "son-of-a," and "nuts." For W. C. Fields's film *The Bank Dick,* the Hays Office suggested that "black pussy"—referring to a cat—be replaced by *black pussycat.* They demanded that the word "slut" be deleted from *For Whom the Bell Tolls.* When Dooley Wilson played "As Time Goes By" in *Casablanca,* the script called for Humphrey Bogart to say "What the (pause) are you playing?" Even a pause implying the word "hell" was considered questionable, however, and the Hays Office asked that movie's producers to revise this line.

"The fight against filth kept us busy," Hays wrote in his memoirs. "The dozens of ways of injecting sex into films led to a veritable game of hide-and-seek, in which we tried our best to keep producers advised on the cutting out of unfit words or scenes before they reached the screen."

Hays's particular bête noire was Mae West. Some thought that the Production Code was created with her in mind. Far from being outraged, the sultry actress and screenwriter seemed to enjoy the challenge of jousting with Hays and his minions. "Censorship *made* me," she once said. Like a low-rent Shakespeare, West sprinkled her movies with as many suggestive remarks as she thought she could get away with and some she knew would never pass muster, as red herrings. This led to a constant game of cat and mouse with Production Code censors. Under pressure from the Hays Office, a song lyric in *I'm No Angel*—"Takes a good man to make me"—was changed to "Takes a good man to break me." The line "I like sophisticated men to take me home" became "I like sophisticated men to take me out." Hays's assistants blue-penciled "tart," "jeez," "punk," and "Lawdy" from that film's script. They also wanted one of West's best-remembered lines—"When I'm good I'm very good, but when I'm bad I'm better"—to be made less suggestive. Thankfully, they didn't succeed.

A watershed moment in pitched battles fought between the Hays Office and movie producers took place during the screen adaptation of Margaret Mitchell's novel *Gone With the Wind*. After reviewing the script for this film, they demanded that a brothel owner become a saloon keeper. Words related to her erstwhile profession such as "chippie," "courtesan," "floozy," "mistress," "slut," "tart," and "whore" had to be deleted. The Hays Office was also disturbed by the many references to another woman's pregnancy, even though she was married. But no problem proved more vexing than Rhett Butler's exit line in the movie's closing scene, "Frankly, my dear, I don't give a damn." Hays's censors objected, of course. In response, MGM suggested some alternatives: "I don't give a hoot," "I just don't care," "It's all the same to me," "It is of no consequence," and "My indifference is boundless." To placate Hays, the studio actually filmed an alternate take in which Rhett Butler tells Scarlett O'Hara, "My dear, I don't care." It was as if Lady Macbeth had said "Out darned spot!" Fortunately, MGM stood its ground and won.

Discussing what the Hays Office would or wouldn't allow on the silver screen became a popular American pastime. According to a widespread but unfounded rumor, the Hays Office would not permit any couple to be in bed on screen unless the man had one foot on the floor. That inspired an enduring euphemism for heavy petting without consummation: *one foot on the floor*. A 2009 magazine profile of the writer-director Rebecca Miller noted that she was suspended from her boarding school "after letting a boy take both feet off the floor while sitting on her bed."

As this suggests, on the euphemistic carousel, one topic is a perennial source of verbal evasion, independent of time and place. You may suspect which one I mean. If any subject has transcended all eras and provided a constant source of new euphemisms it is, how shall we say, coital activity.

3

Speaking of Sex

IN 1638, MY ancestor Robert Keyes had to spend an hour in the Cambridge, Massachusetts, stocks because he'd engaged in "unseemly behavior" with Goody Newell of Lynn. She and Robert then sat side by side for an hour in Lynn's stocks. Why were these two punished this way? Did they kiss? Fondle each other? Make love? Talk dirty? Any of these acts might have qualified for such a vague charge. In the Massachusetts Bay Colony, "unseemly behavior" was a catchall description for activities considered too scandalous to mention aloud.

Several years after Robert and Goody paid their debt to society, a Boston sea captain named Thomas Kemble spent two hours in the stocks for "lewd and unseemly behavior." It seems that Captain Kemble had kissed his wife on their doorstep after returning from three years at sea. The charge was, in other words, a euphemism for what was considered inappropriate physical contact between members of the opposite sex—even when they were married.

There were many other such euphemisms. A few years before Robert and Goody served their sentence, a Massachusetts clergyman condemned marital sex engaged in for reasons other than procreation as "mutual dalliances for pleasure's sake." In 1672, Sarah Roe and Joseph Leigh of Ipswich, Massachusetts, were brought up on charges for "unlawful familiarity." Their crime? Conducting an adulterous affair while Sarah's husband was off at sea. Joseph was whipped for his offense, and Sarah jailed for a month. After that she was ordered to appear before congregants in the Ipswich meetinghouse wearing a sign that read FOR MY BAUDISH CARRIAGE.

During the same period that Sarah and Joseph were enjoying unlawful familiarity in Ipswich, John Wilmot, Earl of Rochester, was carrying on in the court of Charles II. This Oxford graduate was notorious not just for his lascivious behavior and lewd tongue but also for the poems he wrote celebrating sensual pleasures. One got him kicked out of court. In this poem, Lord Rochester averred that King Charles "loves fucking much," that he owned "the sauciest prick that e'er did swive," and that "Restless he rolls about from whore to whore, / A merry monarch, scandalous and poor." Was there anything the Earl wouldn't say?

There was. When it came to his own dalliances, even the exuberantly bawdy Lord Rochester drew the line at being too explicit. A poem attributed to him, "Et Caetera—A Song," included these lines:

In a dark, silent, shady Grove,
Fit for the Delights of Love,
As on Corinna's Breast I panting lay,
My right Hand playing with Et Caetera,

A thousand Words and am'rous Kisses
Prepar'd us both for more substantial Blisses;
And thus the hasty Moments slipt away,
Lost in the Transport of Et Caetera.

She blush'd to see her Innocence betray'd,
And the small Opposition she had made;
Yet hugg'd me close, and, with a Sigh, did say,
Once more, my Dear, once more, Et Caetera.

But Oh! the Power to please this Nymph, was past,
Too violent a Flame can never last;
So we remitted to another Day,
The Prosecution of Et Caetera.

Sexual activity could be the all-time most popular inspiration for euphemisms, many of which are remarkably creative. Much ingenuity and wit are employed when we wish to talk about sex without saying what it is that we're talking about. From courtship to consummation, euphemistic talk abounds.

Courtship

During the past several decades personal ads have become a common mating tool. Making sense of them requires an ability to navigate their euphemistic rapids. "Eligible," for example, is a word commonly used by women to describe the type of man they're looking for ("eligible bachelor"). After studying personal ads, psychologist David Buss concluded that this vague word refers less to a man's eligibility for marriage and more to his status and wealth. As Buss puts it, *eligible* is "a euphemism for the highest-status, most resource-laden man around."

"Professional" is in a league with "eligible," a word that women in particular use to indicate that they're only interested in well-educated, white collar, and, presumably, well-paid men. *Older man* can also be a euphemism for "financially secure." *Financially secure* itself is euphemistic for "wealthy," as is *financially independent. Solvent* suggests if not wealthy then at least not in debt. *In transition* probably means "unemployed." *Unencumbered* is short for "not married or in a relationship" (and perhaps not even paying alimony). It can also refer to having no children to support. *Reliable* is euphemistic for, among other things, "emotionally stable," a sought-after trait mentioned most often by men. *Experienced* could mean any number of things but alludes to sex.

When it comes to personal traits, *good listener* might mean what it says, or it could be a euphemism for "catatonically shy." *Outgoing,* on the other hand, may refer to someone who can't stop talking. As for physical attributes, *curvy, full-figured,* and *classically proportioned* are, of course, synonymous with "overweight woman," one with a *mature figure.* Short men, in turn, can describe themselves as *compact* or *built for speed.* (One bold man began his ad with "Life is short and so am I.") Short women can be *petite* without penalty.

One study of online ads pointed out the ambiguity in some modifiers. Does *self-educated* mean "worldly and well read" or "high-school dropout"? Should *still believes the best things in life are free* be interpreted as "has great spiritual vision and lives in delight of the moment" or "has no money; don't expect gifts"? Only the ad writer knows for sure.

Gay ads historically have had a nomenclature all their

own. This was particularly true during more closeted times. In personal ads after World War II, discreet gay men advertised for "roommates," "bachelors," "servicemen," and men interested in "adventure." Some simply sought "male friendship." *Houseboys* was one euphemism for those on offer, *chauffeurs* another.

Once face-to-face (f2f) contact is made, today's minefield of courting nomenclature grows particularly explosive. At one time, the euphemistic question, "Would you like to come up and see my etchings?" reflected a *Playboy* approach to seduction in which a suave man lured a naive woman into his sexual lair under false pretenses (or so he assumed). *See my etchings* lingers as a euphemism for seduction under false pretenses. An ironic variation on this theme among postwar teenagers was *submarine watching,* or heavy sex play in parked cars involving a gullible girl who was invited by a wily boy to "watch the submarines race" in some isolated setting. (Again, she may not have been so gullible.) While watching submarines race, they engaged in *necking, petting,* or even *boodling.*

Although there's some debate about what kind of activity merits which label, in general *necking* is the milder version of *petting.* Based on her experience, a veteran of the 1950s sex wars had a bit more nuanced explanation: "necking was above the neck, boodling was between the neck and waist, and petting was below the waist." Much was left to the imagination. *Spooning* was an older euphemism for nonspecific foreplay. So were *billing* and *cooing,* or simply *fooling around. Getting fresh* involved what the Victorians called *unwanted attentions.* So did *making a pass at.* Then, as now, men who made passes were thought to be *horny,* a concept that dates back to biblical times when animal horns represented virility and, metaphorically, an erect penis.

Time to Get Up

Whether a man's sex organ stands erect, droops, or stays at half-mast is a subject of intense interest among mating couples and always has been. It's not an easy subject to discuss openly, however. Euphemisms are called for.

"The bawdy hand of the dial is now upon the prick of noon," observes Mercutio in *Romeo and Juliet*. In Shakespeare's time, *noon* was a euphemism for a penis as erect as the hand of a clock at midday — though wouldn't it more likely be 11:45 or 11:30, unless the man was flat on his back waiting to be mounted? *Stand* was another Elizabethan era euphemism for an erect penis, one Shakespeare used to good effect in *The Comedy of Errors:* "When it stands well with him, it stands well with her."

Mae West was the source of a popular erection euphemism. When she was the subject of a kidnapping threat in the mid-1930s, West left Hollywood for a couple of weeks. On her return, a group of friends and fans greeted the voluptuous movie star as she got off the train. One, a young L.A. cop, carried flowers. "These are from the fellas down at the station," said the policeman as he handed her the bouquet. "Then he leant down and kissed me," West later recalled, "and said, 'And that's from me. It's good to have you back with us, Mae.' And I said, 'Oh yeah, and is that a gun you got in your pocket or are you just glad to see me?'" Based on many retellings, *a gun in your pocket* became an enduring allusion to an erect penis.

The antonym of "erection" is a touchy topic, one that has inspired lots of creative euphemisms. Some are based on pencils, appropriately enough, this term having the same root as "penis," which is Latin for "tail." In pre–word processing days, "having no lead in your pencil" was a common metaphor. As so often happens, this type of imaginative imagery has given way to flaccid euphemisms for impotence, first to the quasi-clinical *erectile dysfunction* and later—in ceaseless ads for Viagra and similar drugs—simply *ED*. Pharmaceutical companies, to say nothing of their customers, feel far more comfortable when they have initials rather than words—even euphemistic words—to characterize a man who can't get it up.

Doing It

Referring to the sex act without calling it that has long challenged dramatists, among others. In *Lysistrata,* a group of Greek women tell their husbands that until they stop going to war, "I will not stretch up my slippers toward the ceiling." A later English euphemism for sex was "look at the ceiling over a man's shoulder." Or, "pray with knees upward." In *Othello,* when Iago tells Desdemona's father that "Your daughter and the Moor are now making the beast with two backs," members of Shakespeare's audiences roared with laughter at this evocative image.

In *Filthy Shakespeare,* Pauline Kiernan identified several hundred euphemistic references to sex in the Bard's plays. As this suggests, more euphemisms may have been devoted to sex than to any other topic. This would be hard to prove, however. The ubiquity of sexual euphemisms in our ancestors' speech is difficult to verify because most were considered too vulgar to record. Nonetheless, enough were recorded that we can surmise how many more synonyms for sexual activity must have been used in olden-day conversations than ever appeared in print.

During the early eighteenth century, a Virginia planter named William Byrd kept a secret diary of his sexual activities. By his own account, Byrd accosted maidens, maids, slaves, widows, wives, whores—whoever he could get his hands on (including his own wife, in a pinch)—*fooling* with some, *romping* with others, and *committing uncleanness* with still more, an admission usually followed by the phrase "for which God forgive me." Mostly, though, Byrd *rogered* his many amours, once, twice, thrice, or sometimes not at all. "The maid of the house came into my chamber," he wrote on December 4, 1720, "and I felt her and committed uncleanness but did not roger her."

Six decades later, a strapped English antiquarian named Francis Grose sought to replenish his coffers by publishing *A Classical Dictionary of the Vulgar Tongue*. This 1785 volume and subsequent editions included street terms for sex that could be heard during Grose's time, ones such as "swive," "roger," "hump," "clicket," "dock," and "wap." Grose's dictionary is the first place where "shag" was used this way in print, defined as "To copulate. He is but bad shag; he is no able woman's man." Grose also included slangy phrases such as "basket-making" (defined as "copulation, or making feet for children's stockings"), "buttock ball" ("the amorous congress"), "rantumscantum" ("making the beast with two backs"), and "dry bob" ("copulation without emission").

A century after Grose's slim volume first appeared, a massive collection of American slang compiled by John Farmer and William Henley recorded hundreds of words that referred euphemistically to sexual activity. These ranged from the coarse (*ballocking, belly bumping, under-petticoating*) to the vulgar (*take in cream, feed one's pussy, suck the sugar stick*), the banal (*have connection, be intimate, be familiar*), and the inventive (*go star-gazing on one's back, have a live sausage for supper, get a handle for the broom, dance the mattress jig,* and *do a four-legged frolic*).

Women who were captured and raped by Indians used elliptical words to describe this experience once they were rescued. One Coloradoan who survived such an ordeal in 1878 told a military hearing that she was "insulted" several times by her Ute captors. Under questioning, the young woman elaborated a bit by saying that she'd been subjected to "outrageous treatment." When the presiding officer asked, "Am I to understand that they outraged you several times at night?" she responded "Yes, sir."

Sexual euphemisms no less than any other kind tell us something about their times. In the *Decameron* (1353), Boccaccio used "Put the devil into hell" as a metaphor for sex. Five centuries later, the common expression "forced his attentions on" suggested euphemistically that when it came to sex, dominant men imposed themselves on passive women. Such men *took advantage.* They *had their way.* Women, in turn, *submitted.* They *surrendered.* They *sacrificed their honor.* Or so it was assumed in Victorian times. By contrast what would Queen Victoria make of today's euphemism *friendship with benefits?*

Late in her era *think of England* became a euphemistic way to allude to a certain kind of dutiful sex. It was based on a popular assumption that brides at this time were advised to "Close your eyes, and think of England" when letting their husbands have their way. This advice was so Victorian that it was widely assumed to come from Queen Victoria herself. (It didn't. Among other things, the queen was hardly dutiful.) Wherever this recommendation originated, the image of a compliant young bride lying limply on her honeymoon bed, with eyes shut and a head filled with thoughts of Trafalgar

Square, the Union Jack, and a nice hot cup of tea, was so evocative that *close your eyes and think of England* is still a euphemism for submissive sex.

As sexual euphemisms illustrate better than any others, the hotter the activity, the cooler the language we use to describe it in polite company. Such euphemisms put a placid verbal veneer on the fevered goings-on they describe. In one translation of Herodotus's writing about the Nasamoni of northern Africa, the Greek historian reported, "When a Nasamonian man takes his first wife, it is the custom that on the first night the bride should be visited by each of the guests in turn." According to another translation, the guests "lie" with the bride. Old Testament figures would often *lie* with their wives too, the better to *know* them.

For such a spicy endeavor, the euphemisms we use for sexual activity can be remarkably bland (which is the whole point, of course). In a mid-sixteenth-century book, French physician Ambroise Paré referred to wives being "strongly encountered by their husbands." Pioneering sexologist Ivan Bloch described the case of a late-nineteenth-century British junior officer who visited a superior officer, then "enjoyed his wife on the sofa." This resulted in a *criminal conversation* charge being filed against the younger man, a common euphemism for adultery in England between the seventeenth and nineteenth centuries. *Crim. con.* trials—in which a husband brought charges against his wife's lover—excited much public interest. Reading about them in the press was as close as many respectable Britons could get to consuming pornography.

Of course, it was possible to have a conversation without its being criminal. This is just one of many ordinary words that have been pressed into service as allusions to sex. Consider a sampling of ones that begin with *c: commerce, communion, congress, connect, consort, convene, correspondence, couple, cover. Coital activity* is more specific, as are *coition, carnal knowledge,* and *conjugal relations.* A 1940 study of "Morbid Sex Craving" among women converted *cohabit,* a euphemism for unmarried couples living together, into a much more active concept when discussing a twenty-five-year-old subject who "journeyed to a distant city and cohabited with at least ten of the football squad on the night before the game."

Countless numbers of ordinary words may, or may not, refer to sexual activity, depending on the arch of one's eyebrow. "See" is not an inherently erotic word, unless in the mouth of Mae West inviting Cary Grant to come up sometime and *see* her. Practically any verb can refer to sexual activity in context. Among the many meanings of the word "be" is "fuck." ("I'd like to *be* with you tonight.") "Know" is a perfectly innocent word until used, as it once was, to refer to sexual intercourse. ("She has known man"; "Adam knew his wife...and she conceived.") At one time, this synonym for sex was embellished a bit to *know biblically.* ("They knew each other biblically.") More recently, when a man on the make says "I'd like to get to know you better," a woman at the alert takes precautions.

Even an innocuous word like "it" has erotic overtones when coupled with "do," which is why the song "Let's Do It" was at one time banned from the airwaves. From this perspective, a couple on a bed who are thrashing about, moaning, and shouting ecstatically, "Oh, my God. Yes! Yes! Yes!" are, you know, *doing it.* Sometimes "it" is dropped, leaving *do* as the operative euphemism, as in the woman's magazine article

"Six Guys to Do Before You Say 'I Do.'" Based on such usage, a *Miami Herald* columnist once suggested that this two-letter word should only appear as "d-" in family newspapers.

In the recurring contamination process, though, over time even such innocuous euphemisms can take on the erotic charge of the act they allude to. "Copulate" evolved from a Latin term meaning "join together." (Students in the 1970s, ridiculing the euphemisms of their parents' generation, would ask, "Cop you late? What's that supposed to mean?") "Intercourse" originally referred to interaction between two or more people in the broad sense. At one time, to say "they had intercourse" meant simply "they communicated" or "they interacted" (though that, too, could have sexual connotations nowadays). Today, it would be suggestive in the extreme to say "Jason had some intercourse with Amy."

"Making love" used to refer to little more than some ardent kissy face. In the early twentieth century, it escalated into something more, abetted by D. H. Lawrence's frequent use of this phrase as a euphemism for sex in his fiction. By now, of course, *making love* and its close cousin *lovemaking* are the most genteel of euphemisms for this least genteel of activities. *Sleep with* is perhaps the most venerable euphemism of all, well known to the ancient Greeks and Romans, and featured in a legendary courtroom exchange several centuries later:

"Did you sleep with this woman?"
"Not a wink, your honor."

Go to bed with is a related euphemism, referring to an act that can take place not just on a bed, but also on the floor, in a car, or even inside a telephone booth. Yet what is one to do? As

C. S. Lewis pointed out, when dealing with sex, "you are forced to choose between the language of the nursery, the gutter, and the anatomy class." When discussing this topic in polite company, our options are limited. Slang is out. Childish terms are, well, childish. ("They played doctor.") Clinical words sanitize. One can foreignize, of course, referring to couples who have a *liaison* or a *rendezvous,* which, perhaps due to their Gallic origins, sound somewhat more reputable than their having *an affair* or *an assignation.* In general, though, we are left with all the *it's, do's,* and *be's,* trusting context and knowing looks to convey our meaning.

LADIES OF THE NIGHT

If prostitutes are members of the world's oldest profession, then devising alternative names for them is one of the oldest forms of euphemizing. *Streetwalker*—in use for more than four centuries—is among the most euphemistic. Christian essayist G. K. Chesterton once fretted that referring to women who sold their bodies as simply "ones who walked the streets" condoned this contemptible occupation. Other euphemistic terms that might have concerned Chesterton include *sporting lady, fancy lady, lady of the night, working girl, call girl,* and *party girl.* Perhaps alluding to their status as members of the oldest profession, some prostitutes in his time called themselves *professionals.* When *academy* was a euphemism for "brothel," those who worked there were called *academicians.*

Prostitute first appeared in the early seventeenth century as a euphemism for "whore," one that drew on the Latin verb *prostituere,* or "offer for sale." (A female character in Shakespeare's *Pericles, Prince*

(continued)

of Tyre, says "prostitute me to the basest groom / That doth frequent your house.") *Whore* evolved from the Anglo-Saxon "hore," which some etymologists think may have been a euphemism for a word never recorded. After "whore" took on connotations, sixteenth-century translations of the Bible replaced that word with *harlot.* This term originally referred to a disreputable young man, then was applied to women who liked to kick up their heels, then to prostitutes. In time, "harlot" itself became so contaminated that it could no longer appear in respectable publications.

Another synonym for "prostitute," *tart,* has an interesting etymology. Originally that noun referred to a small pastry, as it still does today. Over time, "tart" was used affectionately for a sweet young woman, then for women considered sexually alluring. After that, "tart" became synonymous with a promiscuous woman. Finally, it referred to women who charged for sexual services, at best "A tart with a heart."

During the American Civil War, *camp followers,* whose ranks included "canteen girls," and "drink sellers," offered soldiers their wares (themselves, mostly). Contrary to popular assumption, the term "hooker" did not originate with camp followers of soldiers commanded by Union General Joseph "Fighting Joe" Hooker. Although it's true that during General Hooker's era, Washington's many prostitutes were sometimes called "Hooker's Division," calling any such woman a *hooker* predates the Civil War by at least a couple of decades. According to lexicographer Stuart Berg Flexner, "hooker" originally referred to prostitutes who worked in Corlear's Hook during the mid-nineteenth century, a section of New York also commonly known as "the Hook." They were *hookers.* Others believe that this appellation originated with the fact that prostitutes said they *hooked* customers. Their brothels were called *hook shops.*

Determining what to call prostitutes has long vexed members of the media. When a play opened in New York in 1934 that included a character called "The Young Whore," one newspaper there changed her designation to "A Young Girl Who has Gone Astray." Three years later, when Bette Davis played a prostitute in *Marked Woman,* her character was called a *nightclub hostess.* In *From Here to Eternity* (1953), the prostitute played by Donna Reed (yes, *that* Donna Reed) was referred to as simply a *hostess.* In the euphemism business, vagueness reigns.

At one time, *model* could be a euphemism for "prostitute." ("Model for hire.") Today, to the dismay of legitimate masseuses, their job title often doubles as such a euphemism. More often, contemporary call girls call themselves *escorts,* a term Amy Fisher—who once worked for an escort service—called "prostitution lite." In the Philippines, *Guest Relation Officer,* or *GRO,* is a euphemism for "prostitute." Teenage girls in Hong Kong, who go on paid "dates" with older men that may involve sex, call this *compensated dating.*

One of the most forlorn euphemisms for compensated sex that I've ever seen was in a news article about South Asian women who'd been laid off from factory jobs. Asked what she and her colleagues were doing now, one said that a young coworker was engaged in "making men happy."

Sex Talk

Early-twentieth-century blues singers vied to see how many sexual allusions they could bootleg into their recordings. In her euphemism-rich "My Handy Man," Ethel Waters probably won this contest when she sang:

He shakes my ashes, greases my griddle,
Churns my butter, strokes my fiddle;
. . .

He threads my needle, creams my wheat,
Heats my heater, chops my meat;
. . .

Waters wasn't the only singer putting euphemisms to song this way. Lizzie Miles's "My Man O' War" included the lines:

He storms my trench and he's not afraid
His bayonets make me cry for aid

And Lillie Mae Kirkman's "He's Just My Size" had:

He's a kitchen mechanic and he makes my biscuits rise
He uses the best baking powder and his biscuit's just my size

Double entendreing this way has kept pace with the times. Only the nomenclature changes, though not always for the better. (See Lady Gaga's "I wanna take a ride on your disco stick" as well as Bloodhound Gang's "Foxtrot Uniform Charlie Kilo," a nonsense title that only means anything if abbreviated, and which features the refrain "Put the you know what in the you know where.") And it isn't just song lyrics. When analyzing Fiona Walker's 1996 novel *Well Groomed*, linguist Kerry Linfoot-Ham found not just the expected candor of sex representation but circumlocutions such as *a lights-out act, the big event,* and *steamy scenes.*

Ever since Erica Jong's 1973 bestseller *Fear of Flying* portrayed a sexually adventurous woman enjoying a "zipless fuck," *zipless* has been the go-to euphemism for spontaneous sexual activity. Based on the popularity of a 1972 pornographic movie by that title, *deep throat* became euphemistic for oral sex (as well as for the secret sources of journalists). Such movies were called "adult entertainment." As a result, the word *adult* became a euphemism for pornography or for sex itself. ("We engaged in some adult activity.")

Because *porne* is Greek for "prostitute," and *pornographos* for "depictions of prostitutes," "pornography" originally referred to writing about whores. Since pornography is seldom discussed openly, least of all by its consumers, euphemisms such as *plain brown wrapper* (for the way pornographic material was discreetly mailed) were common during the pre-Internet era. In the United States, such materials were kept hidden beneath a counter; in the United Kingdom, on a hard-to-see high shelf. As a result *under-the-counter* became an American euphemism for pornography, *top-shelf* its British counterpart. More recently, *sexually explicit media* has established its sterile presence as a euphemism for pornographic material. Some make a distinction between *pornography* (dirty) and *erotica* (clean). Of course, one person's erotica is another person's pornography. Or, to put it somewhat differently, if it turns me on, it's erotic; if it turns you on, it's pornographic.

Initializing has begun to rear its boring head in this area as in so many others. "Oral sex" begat *blow job* which begat *bj.* (In a sexual diary, one young New Yorker talks of "eye-bj-ing" a man.) Other modernisms such as *interrelate, sexual penetration,* and *penile insertive behavior* are also sterilizing our sexual lexicon. Nonetheless, we do have some fun new sexual euphemisms unknown to our ancestors: *donating DNA, exchanging chromosomes,* and *horizontal aerobics.* But Grandpa and Grandma had some colorful terms of their own such as *hoochie coochie, hanky-panky,* and *roll in the hay.* Among Britons, *How's your father?* has long been a euphemism for sex, though no one is sure why.

Hooking up is the most ambiguous of sexual euphemisms, referring to everything from a kiss good night to five-star sex. Recently, this expression has moved more clearly into the sexual column. There was little question about what ABC-TV's Jake Tapper had in mind when — referring to his single date with White House intern Monica Lewinsky — the news correspondent said he'd been looking forward to a "no-frills hookup." (For the record, Tapper confessed that his date with Lewinsky consisted of dinner followed by "a very innocent good-bye.") In the latest twist, "hookup" has become a noun referring to a sex partner. ("I ran into an ex-hookup yesterday.") Or an adjective, as in *a hookup encounter.*

Sex provides unparalleled opportunities for roll-your-own euphemisms, including ones that are spontaneous When an eighteenth-century French noblewoman confessed to her priest that she had "esteem" for a young member of the court, the priest responded, "And how many times has he *esteemed* you?" In *Angela's Ashes,* memoirist Frank McCourt recalled the many nights their mother would tell him and his brothers to go to bed while she took the landlord of their squalid flat a mug of tea in the loft above them. "We often fall asleep before she goes up," he writes, "but there are nights we hear them talking, grunting, moaning. . . . I think they're at the excitement up there."

What was his mother supposed to tell her sons? Parents are faced with the perennial challenge of talking about sex euphemistically with their children. "When a mommy and a daddy love each other very much, they have a special cuddle" is one alternative. Or, "Sometimes we kiss and hug for a very long time." Here as elsewhere, the Internet has pitched in. Musing about what parents might tell their children Lady Gaga means when she says she wants to "take a ride on your disco stick," one blogger suggested they say that "disco stick" refers to a microphone on a stand, "so 'take a ride on your disco stick' means Lady Gaga wants to sing at the mic." Or, that disco sticks are drum sticks hammering out a disco beat, "so saying she wants to 'ride the disco stick' means she wants to play the drums." Or, because disco sticks glow like *Star Wars* light sabers, "saying she wants to 'ride the disco stick' means she wants to fight with light sabers."

Promiscuity

In the not-too-distant past, women whom today we might simply call "sexually active" were called "sluts," "floozies," "hussies," "strumpets," "tramps," or "trollops." They were *loose, fallen, round-heeled, women of easy virtue,* or simply *easy women.* These women *slept around.* They'd *been around the block.* At the very least, they were *promiscuous.*

"Nympho" was a label commonly hung on such women, short for "nymphomania," from the French *nymphomanie,* a term coined in the late-eighteenth century for "a female disease characterized by morbid and uncontrollable sexual desire." Though of dubious scientific validity, this notion caught on with the public. It seemed like an up-to-date, medically sound, and rather titillating way to describe women who engaged in sex freely. The idea that there might be *nymphomaniacs* in our midst excited lots of interest, among men especially. The male equivalent, *satyriasis,* was seldom noted. Aren't all men satyrs? So we liked to think. Men who had many sex partners were just behaving normally. Their female counterparts, on the other hand, had a medical problem.

As Carol Groneman points out in her well-researched book *Nymphomania: A History,* the meaning of this concept changed along with our evolving attitudes toward sex. Groneman considers her subject a metaphor, one that "embodies the fantasies and fears, the anxieties and dangers connected to female sexuality through the ages." Although horror and disgust were the initial response to the notion of nymphomania, by the mid-twentieth century sex researcher Alfred Kinsey had defined a nymphomaniac as "someone who has more sex than you do." Today, some even use "nympho" as a teasing term for women who enjoy sex without guilt. Such women are now considered no worse than *sexually active, sexually expressive,* or *sexually adventurous.* Like priapic men, they might be enjoying some *recreational sex.* They're *sex positive.* You could call them *polyamorous free spirits.* They enjoy *a European lifestyle.*

The euphemisms we use for sexual activity in general have lost their judgmental flavor. "Living in sin" first gave way to *without benefit of clergy,* then *shacking up,* and finally *living together,* which is barely a euphemism at all. Those who engage in the casual encounters that traditionally have been called "one-night stands" can today participate in *short-term mating. Distributive sex* is a lofty term for mating that used to be considered promiscuous. Scholars who study what laypeople call "adultery" or "infidelity" (or "cheating" or "stepping out") call it *extrapair sex.*

The term "sex addict" is a particularly interesting indicator of changing values, since it implies that those who couple compulsively with multiple partners aren't responsible for their own actions. Even though there is little more clinical basis for this notion than there was for nymphomania, it suits our current perspective to imagine that a predilection for constant sex with many partners is a craving that can't be controlled. The concept of sex addiction recast obsessive sexual activity as a disease, not a sin. The fact that, unlike "nymphomania," "sex addiction" can apply to men and women alike is a plus in egalitarian times.

The Solitary Vice

In a rare, delicate reference to female masturbation, a French exile named Moreau de St. Méry wrote about postrevolutionary women in Philadelphia who were stranded in barren marriages, "These women, without real love and without passions, give themselves up at an early age to the enjoyment of themselves." (The Frenchman didn't explain how he knew this.)

This depiction of masturbation was pretty mild for its time. Since fondling one's own genitals was seen as a straight shot to hell or insanity or at least hairy palms, it was called *self-abuse, self-pollution,* or *self-defilement.* (When he first heard of masturbation in the early 1950s, my brother Gene looked it up in an old dictionary. There the practice was defined as "self-pollution," a definition Gene creatively misread as "self-pollination.") The very word "masturbate" most likely derives from a Latin root that essentially means "defile by hand." At best, our ancestors referred to playing with one's genitals as *the solitary vice* or *the secret vice.* Francis Grose defined "toss off" as *manual pollution.* William Byrd called his own self-indulgence *manual uncleanness.* Puritans in Massachusetts considered it "the hideous sin of Onanism." This alluded to Genesis 38:9 wherein, when engaged sexually with the widow of his brother Er, Onan "spilled it [his semen] on the ground." (What Onan most likely engaged in was what today we'd call coitus interruptus.) In the early-eighteenth century, a popular English tract was titled "ONANIA, or the Heinous Sin of Self-Pollution, and All its frightful Consequences, in both Sexes, Consider'd, with Spiritual and Physical Advice to those who have already injur'd themselves by this abominable Practice."

Psychologist G. Stanley Hall warned Victorian era Americans about the consequences of masturbation; these included baldness, chronic coughing, digestive problems, and "a stooping and enfeebled gait." Needless to say, Hall's conclusions were not the result of controlled studies. The eminent psychologist was particularly concerned about hand-in-pocket genital play by boys. He thought that the pockets of their trousers "should be placed well to the side and not too deep," and "habitually keeping the hands in the pockets should be discouraged." Professor Hall probably never heard the vernacular name for this practice — *pocket pool* (or *billiards*) — and most likely would not have been amused if he had.

As tolerance for onanism grew, the flavor of euphemisms referring to this practice lightened up. Following World War II, it was called simply *playing with yourself, relieving yourself, jacking off,* or *beating off.* Soldiers called it *blanket drill.* Men who engaged in this practice were *milkmen.* Or, in England, *wankers.* By now, euphemisms for male masturbation have grown positively playful: *milk the snake, stroke the chicken, crank your shank, yank your crank, varnish your pole.* Men and women alike engage in *killing kittens* (based on another era's warning that "Every time you masturbate, God kills a kitten"). A shorter list for women includes *pet the poodle, flick the bean,* or, in China, *stir the bean curd.*

Since masturbation has come to be seen as a benign, nearly universal, and even desirable entrée on the sexual menu of men and women alike, *self-pleasure* has replaced more pejorative euphemisms. So have *finding out alone, touching yourself,* or simply *self-sexuality.* Or the altogether neutral *sex without a partner.*

Alexander Portnoy — the exuberantly self-pleasuring protagonist of Philip Roth's 1969 novel *Portnoy's Complaint* — loaned out his name as a euphemistic allusion to the kind of autoeroticism that involved a manual aid such as raw liver, his own favorite sex aid. Nearly four decades after the publication of Roth's bestseller, Nancy Franklin wrote in the *New Yorker* about Jon Stewart's "masturbatory" delight in the adulation of his *Daily Show* audience, "as if he were Portnoy and the audience his slab of liver."

If sex engenders so many euphemisms, what about the body parts involved? Wouldn't they be prime candidates for euphemistic lingo too? They are. So are bodies as a whole.

4

Anatomy Class

Since we are all sensitive about the appearance of our bodies (trust me on this), anatomy provides fertile ground for euphemizing. This topic poses considerable linguistic challenges and always has. "In all manners relating to the human body," wrote H. L. Mencken several decades ago, "...euphemisms are common and some of them are very old." At one time, the very word "body" was suspect and gave way to *person*. ("Contraband was found on her person.") A woman who grew up in Michigan after World War II recalled that while in grade school, she and her classmates referred to the *upper peninsula* and *lower peninsula* of their bodies.

For those whose bodies deviate from the norm—which is to say nearly all of us—euphemisms are welcome. Balding men can be said to have *high foreheads*. Wrinkled faces feature *character lines*. Then there's the matter of weight. When it comes to those whom airlines call *people of size*, euphemisms are in constant demand. Ever since the Dutch painter Peter Paul Rubens reverently painted women who would today be considered candidates for gastric bypass, *Rubenesque* has been a polite term for women carrying extra pounds, one with artistic and vaguely erotic overtones. *Voluptuous* does similar duty, as do *shapely, curvaceous,* and the Yiddish term *zaftig.* *Pleasingly plump* lacks sexy flavor, as do *buxom, generously proportioned, big-boned,* and *fluffy.* Such terms do keep us from having to say "fat," though. In a pinch, there's also *ample, plus size,* or *queen size.*

In one of Alexander McCall Smith's mystery novels, Precious Ramotswe, the "traditionally built" Botswana detective, is described as "more traditionally built than ever—a wide expanse of woman, bulging like the continent of Africa itself." When Mma Ramotswe is told politely by her mechanic-husband that the suspension problem in her minivan may be due to "distribution of load," she ponders this message, then says, "And the load, I take it . . . is me?"

For their part, men needn't be "fat" when they can be *burly, hefty, portly, rotund,* or *stocky. Sturdy* and *stout* have the advantage of suggesting *stalwart. Stout* also refers to a rich type of beer and to a courageous sort of man, one who is *stouthearted.*

Calling ample waists *love handles* is not gender linked. Nor is *bay window* for a potbelly, *spare tire* for an expansive midsection, or *well upholstered* for the generally overweight. Such terms are usually reserved for men, however. At the other end of the scale, cadaverous women who verge on anorexia can be called *willowy, svelte,* or simply *slender.* At worst, they are *skinny.* Little women are politely called *petite,* although one small character in a Rona Jaffe novel disdained this adjective as "a euphemism for getting stuck with all the short boys on blind dates."

"Short" is not a nice word. Among men who don't feel tall

enough, it can be seen as provocative, a fighting word even. *Compact* is more tactful, as is *trim* or *diminutive*. (*Vertically challenged* is a gag euphemism that I've never seen or heard in actual use.) One class of neoeuphemisms consists of words that allude to shortness without spelling it out. Terms such as *dapper* or *natty* or *scrappy* have nothing to do with body size per se but are seldom used for taller men. A description such as "He is thin and spry and has a kindly, elfin air" could only refer to a man who is short. *Feisty* is often applied to contentious small men but rarely to tall ones. (The etymology of this term is none too flattering. It is based on "feist," a southernism for a small, yappy dog who has more bark than bite.) At five feet five inches tall, French president Nicholas Sarkozy can be called *feisty* and is. At six feet six inches tall, his equally contentious predecessor Charles de Gaulle was not. Men like de Gaulle are typically described as *stately, distinguished, formidable,* or *imposing. Imperious* is the closest thing to a pejorative allusion to tall men in a society that looks up to them. Tall women are *majestic, regal,* or *Junoesque. Amazonian* is ambiguous, a term that can be complimentary or insulting, depending on tone of voice and curl of lip.

Midriffs

When Moreau de St. Méry spent time in America after the revolution, the French exile was struck by how reluctant American women were to mention specific parts of their bodies, even when seeking medical help. A nursing mother he met in Philadelphia had developed painfully cracked nipples. She couldn't bring herself to tell her doctor what the real problem was, however, instead saying she had stomach pains. According to St. Méry, American women at this time called the section from waist to feet their "ankles"; and from waist to neck, their "stomach."

Deciding what name to give the digestive organ in our midsection has long posed problems. Even though this had been called a belly with perfect aplomb for centuries, that word eventually succumbed to bourgeois sensibilities. "Belly" was a perfectly functional word. It just didn't *sound* respectable. Under Sophia Hawthorne's busy blue pencil, "belly" was changed to *rotundity* or *paunch* any time it appeared in her husband Nathaniel's journals. An Englishman named J. S. Buckingham, who visited southern states before the Civil War, heard a preacher in Athens, Georgia, reword the Genesis 3:14 passage in which the serpent is commanded "upon thy belly shalt thou go," to "upon thy stomach shalt thou go." When a French physician asked a Victorian Englishwoman if she was feeling pain in her belly, the elderly woman grew flustered. After regaining her composure, she told the doctor that he should avoid using that dreadful word when treating English patients. And what word should he use instead? "Stomach," the woman replied.

So *stomach* it was. Once again, a word rooted in Latin (*stomachos*) elbowed aside a sturdy Anglo-Saxon antecedent. Not even belly dancers were exempt. The first English edition of Oscar Wilde's 1894 play *Salome* featured a drawing by Aubrey Beardsley of a topless belly dancer titled "The Stomach Dance." As late as 1962, during a performance of Rodgers and Hammerstein's *Carousel* for Britain's royal family, the line, "Our hearts are warm, our bellies full" became "Our hearts are warm, and we are full."

Why not simply say "our stomachs are full"? Perhaps

because by then the contamination effect had kicked in and "stomach" was a bit outré. Following World War I, H. L. Mencken noted that "stomach" had become an "outlaw" term in England. "No Englishman of good breeding, save he be far gone in liquor, ever mentions his stomach in the presence of women, clergymen, or the Royal family," wrote Mencken. American stomachs were another matter. According to Mencken, his countrymen discussed this body part as freely as they talked about their business. Moreover, he said, in the United States, "stomach" was used "with a degree of respect verging upon reverence," doubling "as a euphemism for the whole region from the diaphragm to the pelvic arch."

On both sides of the Atlantic, some preferred *tummy, tum-tum, breadbasket,* or *Little Mary* when talking about their digestive organ. A half century after H. L. Mencken ruminated on stomachs, lexicographer James McDonald concluded that the English were "now fairly evenly divided between those who talk of *tummies* and find words like *guts* and *belly* offensive, and those who talk of *guts* and *bellies* and find words like *tummy* offensive."

Of course, they could always refer vaguely to their *midriff* or *midsection,* as some do, or resort to quasimedical euphemisms such as *abdomen.* This term has sometimes been used for male genitals, particularly in the form *lower abdomen.* In his 1971 play *The Basic Training of Pavlo Hummel,* David Rabe wrote of a wounded soldier who tells a companion that he's been hit in "the abdominal and groin areas." His companion responds, "Don't you talk that shit to me. Abdominal and groin areas, that shit. It hit you in the stomach, man, like a ten-ton truck, and it hit you in the balls, blew 'em away."

Mammary Glands

Mammary glands are another popular source of euphemism and have been for centuries. Even though *teat* was used freely in the King James Version of the Bible, that Anglo-Saxonism did not pass muster with Noah Webster. In Isaiah 32:12, Webster revised "They shall lament for the teats" to "They shall lament for the breasts."

Breast was an acceptable substitute for "teat" in Webster's time. Even the highly euphemistic Jane Austen used that term in her writing. By the mid-nineteenth century, however, direct reference to women's breasts was considered too likely to bring them to mind. In *Vanity Fair,* William Makepeace Thackeray portrayed two men considering the "frontal development" of curvy Becky Sharp. To fastidious speakers, what was previously known as a "breast-pin" now became a *bosom-pin.* Well into the twentieth century, BBC announcers could refer to "the breast" but not to "breasts." On *The Smothers Brothers Comedy Hour,* Tommy Smothers and Elaine May mocked this sensibility with a 1967 skit in which May's line, "My pulse beats wildly in my breast whenever you're near," is bowdlerized by censors to "My pulse beats wildly in my wrist whenever you're near." CBS deleted that segment.

Alternatives to "breasts" included *bust* and *bosoms* (pluralizing *bosom,* which took in the mammary glands and some chest muscles as well). *Charms* became a rather cheery euphemism for breasts in early-nineteenth-century England, far more appealing than its predecessors *dairies* and *milky ways.* In time, equally vague but less appealing terms appeared, such as *a pair* or *assets.* Or *physique* or *torso.* ("Great torso she's got!") Here as elsewhere, an age-old strategy involves using the name of a respectable body part euphemistically for one that's more suspect: *lungs* for "breasts," *kidneys* for "testicles," or *feet* for sex organs (a common biblical dodge). Employing a term that stands in for other ticklish body parts — *equipment* — busty actress Raquel Welch once commented that her childhood nickname of "Bird legs" gave way to *Rocky,* then *Hot Rocks* "after the equipment arrived."

A multitude of nouns can refer to breasts so long as they are preceded by "pair," "two," or "set." Movie critic Joe-Bob Briggs liked to talk of busty starlets who were cast in movies because of their "two enormous talents." In George Pelecanos's novel *The Big Blowdown,* a man says of actress Carole Landis that "she's got this beautiful set of personalities." Another character had previously said that Landis "has this set of tits on her like..." In common parlance, *tit* became a contraction of "teat" during the Middle Ages. Over time, this three-letter word grew taboo enough that proper speakers thought twice before using terms such as "tit-bit" or "titmouse." Today, *tits* are back, along with *boobs,* as common conversational fare (among friends, anyway). A contemporary breast-cancer-awareness program is called "Save the Boobs." On theboobblog, a big-breasted New Yorker writes of the "titiquette" she wishes men would observe when confronted with her chest. According to the Urban Dictionary, "Proper titiquette dictates that one does not look for longer than one full second." Frustrated by the longer looks men continually gave her own ample breasts, a woman I know tried explaining to a male friend that "big boobs" like hers were nothing more than fatty tissue. "Men love b-i-i-g fatty tissues," he responded.

As long as men and women alike are obsessed with them,

mammary glands will challenge our vocabularies. Despite their increasing respectability, *boobs* and *tits* are still rather risqué terms, as are *jugs, tatas,* and *cowabungas.* Other than "breast" itself—a word that remains dodgy in some circumstances—what can we safely call this body part? When breasts are in the news, journalists must improvise. After a picture of Barack Obama's speechwriter Jon Favreau caressing the chest of a life-size Hillary Clinton cutout circulated on the Internet, columnist Kathleen Parker was reduced to writing that Favreau had been figuratively "captured clutching the prospective secretary of state's, um, pectoral area."

Private Parts

Proper Victorian women went to great lengths to cover their entire anatomy below the chin. They took care not only to conceal but even to avoid looking at certain body parts. These women minded the counsel of German educator Johann Heinrich Campe who once referred to "secret parts of our bodies," ones we should "not merely keep...secret from everyone but also from ourselves." *Parts of shame* some called them. Should there be a need to mention such parts, euphemistic words did important camouflage duty.

Private parts is the most useful euphemism for this group as a whole and has been for centuries. A 1615 book of advice for housewives suggested that for "disease of the private parts," one should "Take a great handful of orpines [an herb], and bruise them between your hands till they be like a salve, and then lay them upon a cloth and bind them to the fundament." This book also included a recipe for a poultice to use when "any man have his privy parts burned." In time, *parts* alone became sometime shorthand for "genitals." More often, it is shortened to *privates. Privities* was a highfalutin' version meant to sound somewhat scholarly.

Loins was good enough for the King James Bible, eventually giving way to the even more euphemistic *crotch, groin, nether parts, down south,* or *down below.* This reflects a sense that certain parts of the anatomy just below the waist are not ones to be proud of. The more clinical term "pudenda" is adapted from the Latin terms *pudere,* which means "to cause shame," *pudendum,* "that of which one ought to be ashamed," and *pars pudenda,* "shameful part." *Genitalia* is another Latin term, one that transformed "genitals"—in use since the Middle Ages—into a word that sounds hygienic enough to be used by doctors and laymen alike without fear of sounding lewd.

Counseling children on what to call their genitalia poses a particular problem for parents who have boys and girls. Some just go with "penis" and "vagina." Others consider those names too clinical and roll their own. One mom settled on *twiggy* for her daughter's vagina, *twaggy* for her son's penis. Another used *lou la* for her daughter, *tink a link* for her sons. *Wee wee bum* and *widger* were the respective euphemisms in one family, *piggy* and *punky* in a second, *peggy* and *winkie* in a third. *Tossle* and *woodle* are used by some Australian parents. Those who rely on *winkie* and *boo-boo* risk problems, however, since the latter is so often used as kid talk for wounds of various sorts.

Some euphemisms can refer both to male and female sex organs. Figs, for example—long considered an unusually erotic fruit—were used that way by Aristophanes in his poem "The Peace":

Pick your figs,
May his be large and hard,
May hers be sweet.

In one of his sonnets, Shakespeare used the word "will" to refer alternately to male and female sex organs. *Gear* is a more recent euphemism for both genders' genitalia. *Thing* can also be used bisexually, as can *whachamacallit,* and the ever-useful *it. Anatomy* refers to either one. ("He pulled out his anatomy." "I caught a glimpse of her anatomy.") *Tail* was once used both for men's and women's genitals. At one time *cock* was synonymous with "vagina" in parts of the American South. In that region, *boody*—an Elizabethan era play on "body"—was first euphemistic for either gender's sex organ, then for women's alone. Although *organ* can swing both ways, it most often swings in the male direction. According to one old story, when a woman on the witness stand in court was asked if the defendant had "introduced his organ," she replied, "It was more like a flute, your honor."

Weaponry

What one calls a penis depends, of course, on where and when one lives. According to classicist J. N. Adams, ancient Romans had at least 120 synonyms for this body part. They included Latin words for "instrument," "branch," "throat," and "worm." One Latin term, *telum,* could alternately mean "penis," "tool," or "weapon." Weapons provided the most metaphors for penis, including the word "weapon" itself, and often figured in double entendre–based jokes. In one, a Roman man being frisked by another tells the frisker that he should be careful lest he find a weapon other than the one he's looking for.

Daggers, lances, stakes, and swords were an especially popular source of synonyms for "penis." (The fact that the sharp points of such implements could prick probably led to that English word being synonymous with "penis" for at least the past four centuries.) Ancient Romans used plants with stalks as metaphors for "penis," including cabbage (*caulis*) and spearmint (*mentula*). *Tool* has also referred to the penis since then and still enjoys great popularity among English speakers, perhaps because in Protestant-ethic cultures this synonym equates sex with work.

Since it's more vague, *member* is even more useful as a euphemism, as in this translation of Montaigne's musing on the penis: "We are right to note the license and disobedience of this member which thrusts itself forward so inopportunely when we do not want it to, and which so inopportunely lets us down when we most need it."

When it comes to naming penises, the United States and the United Kingdom part company. *Willy* is the most popular of many names given English penises, *Dick* and *Peter* that of Americans. As an itinerant preacher discovered to his dismay, "Peter" was so closely linked with "penis" among residents of the Ozark Mountains that when he mentioned Peter's denial of Christ, then shouted, "How many Peters are there here?" he was greeted by shocked silence.

Some men take the initiative and name their own penises. Lyndon Johnson was one. According to biographer Robert

Caro, even in college the future president "displayed great pride in his sexual apparatus," often returning from dates to tell his roommates, "Jumbo had a real workout tonight." In other cases, it's a mate who does the naming. Elmore Leonard's novel *Road Dogs* features a Cuban gangster whose girlfriend calls his penis "little Ricky" when it is limp, "Ricardo" when erect. ("We'll be saying hi to your one-eyed buddy Ricardo.") One inventive woman calls her husband's beneath-the-sheet erection *Omar the tentmaker.*

Johnson is the last name most often used for the male sex organ. According to one theory, this slangy euphemism originated with the name of a large railroad brake lever. Lexicographer Eric Partridge thought it was more likely an abbreviated version of *Dr. Johnson,* a onetime synonym for "penis" that Partridge said might be based on the assumption that "there was no one Dr. [Samuel] Johnson was not prepared to stand up to." Working under the verbal restraints of his times, Partridge said this synonym was for the "membrum virile."

Rodney is sometimes mentioned in the torrent of spam e-mails that offer to help men enlarge and recharge their *membrum virile.* So is *King Kong.* ("Make your King Kong twice larger.") Some of these pitches show impressive euphemistic flair: *Charge your trouser warrior! Invest in your wang! Excite your pistol! Upsize your manhood! Boost your donger's staying power! Tired of having a peanut in your pants? Tired of girls searching for your little friend in bed and not being able to find it? Your little friend looks like a dwarf? Time to decide whether you want a bigger pride. Your big proud friend in the pants will overshadow the Empire State Building. She will not need a magnifying glass anymore to find your instrument. Your instrument will be so large you will be able to touch the ceiling with it.*

Testicles

When testicles are in the news, broadcasters are forced to improvise. I recently watched a TV announcer report that a male basketball player had been bumped "in a painful area." After the *Today* show's Meredith Vieira accidentally kicked cohost Matt Lauer in the groin during taping, weatherman Al Roker exclaimed, "My goodness, right in the peppercorns!"

Of course, it's not just testicles per se but what they represent that requires euphemizing on the air. During news coverage of Illinois governor Rod Blagojevich's audacious maneuvering to avoid impeachment, one CNN analyst said, "There's a term you can use for this. It involves a male part…[what] an old football coach of mine would refer to as 'intestinal fortitude.'" A colleague chimed in, "Or as we would say in Spanish, '*cojones.*'" A few days later, ABC commentator George Will wondered if contemporary political figures had the "kidneys" to make tough decisions. When an Internet commentator subsequently questioned whether Democrats "have the low-hangers necessary to walk away from FOX [News]," he explained in a footnote that *low-hangers* was "a euphemism for intestinal fortitude, cojones, stones, balls, scrotal presumption, gonads, testicles, manliness…"

To name just a few. Other euphemisms for this body part include *marbles, gonads,* and, of course, *family jewels.* No synonym has proved more durable than *nuts,* however. James McDonald thinks this probably is a clip of *nutmegs,* a longtime synonym for testicles. After movie censors decreed that "nuts" could not appear in screenplays, this word was dutifully deleted from one script after another (prompting one frustrated screenwriter to substitute *almonds* for "nuts").

When Jesse Jackson was inadvertently recorded off-camera telling a TV interviewer that he wanted to cut off Barack Obama's "nuts," demonstrating with slashing hands what he had in mind, journalists were faced with a dilemma. Exactly what body part of Obama's could they say Jackson wanted to delete? "His you-know-what" said one cable news reporter. His "manhood" reported another. In her *New York Times* column, Maureen Dowd referred to "a sensitive part of Obama's anatomy." On MSNBC, a commentator said that Jackson had threatened "to do something to Barack Obama [long pause] that wasn't exactly painless, shall we say." According to a blogger, Jackson wanted to "expunge Obama's manhood."

Like modern newscasters and bloggers, ancient Romans sometimes classified this male body part broadly under the term *manhood* (especially when referring to the loss of same among castrated men). "Testicle" is based on the Latin term *testis,* meaning "witness." "Testis" apparently is the common root for "testicles," "testimony," and "testify," presumably because it was a common practice in ancient times for men to clutch their testicles or those of a monarch when swearing an oath. Noting the male basis of these terms, a feminist once proposed *ovarimony* as an alternative to "testimony."

A biblical euphemism for testicles was *thigh,* as when a dying Jacob said to Joseph in Genesis 24:2, "Put, I pray thee, thy hand under my thigh...bury me not in Egypt." Another ancient synonym for testicles—one that appeared in John Wycliffe's 1382 translation of the Bible—is *ballocks,* adapted from the Old English *bealluc.* "Bollocks" was, and is, a swear word in England, one that spawned the adjective *bollocky* or *ballocky.* Although the original version of a venerable song referred to "Ballocky Bill the Sailor," this eventually was sanitized to "Barnacle Bill the Sailor." Another spin-off of "bollocks" was *bollixed up,* a phrase many of us use quite innocently without realizing its racy root.

Stones is a longtime synonym for testicles, one that appeared often in the King James Bible. Noah Webster did not approve, of course, revising a reference to "the sinewe of his stones" in Job 40:17 to "the sinews of his male organs," and "hath his stones broken" in Leviticus 21:20 to "hath his peculiar members broken." By the mid-nineteenth century, many Americans found the once-respectable word "stones" too tainted for common use. This called for a euphemism for that euphemism, leading to confusion among visitors from abroad. During his tour of southern states before the American Civil War, J. S. Buckingham was told of an incident in which a student threw a rock at the president of the University of Georgia, hitting him in the head. Since in his native England "rock" referred to a large stone, Buckingham commented that this student must have been Hercules-like. Oh no, his female host responded, it was but a small rock and did little harm. Only then did the Englishman realize that this woman was using "rock" instead of "stone," presumably because of the latter word's association with testicles.

Men's genitals consist of three distinct parts: the penis, scrotum, and testicles, facilitating the euphemism process. Women's genitals are a bit more complicated, comprising the overall pudenda, the outer labia minora and majora, and the inner vagina and vulva (as well as the hymen and clitoris). Since this is a powerful lot of words to consider, we typically use "vagina" synonymously with them all and devote a lot of ingenuity to developing euphemisms for that touchy term.

Vagina

In an old English tale, an aristocratic young woman went horseback riding, accompanied by her groom, John. Along the way, she fell off her horse, feet flying in the air and petticoats dropping. Quickly jumping to her feet, the young woman asked, "Did you see my agility, John?"

"Yes, miss," replied her groom, "but I never heard it called by that name before."

And what names might he have heard? In Elizabethan times, it could have been *commodity, slit, cut, breach,* or *the king's highway*. In his 1785 *Dictionary of the Vulgar Tongue,* Francis Grose included *money* (defined as "A girl's private parts, commonly applied to little children: as, Take care, Miss, or you will shew your money"), *pitcher* ("The miraculous pitcher, that holds water with the mouth downwards: a woman's commodity"), and *hat* ("A woman's privities: because frequently felt"). In addition to *monosyllable,* Grose sometimes used **** in place of *cunt*. During a long-ago court case that he reported, a woman on the witness stand referred to her gender's *cauliflower*. The presiding judge reprimanded this witness, saying she might as well call that private part an artichoke. "Not so, my lord," she replied, "for an artichoke has a bottom, but a **** and a cauliflower have none."

This woman's invention drew on a long tradition of substituting horticultural euphemisms for the vagina. They include *cabbage, mushroom, split fig,* and *sweet potato pie*. When *papaya* became slang for vagina in Cuba, another name was conjured for that fruit among polite speakers: *fruta de bomba*. (Stories have been told of tourists asking a Cuban fruit vendor for a papaya, only to be angrily told that he was no pimp.) In Japan, *the clam that shrinks* is a vaginal metaphor comparable to English speakers' *the bearded clam*. Other living creatures whose names have provided synonyms for the vagina include not just kittens and beavers but snails as well. In Herta Müller's *The Land of Green Plums,* a Romanian woman travels to Hungary with a bag of smuggled gold "stuffed up her snail." ("I wouldn't buy gold that had been in the snail of some woman," comments the novel's narrator.)

As compared to the more assertive synonyms for "penis," substitute names for women's sexual organs tend to be softer, gentler, more classically euphemistic. The 650 terms John Farmer and William Henley recorded in their late-nineteenth-century compilation of slang included *mossy bank, lamp of love,* and *lowlands.* The same book had just half as many synonyms for "penis." This reflects the fact that in most eras and settings, discussion of the female sex organ is more taboo than discussion of that of the male. A study commissioned by the BBC and others at the turn of this century found that participants considered "cunt" the most vulgar English word in common use. ("Fuck" was third, "prick" seventh.) A survey of ticklish body parts conducted by linguists Keith Allan and Kate Burridge determined that the vagina was the most difficult one for participants to mention by any name. This taboo is illustrated in a passage of Richard Russo's novel *Mohawk,* which depicts a low-life couple insulting each other. The woman repeatedly refers to the man's *weeny.* That man, however, in the author's words, used "a simple four letter word to describe his companion and it is a part of her own anatomy."

"Vagina" originated as Latin slang based on the word for

sheath, the receptacle in which Roman soldiers inserted their swords. (Little girls in ancient Rome were told to call this organ their *piggy.*) From its slangy roots, this term became standard issue after being adopted by medieval anatomists. "So, thanks to similes and early anatomists," writes Catherine Blackledge in *The Story of V: A Natural History of Female Sexuality,* "humans have sex with sheaths and tails. It could have been worse, though; it could have been a combination of the king's highway and cabbage stalks."

In a study of how vaginas are referred to in contemporary England, men proved far more willing than women to use slang synonyms. Women preferred vague euphemisms such as *down below, downstairs, middle,* and, of course, *private parts.* One Englishwoman was embarrassed to discover that when taken to a hospital after injuring her genitals on the crossbar of a bicycle, she couldn't think of any non-euphemistic word for that part of her body. "My mum used to call it a tuppence," recalls another. A third woman's mum apparently placed less value on this body part. "When I went out in my teens," her daughter recalls, "I was told to keep your hands on your half-penny and everybody else's off!"

According to an old jest, one James Joyce incorporated into *Ulysses,* when women of a certain age bathed standing erect, they first washed up as far as possible, then down as far as possible, then washed "old possible." From *bits* to *down there,* when it comes to euphemisms for the vagina, blandness reigns. Gloria Steinem once referred to herself as a member of the "down there generation." A participant in an online woman's forum who still used "down there," added, "I did just think of saying 'down in Virginia,' while pointing my finger downward and slightly lowering my head." Another said she hated the coyness of "down there" or "private bits" and stuck to "vagina." But this word was hard for her little girl to pronounce, one participant found. She first said "bachina," then shortened it to "China," and "we have both been happy with Chinas ever since!!!" her mom reported.

Several mothers who took part in this forum agreed that "vagina" was a bit clinical for their young daughters but were at a loss for a better alternative. "I'm going with . . . 'girl parts' for now," said one. Another reported that her daughter calls it her *stuff.* According to a third mom, since their family calls her son's penis his *peepee,* that's what her daughter calls her vagina. The mother of a three-year-old said that while frolicking in a spray fountain, her daughter announced, "Mommy, my cooch is getting wet!" (This semicommon euphemism could derive from the Arabic *cush* or the Sanskrit *cushi,* meaning "ditch," a synonym for "vagina.")

With so little guidance from society, those who need to refer to this body part sometimes simply roll their own euphemisms. Some of the more colorful inventions include *mussintouchit, pookalolly pie, the love cavern, squishy,* and *split knish.* One woman calls her vagina *Rochester* because that's where she lost her virginity. Another calls hers *the downtown dining and recreation district.*

More recent euphemisms draw on new resources. Due to modern depilation methods, we're now able to talk comfortably about the *wax line, bikini line,* or *bikini zone.* An Oprah-endorsed attempt to have *vajayjay* become the preferred synonym for "vagina" hasn't caught on despite being used in an episode of *Grey's Anatomy* in which a pregnant doctor in labor tells a male intern, "Stop looking at my vajayjay." Euphemisms don't lend themselves to that type of self-conscious coinage. *Vag* (or *vaj*) has gained some traction recently, mostly among younger women. A universally acceptable euphemism for female genitalia has yet to be agreed on.

HAZARDOUS TRAVEL CONDITIONS

My friend Louise discovered the hazards of trans-Atlantic euphemizing when she left San Diego to visit an expat sister in London during the mid-1970s. Her sister invited some English friends to tea. "We were talking about family resemblances (and the fact that I didn't resemble anyone in my family at all)," reported Louise, "and I remarked that my family had been so desperate to find a resemblance that they would say that I 'had Aunt Harriet's fanny.' A dozen china teacups hit their saucers simultaneously as jaws dropped. Finally one woman asked, 'How on earth would they know?'"

What Louise didn't realize was that, while *fanny* refers to the buttocks among Americans, in the United Kingdom it's slang for "vagina."

The names of certain body parts have long posed problems when Brits and Yanks converse. During their Golden Age of Euphemism, Americans called the breast nipple a *cone*. "The American 'cone' is the English 'nipple,'" author Sir Richard Burton told British readers in 1863. "Beg pardon for the indelicacy!" Eventually, Americans reverted to *nipple* for that part of the breast, then made this word do double duty as the suckable part of a baby bottle. In Great Britain, "nipple" refers only to the organic version.

Louise learned about this contrast when she told her sister's British friends about bringing her son Dan home from an adoption agency. She had difficulty feeding him because the bottle that Dan's foster

(continued)

mother had given her had a clogged nipple. "Finally, after an hour of desperation listening to my tiny screaming infant," Louise told her sister's friends, "I resolved this problem by sticking a toothpick into the nipple to unclog it.

"There was that same look of horror," she later recalled. "The guests had been totally confused by the story, as there people have *nipples* and bottles have *teats*. Sticking a toothpick into one's nipple was an image that had them almost swooning with pain. By the way, *nipple* isn't a word used at a formal tea anyway. VERY vulgar!"

Then there's the *pecker*. In Britain this synonym for the nose was featured in a hearty exhortation to be in good spirits: "Keep your pecker up!" Among Americans, for whom *pecker* is slang for "penis," that's an advisory to be ready for sex.

Sexual euphemisms can be no less dicey than anatomical ones along the trans-Atlantic linguistic divide. When my wife, Muriel, studied at the University of Newcastle-upon-Tyne, a classmate who was about to spend time in the United States startled her by inquiring, "If I ask the blokes over there to knock me up, will I go down well?" This young woman thought she was asking Muriel whether inviting young men to call on her would enhance her popularity. But, as Muriel explained, in American parlance, she was saying, "If I ask men to get me pregnant, will I do well at sex?"

The divergent meaning of any number of euphemisms poses problems for English speakers who visit each others' countries. An American tourist who refers to something British as *top shelf,* meaning "first rate," would startle natives for whom *top shelf* refers to pornographic material that news dealers keep high and out of sight.

Names of apparel items can also be problematic, as my friend Louise discovered toward the end of her London tea. "I regaled them with the story of the torrential rains that had fallen in San Diego that winter," she recalls. "At one point, the water was so deep in the street that in order to get to my car, I was forced to take off my shoes, roll up my pants, and wade to it. By now, I was getting familiar with the crashing teacups routine and knew I'd said something wrong again. My sister immediately jumped in. 'She means she rolled up her trousers.' I had treated them to the image of me rolling up my underpants."

"After my intent was clarified, one woman said, 'Well, you *do* come from California.' No wonder I·was never invited back."

Behind

When Lord Methuen was shot in the buttocks during the Boer War, a military communiqué said he'd been wounded in the *fleshy part of the thigh* so as not to suggest that the British field marshal had been facing backward when shot.

For a long time, "arse" was standard English for this body part. The fact that Samuel Johnson included this word in his 1755 dictionary raised few eyebrows. Johnson did delicately define "bum" as "the part on which we sit" (leading one critic to ask, "Do you mean a chair, Doctor?"). This definition may have inspired subsequent euphemisms for the behind such as *sit upon, sit me-down,* and *sit-me-down-upon* that were once popular in Britain. Perhaps coincidentally, the word "chair" itself took on connotations in the nineteenth century and gave way to *seat.*

Although "ass" was initially a politer form of "arse," both words fell victim to language cleansing to such an extent that the animal once known as an "ass" became a *donkey* to many. Instead of calling an obnoxious individual a "jackass," one proper Englishwoman took to calling such a person a *Johnny bum.* According to Francis Grose, this woman "would not say Jack, because it was vulgar, nor ass because it was indecent."

"Buttocks" has proved durable as the most respectable term for this body part. "Bum" occupies a verbal purgatory in England and Canada: not quite respectable nor outrageously offensive. As recently as the Depression era, however, Al Jolson's 1933 film *Hallelujah, I'm a Bum* was retitled *Hallelujah, I'm a Tramp* in Britain.

Referring to the buttocks and the anus has always posed problems during polite conversation. In their survey of ticklish body parts, Allan and Burridge found that the anus (another Latinism) ranked second only to the vagina as the least mentionable anatomical feature. This is an area where foreignisms really earn their keep. Reviewing euphemisms for the buttocks (or "butt") is like a short course in foreign languages. Consider *derriere, heinie,* and *culo.* Even the nursery word *tooky* comes from the Yiddish *tokhes* (from the Hebrew *tachat,* or "underneath"), also known as the *tushie* or *tush.* Such terms can be uttered with nary a twitch of the lip by English speakers who might studiously avoid saying "ass," "arse," "butt," "bum," "buns," "can," "rump," "seat," "tail," "rear end," or even "behind." In a mid-1930s *New York Times* ad, Bonwit Teller responded to an inquiry from a woman who wanted to flatten her figure. "This question is posed most frequently by women who have large *derrieres,*" observed Bonwit.

Another synonym for the buttocks is *keister.* Ronald Reagan was particularly partial to this mock-foreign term that may derive from *kiste,* a German word for a "box" or a "chest." A modern verb, *to keister,* means "to hide something in one's rectum." ("I keistered those joints and sailed right through customs.")

The common use of *bottom* as a euphemism for "arse" has caused much anguish among the world's Bottomleys, Ramsbottoms, Winterbottoms, Higginbottoms, and Hickinbottoms, leading some of them to take refuge in respelled versions such as Higginbotham and Hickinbotham. (The "bottom" in those names actually drew on an earlier use of that word for "bottomlands.") In a yarn recounted by Robert Graves, an English prankster invited a group of notables with bottom-based names to a formal dinner, one at which rump steak was served, then watched in delight as the name of each guest was announced before he made an early exit.

One reason that body parts are so ticklish to talk about has nothing to do with their anatomical delicacy or even their sexual functions and everything to do with the liquids and gases that emerge from them. In an evolutionary anomaly, body parts such as the behind and the genitalia are used both for sex and secretion. This makes them doubly difficult to discuss. If anything, the elimination of body wastes is even more embarrassing to talk about than sex. As a result, it is one of our leading sources of euphemisms.

5

Secretions and Excretions

AFTER HARRY TRUMAN became our thirty-third president, a woman was said to have pleaded with his wife, Bess, to clean up her husband's language. He'd recently called someone's comment "a bunch of horse manure." The First Lady reportedly smiled and responded, "You don't know how many years it took to tone it down to that."

No less than in the arenas of sex and anatomy, when referring to bodily functions we protect ourselves with well-armored euphemisms. Any substance emerging from the body is fair game: gases, liquids, solids. Latin-based words come to the rescue when we need to discuss such phenomena: "urine," "feces," "perspire," "expectorate," "regurgitate," to name just a few. Medical terms such as "micturate" and "specimen" draw on Latin. So do "excrete" and "excrement," both based on *excrementum,* which means "what is sifted out." "Defecate" is another Latinism, one that referred broadly to eliminating impurities, until more than a century ago when it began to emphasize the elimination of human waste. On the eve of this transition, in 1867, James Russell Lowell wrote about the tendency among Britons to restrict language and "defecate it of all emotion."

Words used for bodily functions reflect social standing. Refined people never "spit" but do sometimes *expectorate*—*saliva* or *sputum*, not "spittle." Their noses don't harbor "snot" and certainly not "boogers" but might contain *mucus*. They don't "belch" but do *burp* on occasion. Better mouths never "throw up" and certainly wouldn't "upchuck," "retch," "barf," "spew," "puke," "hurl," or "hug the throne" but at times do *regurgitate, purge,* or, in a pinch, *vomit*. Or, when feeling nauseous, fastidious speakers might simply *be sick*. Should that happen on an airplane, they're grateful for what used to be known as "vomit bags" and are now called *sickness bags,* ones available for use by those who experience *motion discomfort*.

It used to be said that "Horses sweat, men perspire, and ladies glow." As this chestnut suggests, there was once some question about whether refined women perspired at all. Questioning an advisory to wear wool to absorb perspiration, a Victorian era commentator wrote, "But surely a gentlewoman rarely does anything to cause such an unpleasant thing!" Some held the verbal line, however. Imagine Winston Churchill in 1940 offering Britons nothing more than "blood, toil, tears, and perspiration." Or worse yet, "blood, toil, tears, and wetness."

Why such delicacy?

It seems obvious that a disgusting topic such as body waste cries out for euphemizing. Yet bodily wastes are not revolting to animals, nor to children fascinated by their boogers, saliva, and farts. Infants are no more offended by shit than pets are (as any parent and dog owner can attest). One study of three-year-olds found that most actually liked the smell of their own feces. Few adults do. Most find this an extremely revolting substance. Reviewers of the 2006 movie *Black Book* were less appalled by episodes in which hundreds of innocents are slaughtered, including a boatload of defenseless Jews trying to flee occupied Holland for Belgium, than by one scene in which a cauldron of human waste is dumped on the head of a Dutch woman accused of collaborating with the Nazis.

There's no inherent reason that adults should find manure more disgusting than chocolate fudge, or vomit more off-putting than hollandaise sauce. Yet we do. And euphemisms ensue. There is an intimate relationship between disgust and euphemizing. We use euphemisms for any substance that nauseates us, as if sanitizing the word might purify the substance. Scholars of disgust (there are some) have found that the more revolting we find something, the more likely we are to discuss it indirectly. The evasive words we use when referring to such subjects become verbal spotlights. As William Ian Miller writes in *The Anatomy of Disgust,* "Euphemism shows that we are in the presence of taboo and the danger and disgust that attend it."

Windbreaks

Because euphemisms for gas emitted from the rectum are more universal than most, they have proved useful as a tool for tracing the evolution of language. *Break wind* has been particularly durable. In 1552, an English writer used the phrase "breake wynd vpwards." Half a century later, an English translator wrote, "He would give folke leave to break wind downward."

"Fart" was originally a euphemism, freely used by Chaucer ("This Nicholas anoon leet fle a fart, / As greet as it hadde been a thonder-dent [thunder clap]") and by Ben Jonson, whose 1610 play *The Alchemist* included the words "I fart at thee" in its opening soliloquy. At that time and for many decades thereafter, the term "fart" was considered no more offensive than "flatulence" is today. Samuel Johnson included it in his 1755 dictionary, defining "fart" as "to break wind behind," and illustrating its use with lines written by Jonathan Swift that ended, "He farted first, and then he spoke." Well into the nineteenth century, "fart catcher" was slang for a valet or footman who walked behind his employer. As so often happens, however, this euphemism took on vulgar overtones and gave way to even more euphemistic synonyms such as *passing gas,* or, among children, *cutting cheese* (because when the rind of a wheel of cheese is first cut, a pungent smell of fermented gas escapes).

Words referring to flatulence have traditionally made distinctions based on the force of gas expulsion. "Fizzle" was a term medieval English speakers used for a discreet passing of gas. When used this way, it is defined by the *Oxford English Dictionary* as "to break wind without noise." To illustrate that obsolete usage, the *OED* gives this 1601 translation of a work by Pliny the Elder: "they say if Asses eat thereof, they will fall a fizling and farting." This led to today's use of "fizzle" for something that leads nowhere ("fizzled out") and "fizz" for a hissing, sputtering sound.

Other euphemisms for modest wind breaking are more

esoteric. In his novel *The Tongues of Angels,* Reynolds Price writes of a boy at camp in the 1950s where letting loose an "*S.B.D.*"—a "silent but deadly fart"—was considered a high art form. In Price's words, this was "the anonymous invisible outrage that left a room gasping. If no one guessed the culprit within thirty seconds, he got to cry 'S.B.D.!' in triumph and could hit us all, one good hard punch."

At the other end of the scale are powerful farts known to some as *wallpaper peelers.* Among those raised in cities, *painting the elevator* alludes to that type. "In our family," writes educator Bob Burton Brown, "we all know what it means when one of us asks, 'Who painted the elevator?'" Brown's compilation of other such euphemisms includes *cushion creeper* ("I've had about all of your cushion creepers I can take"), *squeaking chair* ("Are you sitting in a squeaking chair?"), and *barking spider* ("About time to call the exterminators. Those barking spiders are back").

Most families have pet euphemisms for flatulence, some rooted in their collective histories. They are a way to acknowledge shared experience and an irreverent sense of humor. Members of one family call farting *coo-coo* because, when a toddler in that clan was told "Excuse you" after she passed gas, the closest pronunciation this girl could come up with was "coo-coo." *Pop* was the term used by another family. ("Who popped?") One woman recalled that she and her sisters referred to farting as *shooting ducks.* "I [once] proudly and loudly announced at a restaurant that my older sister was shooting ducks!" she added. "Mother was not amused. Daddy was."

Elimination

It's only been within the past century that residents of developed countries have enjoyed the luxury of eliminating body waste indoors. Before then, most had to do this outside in an outhouse or on a discreet patch of ground. Telling others where one was going when responding to this call presented a challenge. Women commonly said they were off to *pick a daisy* or *pluck a rose*. Men were more likely to *go visit my uncle* or *see a man about a dog*. A woman who didn't realize what this meant once innocently asked a man what kind of dog he was looking for. "A dachshund with four puppies," the man replied.

These are just a few of the many euphemisms we've used over time for the act of eliminating body waste. As a sometime participant in Friends Meeting for Worship, I'm particularly struck by ones that alluded to this denomination: *bury a Quaker* for defecation ("I need to go bury a Quaker"), and *Quaker burial ground* as the place where this is done. No one is quite sure where this locution originated, or why, though R. W. Holder thinks it might have something to do with the brown garb once worn by Quaker men. In Francis Grose's time, the substance being buried was known to some as *Pilgrim's salve*.

Euphemisms for the elimination of body waste vary by time and place, of course. In Africa, speakers of Swahili may excuse themselves to *go to the prayerhouse*. Bulgarians *go to the thinking place* (leading to a euphemism for what they plan to do there: *think*). Some Spaniards say they'll be *visiting Señor Roca*, referring to the Roca brand of bathroom fixtures widely used in that country. During World War II, members of the

French resistance responded to a call of nature by announcing, *"Je vais téléphoner à Hitler"* ("I'm going to call Hitler") while pinching their nose with one hand and pretending to pull a flush chain with the other.

In postwar London, where public-lavatory doors cost a penny to open, "Where do I go to spend a penny?" needed no further explanation. *Do your duty* is a euphemism that has particular resonance to the British. English novelist Catherine Storr was raised in a family that referred to elimination this way ("You may be excused to do your duty"). When she grew up, Storr was startled to discover that this phrase had other meanings. Referring to Admiral Horatio Nelson's exhortation at the 1805 Battle of Trafalgar ("England expects that every man will do his duty"), Storr wrote that "Nelson's message to his men sounded to me for years like a very public after-breakfast call."

Call of nature has proved the most enduring allusion to this activity. When folklorist Vance Randolph was a child in Scranton, Pennsylvania, his teachers told students that those who felt such a call should raise their hands, then wait to be told, "You may leave the room." The students themselves converted *leave the room* into a euphemism for any bodily function, especially farting. ("Oooh, he left the room!")

Some time later, a Missourian recited a rhyme for Randolph that went:

> *When Nature calls at either door*
> *Do not refuse her,*
> *For many an ail is sure to come*
> *If you abuse her.*

Pee

Jack Garner, Franklin Roosevelt's first vice president, once said that his position "wasn't worth a pitcher of warm piss." "Piss" got changed to "spit" in news coverage, and "spit" it's been ever since. "Those pantywaist writers wouldn't print it the way I said it," Cactus Jack later complained.

Maybe it's something about Texas politicians. To explain his refusal to fire the disreputable FBI director J. Edgar Hoover, Garner's fellow Texan Lyndon Johnson famously said he'd rather have someone inside the tent pissing out than outside the tent pissing in. Not that this concept could be referred to directly by newscasters, then or in succeeding years. After Barack Obama made rival Hillary Clinton his secretary of state, MSNBC's Keith Olbermann speculated about the president's motives: "Let's see how I can phrase this: to make sure that she's *expressing* herself in the tent rather than expressing herself outside of the tent into the tent?"

At one time, "piss" was a perfectly reputable synonym for "urine" as a noun, and the act of excreting it as a verb. In a more earthy, less hectic era, Englishmen called a brief period of time *a pissing while*. The King James Bible referred to men in general as "any that pisseth against the wall." A late-seventeenth-century schoolbook for American students asked, "Why doth a dog being to piss, hold up one leg?" Because of its diuretic qualities, the common dandelion was called a *piss-a-bed* in pre-Victorian England (and is still called a *pissenlit* in France). To this day, we commonly use the semirespectable expressions *full of piss and vinegar, piss poor* (i.e., "doesn't have a pot to piss in"), and *pissed off*. For the most part, though, "piss" has had its day as a reputable term. Nowadays adults *pass water, take a leak, empty their bladders,* and *make room for tea* (or for *another beer*). Men-only euphemisms involve lots of shaking: *shake the dew off the lily, shake hands with my wife's best friend,* or, among English soldiers, *shake hands with the bloke I enlisted with.* Women *water the roses* and *change the canary's water.*

For the past couple of centuries, *wee wee* and *pee pee* have been the euphemisms of choice for most English-speaking children. Kids also *tinkle, make, piddle,* or simply *pee* (based on the first letter of "piss"). Some adults do too. During one of California's chronic water shortages, Senator S. I. Hayakawa (R-CA) proposed this toilet-flushing guideline: "Pee don't, poo do," a nifty use of kid speak to make his point without giving offense. Reliance on nursery words is typical of euphemizers like him. When in trouble, the patrician George H. W. Bush was fond of saying he was in "deep doo doo." After Barack Obama used the expression *wee weed up,* befuddled members of the press finally concluded that this was street slang for "riled up." (" 'Bed-wetting' would probably be the more consumer-friendly term," White House press secretary Robert Gibbs later conceded.)

In an episode of HBO's *The Wire,* a retired policeman named Howard "Bunny" Colvin eats in a restaurant with a former colleague who now does security for Johns Hopkins University and with a university administrator who is recruiting Colvin to do the same work. Midway through their meal, the administrator smiles archly and says sotto voce, "Excuse me while I go to the little boys' room, gentlemen. I need to tinkle." After he leaves, Colvin says to his former colleague, "Tinkle? I never understood why a grown-ass man gotta talk like that. He needs to *take a piss,* whether he knows it or not."

The other ex-cop chuckles, assuring him he'll get used to the way academics speak. When the administrator takes his time returning, this man says, "Wonder what's keepin' him? All he had to do was tinkle." Responds Colvin, "I guess he felt the need to make a dookie too."

Poo

An irreverent dairy near me sells a rich, dark-chocolate ice cream it calls Cow Patty. That's because "patty" or "pie" at one time referred to mounds of bovine excrement. "Chip" did similar duty. What word could be more innocent? "Chocolate chip," "ice chip," "chip on your shoulder." This is where things get dicey, however. Back in olden days, an American boy itching for a fight might announce this fact by placing a chip on his shoulder, daring anyone to knock it off. To fastidious ears today, "chip" suggests a sliver of wood. But the chip in question was more likely to be a piece of dried cow or buffalo dung. Hard as it is to picture a twenty-first-century boy putting dried shit on the shoulder of his Abercrombie and Fitch polo, having a *chip on your shoulder* still suggests prickly belligerence.

Determining the right words to describe solid body waste and its elimination has always been more problematic than choosing ones for liquid waste. According to J. N. Adams, Latin words for urinate such as *mingo* and *melo* were less offensive than ones for defecate: *caco, merda,* and *pedo.* Some editions of the Bible that freely refer to "piss" are coy when it comes to excrement, calling it, among other things, "that which cometh from thee." In a similar vein, two centuries ago Moreau de St. Méry complained that women he encountered in America paid so little attention to personal hygiene that their chemises sometimes displayed "marks of that need to which Nature has subjected every animal."

Change is no less constant in this category of euphemism than in any other. After all, *body wax* was once a euphemism for "shit." When discussing defecation, we resort to face-saving euphemisms, sometimes debasing perfectly good words in the process. "Crap" and "feces" had respectable meanings until they were pressed into euphemistic service (both referred broadly to "residue" or "dregs"). Some of the substitute words in this area vary by profession. Farmers spread *manure,* and waste managers dispose of *biosolids.* Doctors analyze *fecal matter* and *stools.* But to do this they must ask patients to give them a *specimen.* Those who work with wildlife talk of *droppings, dung,* and *scat,* as well as the *casings* of worms and *guano* eliminated by bats, seabirds, and seals.

What's wrong with "shit"? What makes us so averse to using that sturdy old term in polite company? Originally spelled "shite," it is a perfectly good word: terse, forceful, to the point. It has the added benefit of being both a noun and a verb. "Shit" is an integral part of many vivid expressions: "in deep shit," "up shit creek without a paddle," "doesn't know shit from apple butter," "shit or get off the pot," "the shit hit the fan," "get your shit together," "shoot the shit," "shit-eating grin," "shit happens," "shit list," "tough shit," "no shit," "shitfaced," and, of course, "bullshit." Yet, "shit" has become so contaminated by association with the substance to which it refers that in modern times it's one of our most euphemized words. As Donald Rumsfeld said so memorably when he was defense secretary, "Stuff happens." During a presidential press conference, Ronald Reagan said "everything hit the fan." When Reagan's onetime speechwriter Peggy Noonan was recorded saying "bullshit" in a radio studio (off-mic, she thought), Noonan apologized to readers of her newspaper column for using this "barnyard epithet." A guest on National Public Radio later referred to the "big stinking pile" that George W. Bush left behind when departing the White House. In a rare show of wit, Bush himself said that walking his dog around his Dallas neighborhood involved "Picking up that which I had dodged for the past eight years."

Environmental activist Abby Rockefeller thinks that relying on this type of verbal sidestep limits our ability to deal with biosolid disposal. Our reluctance to call a turd a turd makes it harder to find better ways to dispose of human waste. How can you discuss an issue if you can't even agree on what words to use? "Shit" doesn't pass the smell test. Euphemistic terms such as *dung, scat,* or *excrement* sound prissy and evasive. Rockefeller herself settled on "manure" because this word describes its subject clearly while alluding to its potential as fertilizer. "Dirt" does the same thing. So does "soil," as noun and verb. Following the 2008 presidential campaign, political correspondent Jason Linkins observed that a defender of Sarah Palin's pallid debate performance seemed to be saying, "By not soiling herself onstage, Palin was the big winner."

Night soil is a benign-sounding variation on this theme, as is *honey,* used euphemistically when referring to receptacles for human excrement. Thankfully, in developed countries anyway, few of us have need for such *honey buckets* or *honey pots* any longer. This euphemism for "chamber pot" (itself originally a euphemism) lives on in its verbal descendants *go potty* and *potty mouth.*

The Smallest Room

In Judges 3:24, servants of Moab's king, Eglon, wonder why the door to his upper room is locked. They conclude that he must be relieving himself. The way this is expressed varies in different translations. These variations tell us something about changing euphemisms for defecation and the setting where it takes place.

In the King James Bible, Eglon's servants say of Moab's king, "Surely he covers his feet in his summer chamber" (apparently referring to the fact that the king's robes covered his feet when he squatted to defecate, and that his "summer chamber" was where Eglon did this). In other translations, they say:

"Surely he is covering his feet in the upper room."

"He is only covering his feet in the inner chamber of the wall."

"He must be relieving himself in the inner room of the house."

"He is only relieving himself in the closet of the cool chamber."

"It may be that he is in his summer-house for a private purpose."

"Perhaps he is easing nature in his summer parlour."

"He might be using the latrine in the room."

"He must be using the toilet."

As it turns out, Eglon was indeed in what today we'd call *the bathroom* or *the lavatory*, and that was where the

Israelite Ehud thrust his dagger into the vulnerable belly of Moab's king. This wasn't an uncommon fate for history's monarchs. A seventeenth-century historian noted how many of them had been "slain in the draught [outhouse]," including several in Rome who were killed while seated on their "stool of ease." Reading descriptions of such episodes provides an excellent glossary of terms used for this setting at the time of writing. According to an 1841 account, in 1016 an enemy of England's King Edmund Ironside dispatched him with a spear while the monarch was "at the withdraught [outhouse] to purge nature." Three centuries later, James I of Scotland was reportedly murdered while in a monastery *jakes*. A few decades after that, Henry III of France was said to have been stabbed in the stomach while seated on his *chaise percée*, an armchair with a hole in the seat and a chamber pot below. In common use during the Middle Ages among those who could afford them, this convenience spawned other euphemisms such as *necessary chair, withdrawal chair,* and *business chair.* Since so many were housed discreetly within wardrobes, *go to the wardrobe* became a common euphemism for calls of nature. Chaucer used the term *wardrobe* for the setting that he also called a *pryvee*.

Privy chamber was the original designation, one that gave a touch of class to the place where private acts took place. Over time, *privy chamber* was condensed to *privy*. In his 1755 dictionary, Dr. Johnson defined "privy" as a "place of retirement" (alluding to yet another euphemism for this setting, *retiring room*). Early indoor privies consisted of a room barely large enough to accommodate a seat with a hole, dubbed a *closet stool* or *close stool* prior to the Elizabethan era. In a late-seventeenth-century poem Lord Rochester wrote of "Men with Close-Stools, to ease Nature." Eventually this was short-ened to *stool* ("I'm going to the stool"), which left that word behind for the solid waste eliminated there.

This setting has been the subject of some truly inspired euphemisms. My favorites include *a place of general interest, where you cough,* and *where the Queen goes alone.* For reasons that aren't clear, during the Elizabethan era and for centuries thereafter, outhouses were commonly called *jakes.* In Shake-speare's *King Lear,* Kent says he'll "tread this unbolted villain into mortar, and daub the wall of a jakes with him." Nearly two centuries later, Benjamin Franklin charged that the English practice of sending prisoners to settle its colonies was tantamount to "emptying their jakes on our tables." In the colonies, *Cousin John* or simply *John* rivaled *jakes.* A 1735 Har-vard edict warned that "No freshman shall mingo [urinate] against the College wall or go into the fellows' cuzjohn."

Like their forebears in England, upscale colonists some-times called the setting where "necessary matters" took place a *necessary house* or simply *the necessary.* (A Latin-inspired alter-native was *the necessarium.*) In a 1747 letter to his son, Lord Chesterfield noted with approval the example of a man who made good use of time he spent there:

> I knew a gentleman who was so good a manager of his time that he would not even lose that small por-tion of it which the calls of nature obliged him to pass in the necessary-house; but gradually went through all the Latin poets in those moments. He bought, for example, a common edition of Horace, of which he tore off gradually a couple of pages, carried them with

him to that necessary place, read them first, and then sent them down as a sacrifice to Cloacina [the so-called Goddess of Sewers]...I recommend you to follow his example. It is better than only doing what you cannot help doing at those moments.

When a newfangled indoor toilet was installed in the White House during John Quincy Adams's presidency, *Quincy* enjoyed a brief vogue in America as a euphemism for this convenience. ("If you'll excuse me, I need to go visit Quincy.") The word "toilet" first appeared in the mid-sixteenth century. It was based on the French *toilette,* which referred to a sack that held clothing and meant the same thing. Over time, the meaning of "toilet" expanded to refer to the cloth covering of a dressing table, then to the activities that took place at such a table. ("She made her toilet.") By the nineteenth century, this word's application expanded some more, now being used for dressing rooms themselves. It then became more specific yet, referring to rooms that also included bathing facilities. Such bathing rooms were accoutrements of better homes at this time, a setting with sinks and tubs where wealthy homeowners washed up. A separate room housed commodes. This word originally referred to a woman's headdress, a chest of drawers, or a cupboard in a bathroom. Later, especially in the United States, "commode" referred to a toilet that resembled a piece of furniture. Eventually, the two settings were combined as "bathrooms" that began to accommodate commodes as well.

After the Civil War, public toilets in the United States were first called *washrooms,* as they still are in Canada, then *restrooms. Public comfort stations* was another euphemism for such facilities, as was *public convenience,* and, most circumspect of all, *facility.* ("I'm going to use the facility.")

Bathroom remains the most popular American euphemism for the place where we urinate and defecate. It is now so ubiquitous that backcountry campers who are about to squat behind a tree talk of "going to the bathroom." Others talk of animals doing the same thing. ("That damn dog is going to the bathroom on my lawn!") But even this antiseptic term has proved a bit gamy for some. When architect Alexander Kira first published *The Bathroom* in 1966, an American newspaper referred to it as a book about "the watchamacallit."

Another widely used euphemism for this room is based on its modest size. As Queen Victoria once inquired, "Has the railway carriage got a small room to it?" This more common form inspired John Pudney's 1954 book about such facilities titled *The Smallest Room.* "When you're throwing a party," advised a newspaper feature half a century later, "the smallest room in your house can be the most important." Even the euphemism *smallest room* can be dodgy, though. At one time, it was considered disreputable for a male host to direct a female guest there. Doing this service for a member of one's own sex was also questionable. "Would you care to wash your hands?" was much preferred, or "May I show you the geography of the house?" or simply, "May I show you the geography?" Eventually *the geography* became a euphemism for smallest rooms. In mid-twentieth-century England, *geography* was considered an upper-class euphemism; *WC* (for *water closet*), one used by members of the working class. *Lavatory* was another alternative.

Like "bathroom," "lavatory" originally referred to a setting where bodies are washed. Its root is the Latin *lavare* (wash) and *lavatrina* (where washing takes place). When commodes were added to this room, "lavatory" came to mean a place for elimination more than cleansing, especially in England. There was a time when this term was considered vulgar. In a saga from early last century, a young Englishman who'd had too much beer asked his dancing partner, "Where is the lavatory?" Pushing him away, she responded, "On the right of the entrance hall you will find a door with the notice GENTLEMEN. Disregard the warning. Go right in. You will find what you want."

For those of his countrymen who disdained "toilet" as a mealymouthed Americanism, Evelyn Waugh reminded them that "lavatory" was no less euphemistic. After Waugh made this observation in 1956, increasing use of the American term by middle-class Britons led to its use among members of their upper class as well. The Americanisms *restroom* and *comfort station* have never caught on in Britain, though, suggesting as they do boards laid across toilets to accommodate those who are weary, or a room filled with La-Z-Boy recliners.

There are various theories about why so many Britons call this room a "loo." Does it derive from "Gardy loo!"—the exuberant cry of Scottish women emptying chamber pots to the street below (from the French *gardez l'eau*, "watch out for the water")? Or is it a contraction of *bourdalou*, a portable commode resembling a gravy boat that was used by Frenchwomen three centuries ago? Or from the French *lieux d'aisances* ("places of ease")? Or from James Joyce's conflation of "Water-closet" and "Waterloo" in *Ulysses*, possibly as a clip of "Waterloo"? After considering all such possibilities, etymologist Michael Quinion concluded that none is definitive. Another alternative is that British soldiers during World War I mistook the numerical euphemism *100* on lavatory doors in French hotels for "loo." The most intriguing suggestion of all, one noted by linguist Alan Ross, had to do with a Victorian era guest at a lodge in Dublin who was named Louise. As a gag, some lodge-mates moved the nameplate reading "Lou" from her door to the women's lavatory. Word of this prank spread so widely that, in time, Louise's nickname became a popular synonym for "lavatory," respelled *l-o-o*.

Obviously, coming up with euphemistic names for a lavatory inspires remarkable creativity. As with euphemisms for elimination, many families devise their own names for the setting where this takes place. One Maine patriarch passed *bagaduce* along to his kids as a euphemism for "outhouse" ("I'm going to the bagaduce"), possibly because there's a river by that name in Maine. Catherine Storr's family called its outhouse a "euph." That was because when a visitor to their home excused herself to "go outside," Storr's mother offered to keep this woman company and had to be told that "go outside" was a euphemism for "use the outhouse." This incident became a family joke that eventually led to their calling any lavatory a "euph."

FALLEN NAMES

Those of us named Ralph are none too happy about the many euphemistic uses of our name. We're especially sensitive to its use as a euphemism for vomiting. We didn't appreciate it one bit when *talk to Ralph on the big white phone* (i.e., toilet) showed up in a collection of college slang.

Those named John may not sympathize. American Johns must share their name with toilets (based on the phrase "I've got to go visit Cousin John") and customers of prostitutes. Brits call condoms *johnnies*. In the United States, "John" combined with "Doe" is the name of everyman and, therefore, no man at all.

In conjunction with other terms, "Joe" also suggests ordinariness: *Joe Blow, Joe Shmoe, Joe Doaks, Joe Sixpack, an average Joe, GI Joe*. The name "Jack" gets used in a similar vein, as something not worth very much ("isn't worth jack shit") or on the ordinary side ("Jack of all trades, master of none"). At one time, "Jack" was also a synonym for "penis." More than a century ago, *get Jack in the orchard* was slang for sex, as was *Jack in the box. Jack off* is a remnant of such usage.

"Roger" once had the distinction not only of being used as a noun meaning "penis" but as a verb meaning "copulate" ("I Rogered her well"). In his published writing, James Boswell felt constrained to euphemize this euphemism as "R-g-r." By World War II, the erotic connotations of "Roger" had declined enough that pilots felt safe to use it as a radio-transmitted acknowledgment meaning "Message received." ("Roger!")

"Charlie" rivals "John" for its many euphemistic uses. At various times, "Charlie" has referred to cocaine, genitalia, breasts, policemen, homosexuals, and members of the Vietcong. It's also been part of *Checkpoint Charlie, Charlie Girls, a proper Charlie,* and *a Goodtime Charlie*. In a 1936 story, Damon Runyan recast a *Goodtime Charlie* as a *Hoorah Henry*. In Britain, wealthy bon vivants subsequently became known as *Hooray Henrys*.

As with so many euphemisms, what names get repurposed and in which ways depends on where one lives. "Randy" is ruined in the United Kingdom, where it means "horny," but is still a perfectly respectable name in the United States. (When visiting England,

(continued)

American Randys are advised to introduce themselves as "Randall" or "Randolph.") During the late Clinton era, "Monica" suggested a younger woman involved with an older married man and lost favor as a name given to American baby girls. "Lolita" is completely ruined on both sides of the Atlantic due to its association with seductive prepubescent girls (to the mortification of staff members at Britain's Woolworths who hadn't heard of Vladimir Nabokov's novel by that name and called a bed for young girls the Lolita Midsleeper).

That's Disgusting!

Let's return now to the question posed at the beginning of this chapter. Why are we so determined to euphemize words related to body waste?

The reasons seem obvious. They're disgusting! Take shit. This substance smells bad, is sticky and slimy, and emerges from a hole in our bodies when we are in a very undignified position. What better reasons could there be to pussyfoot when discussing this subject? As if we needed to be told, studies of disgust have confirmed that body wastes are among the most revolting substances human beings confront. What disgusts us and why is a topic of some debate, however. There may be more than squeamishness involved.

Research conducted in different parts of the world by medical researcher Valerie Curtis has found a nearly universal sense of revulsion at feces, bodily secretions, rotten food, and slimy worms. Few subjects could tell her why their reflexive reaction to such substances was one of *"Yuck!"* however. Although many anthropologists believe that this is a learned response, Curtis concluded that a sense of disgust is an innate response to toxic matter and could have survival value. From this perspective, revulsion is a lifesaving reaction to disease-bearing materials, including ones found in body waste. This sense of revulsion led to taboos that promoted good health. Both the Bible and the Koran admonish believers to keep themselves clean. Ancient Hindu laws mandate avoidance of such body impurities as "oily exudations, semen, blood, urine, feces, the mucous of the nose, ear wax, phlegm, tears, the rheum of the eyes, and sweat." We've seen how many euphemisms such substances inspire. As we'll consider at greater length in the final chapter, this suggests an intimate relationship between euphemistic discourse and human survival. The need to avoid disease-bearing substances underlies constant verbal dodges, as do the topics of health, healing, and death in general. These subjects provide myriad opportunities for euphemizing.

6

Under the Weather and *In the Ground*

Oɴᴇ ᴏꜰ ᴍʏ least favorite euphemisms is "This may pinch a little," murmured by a doctor or a dentist who is about to do something that's going to really, really hurt. Alternatively, "You may experience some discomfort." Or "A little pressure." Obviously, medical personnel don't want to announce boldly, "This will hurt" or "A little pain," so they resort to *pinch, pressure,* and *discomfort* as euphemisms.

Medical conditions would be difficult to discuss without recourse to euphemisms. The very word "disease" began as a polite substitute for "sickness," one suggesting mere discomfort. (Think dis-ease.) Many substitute "ill" for "sick." Plenty of options have developed over the years for those who would rather not admit they're sick or ill. Instead they might be *indisposed, unwell, under the weather, out of sorts,* or merely *a bit off.* Or, if they want to sound professional, *have a malady.* Nowadays, we're less likely to suffer from a disease, sickness, or illness than a *complaint, condition, episode,* or *event.*

As baby boomers age and the field of medicine expands,

so does the range of associated euphemisms. After spending enough time in hospitals, we begin to talk of *meds* rather than "drugs." Instead of "treatment", we get *therapy*. We may not undergo "surgery" but will have a *surgical intervention*. Yesterday's "face-lift" is today's *aesthetic procedure*. A heart attack becomes a *coronary,* a *coronary incident,* or a *coronary event.* Or, when we really want to toss the medical lingo, a *myocardial infarction.*

Doctors are key carriers of euphemania on the health front. Their professional vocabulary serves the dual causes of medicine and obfuscation. Inevitably, some of that vocabulary seeps into common discourse, not only because patients pick it up from their doctors but also because they see it on the Internet and hear it on radio and television, especially in pharmaceutical ads that warn of "serious, sometimes fatal events." In other words, death.

Using substitute words when discussing health matters is a long-standing practice. This is especially true when it comes to naming diseases.

There's a Name for It

I was always told that my great-grandmother, Myrtie Lacey, died of consumption. Only as an adult did I learn that *consumption* was a euphemism for tuberculosis. In Myrtie's time, tuberculosis was an incurable scourge, the AIDS of its day. The very name of this dread disease was taboo. *Koch's disease* it was called, *Pott's disease, acid-fast disease, apical catarrh scrofula, king's evil, the white plague, pleural pneumonia,* and *phthisis* (Greek for "consumption"). Since TB was the leading cause of death in nineteenth-century America, killing an estimated

20 percent of adults and infecting as many as half of all city dwellers, such verbal coyness is understandable. Medical historian William Rothstein has suggested that during the nineteenth century a reluctance to discuss tuberculosis directly was even stronger than reticence about discussing sex.

In his 1827 novel *Armance,* Stendhal depicted the mother of a tubercular patient who refuses to call her son's illness by its actual name for fear that doing so might hasten his demise. A century later, Franz Kafka lay dying of the same disease in an Austrian sanitarium. In a 1924 postcard to a friend, Kafka complained about how maddeningly vague doctors there were about his condition. As the Czech author explained, when discussing tuberculosis "everybody drops into a shy, evasive, glass-eyed manner of speech." All Kafka could get out of them were vague references to "swelling at the rear" and "infiltration." Two months later, he was dead.

In the case of Emily Dickinson, biographer Lyndall Gordon has concluded that the reclusive poet was a closet epileptic who could only refer to that affliction obliquely. During Dickinson's mid-nineteenth-century era, epilepsy—commonly called "falling sickness"—was considered shameful for men to have and unmentionable for women. Gordon thinks that Emily Dickinson's poetry included frequent euphemistic references to this condition, such as "I felt a Funeral / in my Brain." At other times, the poet wrote of "Fire Rocks" in her body and a "Bomb" in her bosom. At no time did Dickinson refer to having epilepsy (which afflicted two of her male relatives) or even to suffering from an unnamed illness.

A reluctance to discuss diseases openly is part and parcel of the primitive fear that using the actual name of something one dreads, be it a bear or an illness, might summon what is dreaded. At one time, residents of the Solomon Islands near Papua New Guinea called virulent diseases such as leprosy and tuberculosis *the chief* or *the pretty girl,* perhaps hoping to tame their fury with flattering names. A century ago, anthropologists found that smallpox, the most feared disease in New Guinea, was seldom referred to directly. Instead, residents of that region referred to this malady in terms befitting something regal that ruled their lives. "Hence smallpox is spoken of as a king," wrote James Frazer in the *The Golden Bough,* "—a pretty word to hide an ugly thing, and yet an appropriate image, since the disease visits district after district, village after village, like a prince making a royal progress."

At a time when the causes of illness were mysterious and ways to treat them uncertain, renaming such scourges seemed as good a strategy as any. In a sense it still does. By using a mild word such as "shingles" for the excruciating condition herpes zoster, we try to temper its severity. "Flu" is a less ominous-sounding contraction of the dread "influenza," a disease that has caused so many deaths during epidemics, especially the one in 1918 that claimed some forty million lives around the world. Due to a suspicion that it originated in Spain, that strain was called "Spanish flu." It was actually less prevalent in Spain than elsewhere but received more publicity there because that neutral country's press wasn't censored during World War I. Since this strain of influenza appeared first in Kansas, "Kansas flu" would have been a more accurate label. But accuracy is not the intent when diseases are given point-of-origin names such as "Hong Kong flu" and "German measles." Ethnic biases come into play. Depending on which way the political winds are blowing, such designations are subject to change. At the peak of anti-German hysteria during

World War I, "German measles" became *liberty measles* (and "German shepherds," *Alsatians*).

The dysentery so often suffered by tourists is commonly named after settings where it's contracted, perhaps as a form of payback. Geographic euphemisms for this condition include *Bangalore bowels, Bali belly, Basra belly, Bombay crud, Delhi belly, Lahori looseness, Spanish tummy, Thai-del wave, Tokyo trots,* and *Tunis stomach.* Burma's Rangoon takes a double hit, with *Rangoon itch* being euphemistic for a penile infection contracted from a prostitute, and *Rangoon runs* referring to diarrhea. *Montezuma's revenge* is a euphemism for diarrhea contracted in Mexico. A low point in Jimmy Carter's presidency came when the humor-challenged president made a feeble joke about Montezuma's revenge while visiting Mexico City. His hosts were not amused.

AUNT FLO'S COME

Euphemisms for menstruation used to be big on floral themes, presumably because of the "flow" of menstrual blood as well as the redness of so many blossoms. At *flower-time,* medieval Englishwomen endured their *monthly flowers.* "I've got my flowers," they told one another.

Nowadays, Englishwomen are more likely to say "Aunt Flo's come" when alluding to this monthly flow of blood. Personalizing periods this way is particularly popular among modern speakers of English. In this gambit they might say "Harvey's here," "Charlie's come," or "Little Audrey's arrived." Aunt Flo herself might *appear* or *make an appearance.* This notion prompted a popular medical yarn about a woman who told her doctor, "I ain't seen nothin' in three months." In response, he referred her to an ophthalmologist.

A cross-cultural study conducted after World War II by anthropologist Natalie Joffe found that English was especially rich in the range, variety, and imagery of its euphemisms for menstruation. Those who spoke other languages were more constrained. Even Yiddish, so colorful in other figures of speech, yielded a mere handful of pallid references to *the time, a guest in the house,* or *the red king.*

Euphemisms based on the color red are ubiquitous among the many allusions to menstruation: *in the red, a red-letter day, fly the red flag, surf the red wave,* as well as *grandma's here from Red Creek.* Alternatively, *my friend Tom's come over to paint the house red* ("Tom" being an acronym for the "time of month"). Referring to provisional license plates that sport a red *P,* some Australian women say "I've got my P-plates."

Natalie Joffe found that the French were especially partial to red-based euphemisms but used them with imaginative indirection: *tomatoes, cardinals, having the painters in.* Most creatively euphemistic of all was their reference to *garibaldians* (referring to Garibaldi's revolutionary "redshirts") and *have the English,* alluding to the traditional nickname for English soldiers, "redcoats."

But it was Americans who Joffe found had the most "vivid and luxuriant" euphemisms for menstruation. Among the more inventive of a hundred she tallied were *the Red Sea's in, the chick is a communist* ("red"), and *her cherry is in sherry.* These euphemisms were primarily used by men, of course, as was *flying baker.* This referred to the naval alphabet in which "baker" stands for *B,* and the semaphore flag for B is red. That flag also warns of danger, when, say, ammunition is about to be loaded and the message is "Beware. Stay away." Postwar American women alerting men that having their period made them sexually unavailable said *the flag is up.* They were *off duty.*

Americans have uniquely incorporated materials used to absorb the flow of menstrual blood into their euphemisms: *on the rag,*

(continued)

ragtime, riding the cotton pony. In her book *The Body Project,* Joan Jacobs Brumberg depicts a fifth-grade girl in the postwar period who can't join friends sledding because, she says, "I'm practicing Kotex." Brumberg thinks the fact that *feminine hygiene* refers euphemistically to menstruation reflects the way this event has come to be treated as health-related rather than maturational. Traditional rituals of menarche have been replaced by buying one's first *sanitary napkins.* One appeal of this switch, suggests Brumberg, is that it provides a neutral, quasi-professional vocabulary to use when discussing this delicate topic. Thus, the *curse of Eve* and *the monthly blues* give way to *sanitary protection* and *menstrual health.*

On the street, things are a bit different, of course. There, it's *vampire time. Old faithful's back. Bloody Mary. Time to put my plug in.* One woman calls her tampons *spark plugs* (as in "Gotta go change a spark plug"). Another has named her period *Fred,* which makes it easier to tell her husband, "Sorry, honey. Fred's visiting." Then there's the *moon goddess* (who shows up every twenty-eight days). Technological advances have produced their own vocabulary for menstruation of course. The most up-to-date euphemism of all is *rebooting the ovarian operating system.*

From *VD* to *STD*

When Columbus's sailors brought what we now call "syphilis" back from the New World, English speakers called it "Spanish pox." This neatly combined the disease's origins with British disdain for Spaniards. After French soldiers who besieged Naples late in the fifteenth century exported this ailment to France, it became known there as the *Neapolitan disease.* As Keith Allan and Kate Burridge note in *Forbidden*

Words, Italians preferred *French malady.* Poles called it *German disease. Polish disease* was preferred by Russians. Because they believed it was imported from England, Tahitians settled on *British disease.* Turks termed it *Christian disease;* Japanese, *Portuguese disease;* and Portuguese, *Castilian disease.*

You see the trend.

The challenge of naming diseases is tied to political and ethnic rivalries. Nowhere can this be seen more clearly than in the area of sexually transmitted diseases such as the one brought to Europe by Columbus's sailors. Their reputation for licentiousness made the French the most popular nationality of all when naming this disease, especially among the English. In Shakespeare's *All's Well That Ends Well,* Bertram infects a woman with "French Pox." The Bard's contemporaries also called this illness *Malady of France* or *French gout. French crust, French distemper, French aches,* and *Gallic disease* were other popular synonyms favored by English speakers during the Elizabethan era.

An epic poem published in 1530 by Venetian physician Girolamo Fracastoro featured a shepherd infected with "the French sickness." His name was Syphilis. In time, the shepherd's name was applied to the disease itself. It stuck. As the word "syphilis" took on the taint of the malady, however, vaguer terms such as *special disease, social disease, secret disease, vice disease, Cupid's disease, a certain disease, blood disease,* and *blood poison* emerged. Doctors sometimes called syphilis *specific stomach* or *specific ulcer. The great pox* was another name bestowed on this ailment, to keep it from being confused with smallpox. *Pox* alone was often a euphemism for the sore-inducing malady. When Shakespeare wrote "A pox on't" in *Cymbeline,* syphilis was what he had in mind.

The most generic name for such maladies was *venereal disease*. Before Columbus set sail, "venereal" simply meant "of Venus" and alluded to sexual matters in general. By the mid-seventeenth century, it referred more specifically to sexually transmitted diseases. Despite the spread of these diseases during World War I, and despite pressure from the Army Medical Corps, American newspapers would refer to this subject only in the most evasive terms. Even "venereal disease" was considered too suggestive for public consumption. A 1919 article in the *New York Tribune* discussed *preventable diseases, social diseases, certain dangerous diseases, communicable diseases,* and, simply, *diseases.* London's *News of the World* subsequently used the term *a certain illness* when reporting on this subject. For the movie version of *A Farewell to Arms* (1932), British censors changed "venereal disease" to *imaginary disease.* As late as 1961, a line in the *West Side Story* song "Gee, Officer Krupke" that went "No one wants a fella with a social disease" did not make the journey from stage to screen.

A satisfactory alternative eventually presented itself in predictable form: an abbreviation. Shortening "venereal disease" to *VD* provided a suitably vague name for this lethal scourge. That approach came to the rescue again when "sexually transmitted disease" became *STD.* After an unusually virulent new form of STD appeared in the early 1980s, the question of what to call it was complicated by the fact that this disease primarily affected homosexuals, intravenous drug users, and immigrants from Haiti. An early candidate was *GRID* (for gay-related immunodeficiency). In addition to being inaccurate, this acronym had a stark, ominous sound, bringing to mind gridlock or power grids. Donald Armstrong of New York's Memorial Sloan-Kettering Cancer Center apparently was the first to suggest calling the disease AIDS, an acronym of its technical name, acquired immuno deficiency syndrome. This benign term for a deadly scourge made it an ideal euphemism. "It has an almost saintly sound," observed David Black in *The Plague Years,* "as though it were the Saint Francis of epidemics."

Medspeak

When a new strain of influenza appeared in Vera Cruz, Mexico, in 2009, the Centers for Disease Control and Prevention simply called it a "febrile respiratory illness." *Mexican flu* was more popular among Americans but not Mexicans themselves. Since it apparently originated in pigs, this viral infection soon became known as *swine flu.* Unhappy hog farmers suggested *hybrid flu* as an alternative. The technically correct *H1N1* was finally settled on as the least controversial option.

Abbreviations and acronyms are the quintessential modern form of euphemism for medical conditions: SARS (severe acute respiratory syndrome), GERD (gastroesophageal reflux disease), COPD (chronic obstructive pulmonary disease), etc. Cattle ranchers, understandably, would much rather we call mad cow disease *MCD* or, better yet, *BSE,* an abbreviation of bovine spongiform encephalopathy. This trend to identify maladies by initials owes a lot to pharmaceutical copywriters. An ad for Orencia refers to rheumatoid arthritis as *RA.* Plavix treats *PAD* (peripheral artery disease). Flomax is for "BPH, also known as an enlarged prostate." (*BPH* actually stands for benign prostatic hyperplasia.)

Cancer is not named in such ads, of course. This word is simply too ominous. Ironically, its root is something of a euphemism or at least a metaphor. Twenty-five centuries ago,

Hippocrates compared the veins snaking out from tumors to crabs, *karkinos* in Greek. Its Latin translation was "cancer." That disease has supplanted tuberculosis as our most dreaded and hence most unnamable scourge. Its many euphemistic designations include the initial *C*. During a remission from the lung cancer that eventually killed him, swaggering John Wayne said he'd beat "the big C." Australian linguist Kate Burridge once heard a cancer patient described as "having a touch of the c's." *The c-word* is a close cousin. *The terrible sickness* is a street euphemism for cancer; *a long illness* or *a lingering illness*, the obituary writer's staple. Generically, any tumor can be called a *lump*, a *growth*, or a *mass*. Among medical personnel, it can be referred to as a *protuberance*, a *neoplasm*, or a *carcinoma* if it's malignant. *Mitotic disease* or *mitosis* (referring to cell multiplication) has become a common medical term for what we're hesitant to call "cancer."

When Ulysses S. Grant died of throat cancer in 1885, his doctors characterized the ex-president's affliction as an "inflammation of the epithelial membrane of the mouth." Previously, they'd discussed his condition in terms of "epithelioma," "malignancy," and "infiltration." Using medical lingo this way is a longtime strategy for trying to avoid alarming patients and those concerned about them. When an elderly W. B. Yeats returned to Dublin from a vacation in Spain, he carried with him a letter from his Spanish doctor to his counterpart in Ireland that read, "We have here an antique cardio-sclerotic of advanced years." At Yeats's insistence, his Irish doctor read him this ominous diagnosis aloud. When the doctor tried to mumble a bit, Yeats demanded that he read it again, slowly and distinctly. "After all, it's my funeral," said the poet. As the doctor repeated the diagnosis, Yeats rolled its key words on his tongue, keeping cadence with one finger: "cardio-sclerotic... cardio-sclerotic...cardio-sclerotic." He then said, "Do you know, I would rather be called 'cardio-sclerotic' than 'Lord of Lower Egypt'!"

Perhaps it's clear-eyed literary types such as Yeats who are best qualified to break through the euphemistic jargon of modern medicine. Novelist Diane Johnson, whose husband is a physician, compares contemporary medspeak to the magic language shamans use when casting spells. The professional vocabulary of today's doctors is rooted in Latin and fertilized by science, creating an aura of mystery that can be wielded strategically. In some cases, a physician might want to brace up a patient with words that sound frightening. Telling one with a mild heart murmur that he has *mitral valve prolapse* could help scare him straight into a healthier lifestyle. Alternatively, a doctor can use medspeak to soothe and mollify. Certainly, *a little spot on your lung* sounds far less menacing than "a possible tumor."

One doctor told Johnson that he was advised to use scientific-sounding euphemisms in front of patients to keep them out of the loop. Thus, an alcoholic discussed among interns in that person's presence would suffer from *hyper-ingestation of ethynol.* Syphilis can be called *sigma phi,* shorthand for this illness based on Greek letters. For their own convenience, and when discussing cancer around patients, doctors routinely initialize it as *c.a.* Initials abound in medspeak. Not just *ER* and *OR* but *MI* (myocardial infarction), *NAD* (no acute distress), *LOC* (loss of consciousness), and *DNR* (do not resuscitate). A patient is a *pt,* a headache an *HA.* Patients "brought in by ambulance" are *BIBA*. *TLC* refers to the type of palliative care given to the terminally ill. Such abbreviations don't just save time but "are used to covertly convey confidential information in a less than confidential setting," one doctor tells me. Thus, a physician who says, "This SOB pt complained of DOE five days PTA" simply means, "This short-of-breath patient complained of dyspnea on exertion five days prior to admission."

Not all initials are professional code, of course. Some are a cross between slang and black humor. Before it became a popular online abbreviation, *LOL* was a euphemism for "little old lady" in hospital corridors. When they can't determine what—if anything—is wrong, some doctors say a patient has *TEETH* ("tried everything else; try homeopathy"). Out of public earshot, medical personnel use abbreviations like *FLK* for "funny-looking kid" (one with an odd appearance but unspecified malady), *FFFF* for "female, forty, fat, and flatulent," *COP* for "crotchety old patient," and *DDD*—"definitely done dancing"—for those who are failing. They are *PBAB*, "pine box at bedside"; or *GFPO*, "good for parts only" (i.e., transplantable organs).

There is a stark contrast between the bland euphemisms doctors use with patients and the black-humorous ones they use among themselves. Depending on the setting, some common in-house terms include *gomer* for a sorry, disheveled type of patient, *grume* for a smelly one (from "grumous," a medical term for coagulated liquids), *groupie* for emergency room regulars, and *buff up* for improving the appearance of a patient about to be released. ("Buff" also refers to cleaning up medical records to discourage possible lawsuits.) Other euphemisms heard in hospital corridors include *code brown* (fecal incontinence), *wallet biopsy* (checking patient's ability to pay), and *positive suitcase sign* for patients who arrive at the ER with a packed suitcase, suggesting no sense of urgency on their part. To understand some of these terms, one needs to be up on dated pop-culture allusions. *Zorro belly* refers to a patient whose abdomen has many scars from previous surgeries. A *Camille* is one who continually feels on the verge of dying and lets everyone know this, loudly. A *dying swan* feels the same way but doesn't make as much fuss.

In some hospitals, *coded* is a euphemism for "died" ("That woman in 304 coded last night"), drawing on the code nomenclature commonly used in this setting, such as "Code Blue" for heart failure. One doctor was startled to hear "demise" used as a verb when he was told that a patient had *demised*. Professionally speaking, doctors' patients don't die, they experience a *negative outcome*, one that might have resulted from a *therapeutic misadventure*. Most often, doctors, like the rest of us, simply say a patient *went* ("she went peacefully") or that they've *lost* a patient. The latter led one immigrant doctor to observe how odd this seemed to him when he arrived in the United States: "I wanted to say, 'Well, we didn't really lose your husband,'" this oncologist told medical researcher James Sexton. "'We know where he is. It's just that he's not breathing any more.'"

Through liberal use of euphemisms, doctors shield both patients and themselves from trauma. Thoughtful physicians recognize that the many evasive expressions they use for disease, dying, and death are for their own benefit as much as that of their patients. As one put it, "Euphemisms...mitigate the macabre, but more for practitioners than for patients." Surprisingly, studies have found that physicians are more afraid of dying than the average person. It has even been suggested that studying medicine can be a counterphobic way to deal with this fear. In the words of one young doctor, "I think it is the innate fear of one's own death that draws a person into medicine because he feels that it is as close as he can come to conquering it." Practicing medicine gives physicians powerful tools to try, particularly a sense of scientific detachment in the face of death as well as a sanitized vocabulary to discuss this issue. In the ways they talk of dying, doctors are no less euphemistic than the rest of us.

Never Say "Die"

When it comes to death, the euphemistic fog becomes nearly impenetrable. The dead are *no longer with us.* They *left the building. Kicked the bucket. Bought the farm.* They've *gone home,* or *south,* or *west,* or to *the last roundup.* They've *laid down their burden.* They're *pushing up daisies.* Noting that the equivalent French expression *manger les pissenlits par la racin* literally means "eating dandelions by the root," Hugh Rawson comments in his *Dictionary of Euphemisms and Other Doublespeak,* "It would be the French, of course, who would think of death in edible terms."

It wasn't always so. When death was more routine, so were the words we used to discuss it. Imagine a marriage ceremony that included "Till a fatal event do us part." Or a prayer that went, "If I should expire before I wake."

In the unsentimental Middle Ages, death was discussed

freely, openly, candidly. Confronting death directly in word and spirit seemed to help our medieval ancestors cope with its prevalence. Works of art—paintings, statues, stained glass windows—brimmed with images of the dead and dying. Dancing skeletons were a common motif in the folk art of southern Europe (and still are in Mexico and other countries south of the U.S. border). Some early clocks were shaped like skulls to remind their owners that time was slipping away; death was on its way. Icons on tombstones didn't gloss over what lay beneath them; they glorified it. A British church luminary named John Wakeman, who died in 1549, was buried beneath a monument adorned with a mouse, snakes, and snails feasting on his corpse. Well into the eighteenth century, skulls were the most common icon on New England gravestones.

This willingness to face death squarely extended to language. One 1615 book for housewives discussed how to deal with "Child dead in the womb" and offered counsel for a woman who "by mischance have her child dead within her." A comparison of the 1662 Church of England funeral liturgy with its revision in the year 2000 found revealing differences. In the 1662 version, reference was freely made to "the Grave," "the Body," and "the Corpse." Three-hundred and thirty-eight years later, "the corpse" became *the deceased*. Prescribed proceedings three centuries ago included this biblical passage: "And though after my skin worms destroy this body, yet in my flesh shall I see God." Its modern counterpart deleted those words. Typical of the newer liturgy was the passage "Like a flower we blossom and then wither: like a shadow we flee and never stay." Guy Cook and Tony Walker, who compared the two versions, dryly noted "an absence of reference to the physical facts of death" in the contemporary Anglican funeral service, which they attributed to "an unwillingness to confront the physical nature of death." In America too, as Gary Laderman notes in *The Sacred Remains: American Attitudes Toward Death, 1779–1883,* modern Protestant theology treats the physical remains of the dead as "persona non grata, so to speak." Avoiding direct contact with dead bodies, Laderman concludes, "became a fundamental dimension of life and death in American culture during the twentieth century."

Before the twentieth century, death usually occurred at home, the dying person surrounded by relatives, friends, and neighbors, including children. Contact with dead bodies was commonplace. Decades after the fact, suffragist Frances Willard recalled being held aloft by her father when she was four (in 1843) so she could get a good look at the body of a next-door neighbor laid out in his Oberlin, Ohio, home. Following the advent of photography, pictures were taken of the dead as a remembrance for those left behind. For an event this ubiquitous, there was no need for flowery, evasive language. Folks died. They were dead. Their bodies were corpses.

As recently as the mid-eighteenth century, there was little attempt to sanitize the language on tombstones. What could be simpler than this inscription on a Beverly, Massachusetts, tombstone:

HERE LYES THE BODY OF Mr. John Blowers
WHO DIED JULY Ye 13th 1748
IN THE 38th YEAR OF HIS AGE

Gradually, however, the words chiseled into granite began to change in concert with a shift in our attitudes toward death. For a time, the two concepts — approach and avoidance —

coexisted, as can be seen in another Beverly tombstone inscription:

In Memory of Mrs. LOIS BARRETT consort of Mr.
THO BARRETT, who departed this life Sept 5th
1789, aged 29 years. Also Betsey their Daughter who
died June 9th 1796, in the 7th year of her age.

From infancy to riper years I grew
Perhaps as certain of my life as you;
But now in silent accents hear my cry,
You soon like me within the Tomb shall lie.

During the early nineteenth century, the words and icons on tombstones became more euphemistic. Now the dead had commenced rather than completed a journey. They *passed over.* They'd *gone to a better place.* They *went home.* Death was "God's call," the prominent clergyman Henry Ward Beecher assured antebellum Americans. "Come home." Soothing words such as these were translated into optimistic inscriptions on tombstones accompanied by sculpted angels, cherubs, lambs, and urns with willow branches.

As mortality declined and a sense of propriety rose, squeamishness about death created fertile ground for euphemizing. This shift could be seen in newspaper *obituaries* (a euphemistic name for what used to be called "death notices"), with their increased emphasis on evasive language. An analysis of obituaries in Irish newspapers during the 1840s found a steep decline in the use of words such as "die" and "death." As for tombstone inscriptions, the new vocabulary clustered around themes such as embarking on a journey (*gone to her eternal rest*), entering a better world (*abode of peace*), taking a rest (*from the labors of a well-spent life*), and earning a reward (*enjoyment of that peace and bliss that await the virtuous and the good*).

On both sides of the Atlantic, the concept of a "good death" emerged, one that took place in the presence of loved ones, the dying person confident of salvation, while murmuring a few memorable last words. Such deathbed scenes were featured prominently in Victorian literature. Death was being sentimentalized.

In America, the Civil War interrupted this process. How good can a death be when it's far from family, in the midst of horror and carnage, with no loved one present to record last words, even if any were murmured? No terms softer than "die" and "dead" had enough gravity to describe the nearly seven hundred thousand soldiers who died during this conflict, 2 percent of the entire population (equivalent to six million fatalities today). As Drew Gilpin Faust recounts in *This Republic of Suffering: Death and the Civil War*, Yankees and Confederates alike became consumed with what they called a "harvest of death." In this context, using euphemisms for dying would have seemed nearly obscene.

Letters from the front to families of the dead relied on phrases such as "I was a witness to his death." They assured parents that their son "was not afraid but willing to die." Anticipating his own demise, one Confederate soldier who was mortally wounded during the battle of Gettysburg wrote his mother, "I died like a man."

Nurses did their best to fill in for mothers far away. Clara Barton carried a notebook in which she recorded the names of dying soldiers and any last words they might utter. A ballad at the time paid tribute to battlefield nurses like her:

Bless the lips that kissed our darling
As he lay upon his death bed,
Far from home and 'mid cold strangers
Blessings rest upon your head

★ ★ ★

O my darling! O our dead one!
Though you died far, far away
You had two kind lips to kiss you,
As upon your bier you lay.

Following the war, as Americans tried to put its horrors behind them, death-related euphemisms returned with a vengeance. Obituaries, once graphic in their descriptions of death and its causes, now reported that the deceased died of "short," "protracted," or "lingering" illnesses. Depictions of deathbed scenes that used to be common in such news accounts became a thing of the past. This was symptomatic, concluded Janice Hume in her book *Obituaries in American Culture,* "of a society running away from death." Our forced embrace of death during the Civil War prompted an unwillingness to even discuss the topic directly afterward. "Corpses" now were *cadavers;* "tombstones," *markers;* "coffins," *caskets* (adopting the name of jewel boxes). Nathaniel Hawthorne considered the latter "a vile modern phrase, which compels a person of sense and good taste to shrink more disgustfully than ever from the idea of being buried at all." Richard Meade Bache, whose father, General George Meade, commanded Union forces at Gettysburg, seconded Hawthorne's motion. "What trifling with a serious thing it is to call a coffin a *casket!*" wrote Bache.

What would Bache and Hawthorne have made of the fact

that by the turn of the century, undertakers had promoted themselves first to *funeral directors,* then to *morticians* (a term introduced in an 1895 issue of *Embalmer's Monthly*), presumably because it sounded like "physician." Throughout the twentieth century, members of the burgeoning funeral industry struggled to banish "death" and related words from their lexicon. The onetime "death certificate" was now a *vital statistics form*. Those who used to "die" now *expired*. They were *deceased,* not "dead." Their *remains* weren't "hauled" to funeral homes; they were *transferred*. The "hearses" used for this purpose became *professional cars*. Bodies that used to be "buried" during "funerals" were now *interred* during *services*.

The most fertile ground for euphemizing is one where open discussion of a topic is taboo. So it was with sex in the Victorian era, and so it became with death thereafter. This topic was driven underground, as it were, becoming the great unspoken. Children who could easily hear sexual issues discussed in some detail on radio and television seldom heard the end of life discussed openly. In a society where death is treated as a taboo topic, observed Elizabeth Kübler-Ross in 1969, "discussion of it is regarded as morbid."

Dying came to be seen as rather indecent, nearly obscene, and "death" akin to a four-letter word. Postwar advice books counseled parents to avoid talking about this subject with their children. A mid-twentieth century survey of 126 British parents found that nearly half—fifty-six—said they'd never discussed death with their offspring, and forty-two said they'd only done so euphemistically. *Went to sleep* became the most common euphemism for "died" when parents talked to their children about this subject. As a result, said one hospice social worker, not only did it not surprise her when children feared sleeping, but "it amazes me that children ever go to sleep at all."

Euphemisms are important bricks in the walls we've built to keep the dead from making us uncomfortable. Having done our best to avoid actual contact with the dying and dead, it would stand to reason that we'd replace associated expressions considered too stark and direct with soothing alternatives. *Passed away* is the most prevalent synonym for "died," or simply *passed*. A writer in the *New England Journal of Medicine* went further, proposing that we call the dead *nonliving persons*. The *British Medical Journal* published a suggestion that bodies with organs eligible for transplant be called *non-heart-beating donors*. Those suggestions didn't take, but doctors do still talk of *losing vital signs* and *negative patient-care outcomes*.

Our discomfort with this topic is reflected in the sheer volume of alternative words for death and dying. Some are quite inventive. Linguist Louise Pound once compiled hundreds of death-related euphemisms such as *counting daisy roots, left a vacant chair,* and *turned up his toes*. Whimsically macabre versions included *food for worms* and *crow bait*. Some were unique to particular professions, as when butchers *dropped off the hook,* actors took one *last curtain call* ("curtains"), or reporters *went 30,* "30" being the numeral typed by journalists to indicate that they'd reached the end of their copy. Since Pound created her list, this process has continued. Boxers *take the last count,* gourmands *lay down their knife and fork,* gamblers *cash in their chips,* computer programmers *go off-line*.

Growing interest in death and dying during recent decades, spearheaded by authors such as Elizabeth Kübler-Ross (*On Death and Dying*) and Sherwin Nuland (*How We Die*), suggests a greater willingness to face the topic squarely in print. This willingness is not reflected in everyday discourse, however. Collecting new death-related euphemisms such as *taking a dirt nap, biting the biscuit, in the crisper,* and *reformatted* keeps website proprietors busy. Oldies but goodies remain in constant use. When Barack Obama's grandmother died on the eve of his election as president of the United States, Obama announced that "she has gone home."

With today's trend toward nontraditional funerals, some involving green or woodland burials in natural cemeteries, a new euphemistic nomenclature of death is emerging. Bodies are buried in *alternative containers;* boxes or bags used instead of coffins. The increasing preference for cremation has led to *inurnment of cremains.* Online funerals are the latest development, attended by distant parties with the help of what some call "cremation cams." Virtual cemeteries are another modern wrinkle, as are memorial websites and online grieving communities created by friends of the deceased. Funeral directors have had to step lively to keep pace with this rapidly changing scene, recasting themselves as *funeral facilitators, grief facilitators,* or *memorial counselors* who engage in *memorialization* activities.

Another modern wrinkle is elaborate memorialization of dead pets by bereaved owners. Of course, the word "owners" is an offensive anachronism to animal rights advocates who propose *guardians* as a preferable designation for this group, and *companion animals* for what most still call "pets." Many of these advocates are vegetarians who also think we should restore candor to the language surrounding edible animals by calling poultry, *birds* ("You gonna eat that bird?"), and meat, *flesh* (as in *flesh eater*). From this perspective, many of the words we use for meat are euphemistic, evasive terms relied on to distract us from what we're actually putting in our mouths. Those who would have us dispense with soothing words for meat are rowing against the tide of history, of course. When it comes to food consumption, the trend is to euphemize more rather than less — especially the names of foods that make us a bit queasy.

7
Comestibles

Every year, an "oyster fry" is held in Virginia City, Nevada. Why, you may wonder, does a landlocked town hundreds of miles from the closest oyster bed host this festival? Because sometimes an oyster is not really an oyster. In this case, it is the renowned Rocky Mountain Oyster, aka calves' or lambs' testicles, rolled in cornmeal and fried in sizzling oil.

Rocky Mountain Oysters have been a western treat since America's frontier days. The custom of eating them in a gala atmosphere lives on in numerous festivals that celebrate ranching traditions. Some requirements of that tradition are described in the introduction to an old Montana recipe for this delicacy:

> When the branding crew leaves in the morning to go brand calves, send along a clean bucket for collecting the R.M. Oysters as the bull calves are castrated. Also send instructions to cover them with cold water, and

keep them in the shade. These instructions will probably be ignored unless you are taking lunch out to the branding crew, but it won't really matter as the oysters will keep well until the crew returns.

A 1905 cookbook I inherited from my South Dakota–raised grandmother includes a recipe for Fried Oysters that are clearly of the inland variety, although this is not spelled out. *Oysters* alone can be a euphemism for this frontier treat. *Fries* is another, for fried testicles, usually of lamb. Alternatively, the testicles of lamb or calves are sometimes called *external kidneys*.

This artful renaming of testicles is part of a long tradition of euphemizing the names of foods that turn our stomachs or are considered taboo. As early anthropologists discovered, food rivaled sex as an inspiration for substitute words among the groups they studied. A century ago, Ivor H. N. Evans found that the Sakai people in what is now Thailand changed the names of animals when eating them because they believed such creatures had souls. Thus, when being consumed, a porcupine became *the thorny one;* a coconut monkey, *no tail;* a mouse deer, *big eyes.*

Culinary renaming practices vary from culture to culture, of course, and from epoch to epoch. Some contemporary consumers of meat don't flinch at calling inner organs by their proper names. An Asian market I frequent sells intestine of pig as "pig's intestines." I've never found that cut of meat by this or any other name at my local Kroger's, however. Nor does this supermarket sell tripe (stomach lining of various animals), which might have done better with a different name. Ditto for scrapple, the Pennsylvania Dutch staple made from pork trimmings and cornmeal mush. These products need to be sent back to the naming committee. Haggis, a Scottish favorite that consists of chopped inner organs of sheep combined with spices and filler such as oatmeal and suet baked in a lamb's belly, has enjoyed somewhat more success. According to the *Concise Encyclopedia of Gastronomy*, "As a rule one does not attempt to make a haggis; one just buys a haggis and does not inquire too closely as to how it was made."

A WEE DROP

For the past three decades, author Paul Dickson has conducted meticulous scholarship on synonyms for drinking and drunkenness. With the help of sources ranging from linguists to bartenders and emergency room personnel, Dickson compiled more than three thousand synonyms that he published in *Drunk: The Definitive Drinker's Dictionary* (2009). Dickson calls this book "a celebration of the English language and its euphemistic splendor." Its entries range from the mundane (*tipsy*) to the arcane (*all geezed up*) and the colorful (*at peace with the floor*).

Paul Dickson is just the latest author to collect words we substitute for liquor, drinking, and drunkenness. Examining these words has fascinated predecessors ranging from Chaucer to H. L. Mencken. On the Internet, the creator of a website called the Drunktionary posted more than five thousand synonyms for drunkenness, then watched this number grow with reader contributions.

Such lists brim with euphemisms. In its most basic form, liquor becomes a mere *beverage*. With elaborate decorum, drinkers *lift an elbow* to down a *libation, some spirits,* or *schnapps*. They have *an eye-opener* to start the day and a *nightcap* to end it. In between, they might enjoy *a pick-me-up, a nip, a little snort, a wee drop, a restorative,* or—in a pinch—some *cough medicine.*

Such euphemistic talk camouflages what is still seen by many as a shady activity, one that too often leads to—ahem—*inebriation.* At best, *having a glow on;* at worst, *smashed. Under the table. Schnozzled. Pie-eyed. Stewed to the gills.*

Mencken noted how much more common, and colorful, drink talk is in the United States than in the United Kingdom, a fact acknowledged by a British reviewer of Mencken's *The American Language,* who envied such Americanisms as *piffled, tanked, slopped, snooted, het-up,* and *frazzled.* One problem confronting those who write about this topic in Great Britain is the fact that its strict libel laws don't necessarily consider accuracy an acceptable defense. A British politician once won a substantial settlement from a journalist who'd called him "drunk" in print, even though this was apparently true. Had the reporter taken refuge in press dodges such as *outgoing, ruddy-faced,* or *tired and emotional,* he could have saved himself, and his employer, a lot of money.

Paul Dickson points to the ridiculousness of those who drink too much as a powerful motivator for creating camouflage words. "Drinkers and those who fuel them feel more comfortable euphemizing their condition," he writes. "Better to say that one was 'a little squiffy' last night than to admit intoxication."

And what of the plaintive morning after? Being hung over has its own euphemistic glossary: *flulike symptoms,* say, or *under the weather.* At one time, this condition was called a *Dutch headache.* Global euphemisms for a hangover collected by essayist Joan Acocella include *hair ache* (French), *carpenters in the forehead* (Danish), and *made of rubber* (Salvadorans). Acocella found many ways to say "hangover" in Ukrainian, but few in Hebrew.

(continued)

During Prohibition, there was widespread concern that the colorful euphemisms surrounding drinking might disappear. A 1916 article in the *Sunday Oregonian* fretted that "Hereafter Only Prunes will be 'Stewed.'" If anything, the opposite was true. According to Paul Dickson, the period from 1920 to 1933 when liquor sales were illegal constituted a "Golden Age" of euphemistic talk about drinking. In one 1922 U.S. District Court case, a lawyer asked a witness if he'd been "keyed up." The witness responded that he'd been "pretty well organized" and "about soused." The judge then had his say: "All these countless slang expressions will not be tolerated in this court. If the man is drunk, all right. I do not know the legal meanings of 'soused' and 'keyed up,' 'organized,' 'polluted' and expressions of a like nature, but I do know what 'drunk' means. A man is drunk who is not his normal self, under the influence of liquor."

The lawyer then asked his witness if he'd been drunk. "Yes," the witness replied, "Yes."

Gastronomic Red Herrings

Which foods are considered tasty and which ones repulsive depends on who you are, where you are, and when. Without flinching or euphemizing, ancient Romans ate all manner of food that we shun today. One of the earliest known cookbooks, two millennia old, included Roman recipes for pig's paunch, cock's testicles, capon's kidneys, hare's liver, and sheep's lungs, as well as flamingo, parrot, cuttlefish, tooth fish, horned fish, conger eel, stuffed dormouse, and fish-liver pudding. Roman gourmands were also quite fond of sow's vulva. Like contemporary Americans, Romans would not eat horse meat.

Culture dictates food taboos. There is nothing inherently wrong with eating any digestible food; only what society tells us is wrong. Westerners are as horrified by the idea of eating dogs, as Indians are by our custom of consuming cows. The horse meat that Americans shun is a staple of French cuisine. My wife's grandmother, raised with rural Ukrainian eating customs, considered lettuce "pig food." What's considered yummy in one society can be seen as yucky in another, and our naming practices fall in step. Pig-eating English speakers call this animal's flesh "pork." Those who consider that meat impure say it comes from "swine."

Why certain foods are taboo in some cultures but not in others is the source of much debate. Why do so many of the world's people gladly eat rat meat, but we don't? Where does the love of blood sausage in some cultures and the revulsion for that dish in others come from? Does the name alone keep many people from eating oxtail? No one is quite sure. For our purposes, let's focus on the simple fact that certain foods are prime candidates for renaming in cultures that find them off-putting. Westerners are more likely to eat seaweed at a Japanese restaurant when it's called a *sea vegetable*. The lowly crayfish sells better as a lordly *rock lobster*. American soldiers are happier when served *chicken Francesca* than when chicken and gravy is on their menu.

The results are what Keith Allan and Kate Burridge call gastronomic red herrings, euphemistic names intended to distract us from what we're actually eating. Even the innocuous term "giblets" helps conceal the fact that it's the inner organs of poultry that we're cooking. Some starving Europeans who ate cats during World War II called them *country rabbits*. Poverty-stricken Americans who took to eating armadillo during the Depression sarcastically called it *Hoover hog*. A few decades earlier, Americans who were sick of eating dried beans took to calling them *Alaska Strawberries*.

Fooling around with the names of food is a long-standing practice that's tightly tied to both taste and taboo. Because food taboos are so focused on meat, euphemizing kicks in to high gear when it comes to naming animals and parts of animals considered edible. In that regard, we're not much different from Thailand's Sakai who would eat the flesh of animals they'd killed only after renaming it. Like them, we don't eat cows but do eat *beef*. Not calves but *veal*. Not deer but *venison*. Not pig but *pork*. Not sheep but *mutton*. (Lamb, surprisingly, seems to have escaped this renaming process.)

One needn't be a vegetarian to conclude that manipulating the words we use for animal flesh may reflect our ambivalence about eating once-living creatures. It's not just cuts of meat that are euphemized but also the way they're retrieved from the animals we used to "slaughter" but now *process*. As a Costco spokesman reminds us, "converting live animals into food is not a pleasant task."

Modern culinary euphemisms reflect squeamishness about food preparation, especially when animal flesh is involved. It wasn't always so. Before the late-nineteenth century, animals were routinely slaughtered at home. Until then, an ability to butcher meat was one of the domestic arts. An English cookbook advised seventeenth-century English housewives that "in all manner of meat except a shoulder of mutton, you shall crush and break the bones well; from pigs and rabbits you shall cut off the feet before you spit them, and the heads when you serve them to table." Victorian women who might have swooned after watching five minutes of *Sex and the City* didn't flinch when *Mrs. Beeton's Book of Household Management* told them to prepare the main ingredient of Turtle Soup thusly:

> Cut off the head of the turtle the preceding day. In the morning open the turtle by leaning heavily on the shell of the animal's back, whilst you cut this off all round. Turn it upright on its end, that all the water, &c. may run out, when the flesh should be cut off along the spine, with the knife sloping towards the bones, for fear of touching the gall.

Now we're getting into sticky territory. Once we delve too far inside the corpses of edible animals, naming their organs becomes problematic. Ever since thymus glands were dubbed *sweetbreads* by some clever cook, the practice of renaming dubious cuts of meat has generated unusually imaginative euphemisms. (According to the *Oxford English Dictionary*, the first recorded use of "sweetbread" was in a 1565 animal thesaurus that referred to "the sweete breade in a hogge.")

Renaming inner organs became a pressing concern during World War II when so much of the outer flesh of slaughtered animals was reserved for men and women in uniform. Left for those at home were the entrails: livers, kidneys, brains, lungs, intestines, stomachs, testicles, and hearts that few Americans wanted to eat. Making matters worse were the names they were given: organ meats, inside meats, and offal, which includes appendages such as tails and feet and sounds a lot like "awful." Who wants to eat that? Historic British alternatives such as "humbles" and "nasty bits" were no improvement.

In order to keep their protein consumption up, Americans on the home front needed to be encouraged to eat more inner organs of animals. The government therefore convened a distinguished group of social scientists that included anthropologist Margaret Mead to determine how disdain for this type of meat might be overcome. One thing they quickly discovered was that when consumers were served cooked offal that wasn't named, they were far less put off than they were when this meat was named. That's why the team proposed dubbing these organs *variety meats*. This appealing new name led to a modest uptick in sales of such meats that didn't continue following the appearance of pork chops, pot roast, and T-bone steaks after the war.

Although the name "variety meats" didn't catch on with the public in any lasting way, some offal-cooking chefs still use it. A website called the Cook's Thesaurus includes a section on variety meats. This also was the name of a 1982 cookbook that offered recipes for dishes made from the inner organs as well as from the head, feet, ears, and tail of various animals. Of necessity, many such recipes have French names. That's partly because variety meats have long been a staple of Continental cuisine, partly because English-speaking consumers are more likely to eat something like kidneys if they're called *rognons*, and appear in dishes such as *brochettes de rognon, rognons au Madère, rognons Bretonne,* or *rognons de veau Clémentine*. If and when Americans begin to eat horse meat, it will most likely be as *viande de cheval*.

Continentalizing

In his novel *Nobody's Fool,* Richard Russo depicts two elderly women eating lunch at the Northwoods Motor Inn in upstate New York. Mrs. Gruber has ordered snails, but after sampling one wishes she hadn't. In fact, Mrs. Gruber has just spit her first bite into a napkin.

"What was there about the way it looked that made you think it *would* be good?" asks her companion, Miss Beryl. Russo continues:

> Mrs. Gruber had not responded to this question. Having spit the snail into the napkin, she'd become deeply involved with the problem of what to do with the napkin.
>
> "It was gray and slimy and nasty looking," Miss Beryl reminded her friend.
>
> Mrs. Gruber admitted this was true, but went on to explain that it wasn't so much the snail itself that had attracted her as the name. "They got their own name in French," she reminded Miss Beryl, stealthily exchanging her soiled cloth napkin for a fresh one at an adjacent table. "*Escargot.*"
>
> There's also a word in English, Miss Beryl had pointed out. Snail. Probably horse doo had a name in French also, but that didn't mean God intended for you to eat it.

When it comes to euphemizing food names, French is a godsend. Those who would not eat a dish under its plain English name might if it's given a Gallic verbal equivalent. If you're squeamish about eating calves' brains but want to try them nonetheless, perhaps in a butter sauce, they might go down better as *cervelles de veau au beurre noir*. "Swollen goose livers" would not do well on menus, but *pâté de foie gras* has done just fine.

Among menu writers, the urge to draw on other languages, especially French, has been nearly irresistible. Restaurateurs were once advised that this was an effective way to "continentalize" their bills of fare. The results are an amusing mishmash of misspelled or misapplied Gallicisms such as the entry on a World War I era Chicago menu for *Beef Broth à l'Anglaise* ("Beef Broth in the English manner"). This was on the *Carte du Jour* of the Auditorium Hotel where my great-grandfather Horace Scott often dined. On July 13, 1916, the Auditorium also served *Consommé Emanuele, Strained Chicken Gumbo en Tasse, Onion Soup Gratinée, Stuffed Celery à l'Auditorium, Planked Bluefish Maitré d'Hotel, Sea Bass Sauté aux Fines Herbs, Breast of Guinea Hen à la Windsor,* and *Larded Sirloin à la Nivernaise.*

Continentalizing menu writers have cleaned up their acts somewhat since Horace Scott dined at the Auditorium but not altogether. In contemporary restaurant lingo, "soup" becomes *potage;* "spaghetti," *pasta;* its sauce *marinara.* At a trendy New York restaurant, the once-humble "mushroom soup" has been upgraded to *cappuccino of forest mushrooms.* In recent decades arcane foodiespeak has incorporated ostentatious Gallicisms on upscale menus in a kind of fusion argot: *Entrecôte au Poivre Madagascar; Stuffed Tomato aux Herbes; Ravioli en Parmigiana, en Casserole; Thyme Fumet Essence; Fraises Charles Stuart; Strawberry Pots de Crème; Short Ribs Provençale with Crème Fraîche Mashed Potatoes; Petites Native Frog Legs Provençale served with Concasseed Tomatoes, touch of Garlic and Spicy Butter.*

Exotic-sounding food names abound on restaurant menus for one simple reason: they move product. In extensive studies of this phenomenon, Cornell University's Brian Wansink has repeatedly found that menu items with euphemistically elegant names are more likely to be ordered by customers.

Restaurateurs already knew this, of course. Squid does better when called by its Italian name, *calamari*. Shrimp sounds even more tempting as *scampi* (which is actually Italian for certain types of lobster). When celebrity chef Mario Batali realized that American customers were unlikely to order the seasoned pork fat Italians call *lardo,* he instructed his waiters to call it *prosciutto bianco.* Giving foreign names to dubious dishes is key to getting Americans and Britons to try such fare. "You lie to them," Batali told a reporter. "We mislead them."

Due in part to the leadership of adventurous chefs like Batali and Fergus Henderson, once-reviled cuts of meat have begun to enjoy a renaissance, almost an offal chic. Henderson fired the first salvo in this counterattack with a 1998 cookbook called *The Whole Beast: Nose to Tail Eating.* This was the year that Mario Batali's flagship restaurant Babbo opened in New York. Over time its menu featured delicacies such as *fennel-dusted sweetbreads, tripe alla parmigiana, pig's foot Milanese, lamb brain Francobolli,* and *testa,* headcheese made from boiled pig brains. In Oakland, California, the Oliveto restaurant has enjoyed some success serving *sheep's milk ravioli with goat sugo* and *goat chops fried Milanese style.*

Under its own name, goat is a popular meat in many parts of the world. Although it's featured in some nouveaux restaurants such as Oliveto, few Americans will eat goat no matter what it's called. Most associate it with either smelly, obstinate barnyard animals or cute ones at petting zoos. Goat meat itself is thought to be tough, bad tasting, and low class. These were the findings of a survey of six hundred Floridians. At the outset, few expressed any interest in sampling this meat. When taking part in a blind taste test, however, more of them liked barbecued goat better than barbecued beef that was prepared the same way. The University of Florida professors who conducted this study concluded that the name "goat" was central to this meat's image problem in the United States. They thought changing its name to *chevon*—a euphemism vaguely reminiscent of *chèvre*, French for goat (and goat milk cheese)—might help create a market for the meat. Goat ranchers use *chevon*, and that name tested well among study participants. If the flesh of calves can be called *veal* and that of pigs *pork*, reasoned the professors, why can't goat meat be called *chevon*? In the two decades since this study was conducted, that name hasn't caught on. To Americans, goat meat remains "goat," not *chevon*.

Relying on foreignisms to sell food can be sabotaged by news headlines, of course. Foreign-based food names are an obvious target when countries come into conflict. Remember *freedom fries*? That short-lived attempt to rename "French fries" during the war in Iraq was too contrived even for those who wanted to give France the back of their hand because of its opposition to this war. At the peak of anti-German hysteria during World War I, sauerkraut (the root of the nickname "krauts" given to German soldiers) was renamed *liberty cabbage*. This euphemism did not survive the 1918 armistice. Nor did one for Hamburg steak: *liberty steak*. Australians tried various ways to avoid saying "German sausage" at this time, calling it *Belgian sausage, Devon sausage,* or *Windsor sausage*. None took.

The Power of Positive Euphemizing

Deep in the waters off Chile swim schools of *Dissostichus eleginoides*. Chileans call these fish *bacalao de profundidad,* or "cod of the deep." English speakers called them *Patagonian toothfish*. With their bulging eyes, pronounced underbite, and pointy teeth that resemble a giant saw, these huge fish — which grow to be six-feet long and longer in a fifty-year lifespan — are unusually ugly and off-putting. Until recently, the Patagonian toothfish was rarely consumed by anyone. Chileans themselves did not care for its bland, oily flesh.

In 1977 a Los Angeles–based fish importer named Lee Lantz saw a Patagonian toothfish that had been caught by accident splayed on a Valparaiso dock. Several days later, he saw another one at a Santiago fish market and bought a filet. After cooking and eating his filet, Lantz wondered if this omega-3-packed fish might suit the American palate better than the Chilean. Its name was a problem, though. Following much rumination, and after passing on "Pacific Sea Bass" and "South American Sea Bass," Lantz settled on *Chilean sea bass*. Under this moniker, it was bought first for fish sticks, then by Chinese restaurateurs, and finally by chefs at upscale restaurants such as the Four Seasons in New York. Within a few years of its renaming, Chilean sea bass became so popular that stocks of this slow-growing fish were depleted by what author G. Bruce Knecht in his 2006 book *Hooked* called "an unsustainable feeding frenzy." A boycott campaign dubbed "Take a Pass on Chilean Sea Bass" prompted many restaurants to stop serving this now-too-popular fish.

Patagonian toothfish is not the only fish whose stock soared following a strategic renaming. The same thing happened to the popular *orange roughy*, which was once the unpopular "slime head." Yesterday's "muttonfish" has enjoyed far greater success as today's *snapper*. What used to be known as "dolphin fish" (no kin to the mammal by the same name) has been successfully reborn as *mahi mahi*. *Tuna* is far more popular under that name than it was under its previous name, "horse mackerel."

Might Asian carp enjoy the same fate? This big, bony invasive species began driving native species of fish out of American waterways two decades ago. Various remedies have been attempted to address that problem, including construction of electrified underwater barriers. The state of Louisiana, however, has taken a more ingenious approach: enlisting Baton Rouge chef Philippe Parola to come up with tempting ways to prepare this unappealing fish. According to Parola, the deboned flesh of Asian carp resembles a cross between scallop and crabmeat. Parola and Louisiana's Department of Wildlife and Fisheries realize that the original name of this ugly fish has negative connotations, however. That is why a central part of their strategy is to give the Asian carp a brand-new, more tempting moniker: *silver fin.*

Most fish were given their names by fishermen, locals, or scientists who weren't thinking about how the names would look on a restaurant menu. They just went with fun appellations such as *elephant fish, sea squirts,* and *dogfish.* At one time in England, a class of long, eel-type fish was called pintle fish, "pintle" being slang for "penis." Medieval Frenchmen called one particularly repulsive fish with a dark, puckered mouth *cul de cheval,* "horse's ass."

You see why renaming certain foods can be so imperative to those who sell them. And it isn't just living creatures. The same University of Florida group that confirmed Americans' aversion to goat meat also found negative associations with the muscadine grape based on its name alone. Foods made with soy products sell better when the word "soy" is not prominent on the label. Other fruits and vegetables with similar problems have been given successful verbal makeovers. Sales of what used to be called the Chinese gooseberry took off when it was renamed *kiwifruit*—after the flightless bird that is New Zealand's national symbol—by a produce exporter, half a century ago. (An earlier attempt to rename it *melonette* was fruitless.) The lowly cremini mushroom, beloved by few in a large form that used to be discarded, became a bestseller when reintroduced as *portobello* or *portabella*. If you want to get technical, *mushroom* is a euphemism for a species of fungus called *Agaricus bisporus*.

When the unfortunately named rapeseed oil had trouble competing with products that had nicer names, a Canadian strain low in saturated fat was dubbed *Canola* (i.e., "Canadian oil") in 1978 and has done rather well since. Incidentally, the "rape" in rapeseed oil has nothing to do with sexual assault. It is a linguistic anomaly based on the Latin term *rapum* for "turnip," a relative of rapeseed.

Many of today's food-based euphemisms are the result of emerging health concerns. An organic sweetener sold as an alternative to white sugar is dubbed *evaporated cane juice*. This sugarcane product is somewhat less refined than the kind we usually put on our Rice Krispies, but it is sugar nonetheless, even if that word appears nowhere in its name. *Turbinado* is another less-refined sugarcane product with a name that obscures its origins.

As with euphemisms in general, those involving food reflect social changes. Today, they emerge primarily from fertile brains in corporate marketing departments. One market study confirmed how much antipathy there was to the name and notion of prunes. As a result, the California Prune Board petitioned the Food and Drug Administration to allow them to relabel their product *dried plums*. "If you call a dried plum a dried plum instead of calling it a prune, it sells better," Senator Barbara Boxer (D-CA) argued in a letter to the FDA. "So I'm all for that. I think we're talking about jobs, we're talking about all kinds of good things that can happen once we can sell this product as a dried plum."

Although it approved the name change, the FDA disallowed "Dried Plum Juice" on the basis that the term was rather oxymoronic. The California Prune Board then reintroduced itself as the California Dried Plum Board. Ketchum, a public relations firm it hired, created a dried plum team that courted media coverage with all the intensity and inventiveness of political strategists. Members of a Ketchum "war room" bombarded the press with news releases, satellite feeds, sound bites, slogans, and Internet posts calling attention to this fruit's new name. Ketchumites called their campaign the "Federal Witness Reidentification Program." Sales of prunes/dried plums in the United States were soon up over 5 percent.

As the dried plum/prune saga shows, in the modern era, renaming foods is often a matter of carefully researched euphemizing. This illustrates the penchant for renaming engaged in by merchants who long ago replaced shamans and priests as our primary suppliers of euphemisms. For those with something to sell, effective renaming can result in higher profits. More revenue. A better bottom line. These are just a few of the euphemistic ways they, and we, refer to one of our deepest sources of anxiety: money.

8

Show Me the Liquidity

When the editors of a collection of personal essays about money had trouble recruiting contributors, they approached a man who'd already written about his drug addiction and nervous breakdown. Surely this author would have no difficulty writing about money. He did. The writer begged off, confessing that there was no way he could discuss the subject candidly.

He is not alone. Money is one of our most taboo topics. I know many more people who will tell me about their sex lives, their loneliness, or their fear of dying than will reveal how much they earn, own, and owe. Therapists commonly find that nothing is harder for patients to talk about than money. In a survey of women's attitudes, *Ms.* magazine discovered that those polled considered money "the ultimate intimacy," more difficult to deal with openly than sex.

When human beings were more self-sufficient and their commerce was based on barter more than on cash, there was little demand for money-based euphemisms. If trade consisted of exchanging ten ears of corn for two loaves of bread, what need was there to euphemize? As the cash economy grew, there was every reason. When financial transactions became central to life in general, money became the measure of one's worth — in many senses of the word. If having enough money could make you feel more worthwhile, an understandable fear of having too little could make you feel less worthwhile, worthless even. Alternatively, in an egalitarian context, having too much money can feel embarrassing. Therapists have a word for anxiety about being too rich: "affluenza." When in college, my son found that even his wealthiest classmates called themselves "upper middle class."

In some African societies, the number of cows owned is a measure of social standing. Among the Saami (Lapps), it's reindeer. To us, cash is the primary yardstick measuring where we stand. In a society that's prone to use wealth as a sign of personal value, making our financial status public tells the world a lot about who we think we are. Too much, perhaps. How could this topic make us anything but anxious? In the financial realm, no less than any other, anxiety is the primary incubator of evasive language.

Money Talks

Money has long been a popular source of slang that allowed us to avoid using the m-word: *bread, dough, moolah, scratch.* Now, we're just as likely to use euphemistic synonyms: *funds, finances, resources, currency.* Those who don't have enough money are *financially insecure.* They have *limited means.* They're *a little short.* When my son tells me about a friend who's strapped, he says she's *under budget constraint.*

In past eras, money wasn't as rich a source of euphemisms for the simple reason that there wasn't enough of it around to merit verbal evasion. Once there was, and once we discovered how uncomfortable this topic made us, euphemisms flowered. "Money management" became *wealth management.* "Income" became *revenue.* "Wages" were transformed into *salaries,* then *compensation* or *remuneration.* Those doing short-term work received *stipends.* College professors who wouldn't be so crass as to expect payment for making a presentation were happy to accept *honorariums,* preferably ones that included a *per diem.* Once again, euphemisms were put to work on behalf of gentility.

Like any euphemisms worth their salt, the ones we use for money soften blunt terms that once were common. You're no longer "tapped out"; you simply have *cash-flow problems.* Business losses have become little more than *revenue deficiencies* or *revenue gaps.* Those who used to "go bankrupt" now *file for Chapter 11* or *Chapter 13.* They aren't "broke"; they're *insolvent.* Their ledger books show *negative net worth* due to *downward adjustment.*

As money, commerce, and the workplace have crept in to so many aspects of contemporary life, so have associated euphemisms. These euphemisms have proved very handy not just for masking anxieties but also for surrounding our financial transactions with verbal fog. Who wouldn't prefer to *leverage* a major purchase than "go deeply in debt" to do so? When *New York Times* columnist Thomas Friedman argued that automakers should have "limits on the leverage they can amass," I believe he meant that they should not be allowed to take on too much debt. Those who do this may have to *deleverage.* I'm old enough to remember when that was known as "paying off loans."

The modern economy is rife with this type of verbal

camouflage. I recently read about a new business that was said to be *in start-up mode* (i.e., it had no customers). Its owners were in a *pre-revenue* state. They were experiencing a *shortfall.* Or, as the president of a struggling college once reported, its financial standing had some *soft spots.*

Those who write annual reports are masters of this type of doublespeak. These reports brim with euphemistic language such as *a challenging economic environment* (recession), *nonperforming assets* (bad loans), and *downward adjustment* (losses). Bad investments are *nonstrategic* or *long-term buys* (i.e., they might pan out over time, but don't bet on it). *Strategic reviews* are under way. *Unforeseen events had a negative impact on earnings* (they suffered a loss). *Profitability was reduced* (more losses). Companies then endure *substantial write-offs* (big losses). In a classic oxymoron, these firms suffer *negative growth* (they shrink).

The peculiar nomenclature of modern finance has become so pervasive that it's easy to overlook its euphemistic roots. Such manipulation of language goes beyond easing discomfort with soothing words. In some cases, it leaps from benign face-saving into a realm where wrongdoing is facilitated by verbal flimflam. In this sphere, brokers who pad their commissions by unnecessarily buying and selling stocks are said to be *churning,* as if they were making financial butter. What's "price-fixing" to you is *parallel pricing* to executives who engage in this illegal practice. Those who buy troubled companies and strip out valuable resources *unbundle* them. At one time, this involved *leveraged buyouts* (i.e., assuming massive debt to purchase a company that then becomes liable for the debt). When this practice was given a bad name by the likes of Michael Milken and Gordon Gekko, those doing it relabeled their companies *private equity firms* and continued to borrow

money to buy businesses they could bleed of resources before reselling them.

Such verbal dodges make shady practices sound positively sunny. There are many more. Corporate spying might be called *competitive intelligence gathering* and is. Copying someone else's product is *reverse engineering.* Even those guilty of actual malfeasance can hide behind a curtain of euphemisms such as *double-entry bookkeeping* and *creative accounting.* An acknowledgment of fraudulent accounting consists of a mere *restatement of earnings.* A bribe given or taken goes by many names: *commission, consideration, contribution, consultant's fee, donation, gift, incentive, inducement,* or *rebate.* The bribed party was *taken care of.*

Even victims of misconduct rely on euphemisms to avoid admitting their plight. Businesses that don't like to talk about shoplifting and employee theft call this problem *inventory shrinkage* (*shrink* for short: "Our shrink is down from last year"). Those who try to catch shoplifters, yesterday's "store detectives" and "floorwalkers," are today's *loss-prevention specialists.* They engage in *corporate-asset protection.* Stolen goods are *temporarily displaced inventory.* After being robbed, one bank posted the loss on its books as an *unauthorized withdrawal.*

Such euphemisms don't just save face; they hide financial fragility. Only when an economy collapses do we realize how many euphemisms helped pave the way for dubious transactions.

Hard Times

What we used to call hard times provide a hothouse of evasive terms that camouflage what's actually going on. *Softening* of the economy is one of my favorites. When the Dow Jones Industrial Average sank 508 points on October 19, 1987, nearly 23 percent of its total value, some called this calamitous event an *equity retreat*.

A century and more ago, stock market crashes were called "panics." Since the word "panic" itself may have contributed to the fear that fueled such events, it was replaced with *depression*. This was thought to be a less ominous synonym. After the Great Depression took care of that one, *recession* was conjured as an alternative, at least for milder economic retreats. When *recession* took on negative connotations of its own, we resorted to *slump, slowdown,* or—most popular of all—*downturn* (George W. Bush's preferred euphemism for the economic crisis that commenced in his second term).

Correction has proved to be a durable euphemism for economic reversals since the *New York Times* began using the word that way during the early 1950s. Thereafter, a declining stock market was one being *corrected,* like a second grader's homework. Markets of all kinds went through *corrections*. This term has an aura of normality, a sense that mere *adjustment* is going on, not only anticipated but healthy. As millions of homeowners began losing their houses to foreclosure, Treasury Secretary Henry Paulson blandly referred to the *housing correction* he saw under way, one that would puncture the artificial *bubble* it was based on.

That bubble came to be, in part, because of the ease of borrowing money using homes as collateral. If the house was already mortgaged, such borrowing would call for a second mortgage. That term became passé, however, and for good reason. "Second mortgage" sounds forbidding, like an added ball and chain. *Accessing home equity,* on the other hand—

tapping it, *putting it to work*—sounds like discovering diamonds in your backyard and was perceived this way by millions of homeowners. They *monetized their assets.*

Banks began to market home loans aggressively in the 1980s, using soothing terminology devised by copywriters they hired away from product manufacturers. Those who might not qualify due to a bad credit history were upgraded to having *less-than-perfect credit.* This phrase was used to describe high-risk homebuyers who were then offered *subprime* loans. Unlike, say, "junk bonds," the term "subprime loan" in no way reflected the riskiness of that type of credit. The fact that high-risk loans were now broadly called *loan products* or *financial products* helped make them easier to sell. A product sounds tangible, like a bagel, say, or a bicycle. Many loan products were mortgages that had been carved into *tranches* (Franco-financial for "slices"), then bundled into *collaterized debt obligations* (CDOs). These loans were said to be *securitized.* This had a reassuring sound. Something that's *securitized* is secure, right? Wrong. Bundling risky loans with safe ones to make them safer was like combining E. coli–infected ground meat with a clean batch in hopes that the clean batch would purify the contaminated one.

"Risk" itself was a word seldom heard in the process, though *downside potential* did sometimes get mentioned. When, despite all the swaps, securitizing, and collateralizing going on, many of these debts proved to be uncollectible, what used to be called "bad loans" were converted verbally into *illiquid assets.* The subsequent drying up of credit became a *liquidity crisis.*

The economic collapse that got under way in 2007 was like a short course in an esoteric vocabulary camouflaging the financial monkeyshines involved. If such terms put you to sleep, that was exactly the point. They'd done their job.

Cagey, jargony euphemisms were integral to the boom that led to the bust of 2008. Arcane verbal evasions helped keep what was actually going on hidden behind a euphemistic curtain. It might be something of a stretch to say that evasive language facilitated the financial shenanigans we've witnessed in recent years, but only somewhat. Calling dubious loans made to bad credit risks *subprime loans* certainly helped bankers make them. Didn't they know better?

Of course they did.

Among themselves, those who engaged in financial doubletalk used starkly different terminology. In-house, vague euphemisms gave way to vivid slang. At the peak of the lending binge, mortgage brokers talked cynically of the "liar loans" they knowingly made to borrowers who faked their creditworthiness. At an extreme were "ninja loans," an acronym for loans offered to those with no income, no job or assets. Such insider lingo was far more colorful, blunt, and candid than the deceptive euphemisms foisted on outsiders. *Haircut* transactions were ones with reduced profit. A *clawback* process was one in which excess payments were retrieved from the party to whom they'd been made. *Cramdown* settlements were ones crammed down creditors' throats by judges. Their insolvent customers were *upside down*. Those who owed more on a mortgage than their property was worth were *underwater*. A rapidly declining asset was a *falling knife*. *Zombie banks* were ones with insufficient assets that continued to do business anyway. Perhaps more public use of such candid terms might have helped avoid some of the worst excesses whose skids were greased by misleading euphemisms.

Fooling around with verbiage is part and parcel of the modern market economy. No one has a more pressing need to make touchy topics discussable than those who have products to sell.

Commerce

To us, a foundation is an organization that gives away money. To our grandmothers, it was an undergarment that nipped and tucked their body's bulges. In the early 1920s, purveyors of brassieres and corsets had concluded that a softer, vaguer word might help them sell these products, or at least make them easier to advertise. Thus, *foundation garments* aka *foundations*. According to the U.S. Patent Office, this term incorporates devices intended to "protect, compress, support, restrain, or alter the configuration of the body torso or a portion thereof, e.g., the female mammae, or those portions of the body lying below the mammae and extending along a line below the abdomen portion of the body to the region of the thighs."

Today "foundation garments" has a musty, dated sound. The need for their assistance remains, however. For women who might like a little such help but are loath to sound like grandma, *body shapers* have come to the rescue. *Shapewear.*

Men's issues along this line have given birth to gender-appropriate euphemisms. What was once known as a "suspensory" sold better as an *athletic supporter,* even among nonathletes. In 1897 the Patent Office approved a version of this product that was called a "jock strap." Symptoms of the fungus tinea cruris that commonly collects in men's groins was subsequently called "jock-strap itch" by merchants who proposed to cure it. That term was eventually shortened to *jock itch* in the vernacular.

Products related to the body and its functions cry out for innocuous names. This is especially true when they need to be discussed in advertisements. As ad critic Leslie Savan puts it, "the more scatological the product, the more euphemistic the spot." Thus "constipation" became *irregularity* (or, better yet, *occasional irregularity*) among those who sell laxatives. To deodorant makers, "sweat" was transformed into mere *wetness*. After Listerine popularized an obscure medical term that blends the Latin *halitus* (for "breath") with the Greek *osis* (for "condition"), *halitosis* stood in for "bad breath" in its ads. "Ringworm" in the feet (tinea pedis) is another affliction that became easier to talk about when the manufacturers of Absorbine Jr. renamed it *athlete's foot* in 1928.

After World War I, a women's deodorant called Odo-Ro-No recast body odor as *BO*. This abbreviation did not catch on until Lifebuoy Health Soap began to warn consumers about its dangers a few years later. In ubiquitous radio spots, "Beee-Ohhhh!!" was said sonorously by a deep-throated announcer, to the accompaniment of a foghorn. Customers were warned that BO in thirteen key body areas stood between them and social success. Eradicating BO with Lifebuoy "can help you win friends wherever you go" a magazine ad assured readers. Another ad featured illustrated panels of a driver and his fiancée nearly getting hit by a truck. "Hal didn't suspect—and Martha didn't either—that a scare can bring on *NERVOUS B.O.*" read the accompanying text. This near-crash and ensuing body odor provokes a crisis in their relationship. "Should I speak to Martha?" Hal wonders. "After all, a man expects the girl he's marrying to be dainty." Martha herself wonders if she ought to say something about Hal's BO because "a girl expects the man she's marrying to be careful." On the advice of Martha's mother and Hal's doctor, both start using Lifebuoy. With BO vanquished, their relationship is saved.

The flourishing personal-care industry that grew up during the past century not only promised to help mask and eliminate body odors but also gave birth to a brave new world of euphemisms. *Personal hygiene* products such as Lifebuoy promised *personal freshness*. Menstruating women were offered *everyday freshness, sanitary protection,* and *feminine hygiene. Toilet tissue* replaced *toilet paper* among those selling it. Better yet, *bath tissue.*

The expansion of commerce during the past century has led to an explosion of newly minted, constantly updated euphemisms in every sphere of the marketplace. Along the way, words have been continually upgraded and degraded. "Cheap," for example, was originally an abridgement of *good cheap,* meaning simply "good bargain." In time, this term took on connotations of poor quality and gave way to euphemisms such as *inexpensive* and sundry successors: *economy, budget, thrifty, frugal, reasonable, affordable,* and, especially, *value.* "We're not here to sell cheap food," says a Whole Foods executive, "but we've been working hard on our value flank." Along the way "day-old" baked goods were renamed *yesterday's fresh.* "Spoiled" produce became *distressed.* "Used" merchandise (itself a euphemism for "secondhand") was now *preowned* or, better still, *vintage.* What once were called "junk stores" became *thrift shops,* then *resale stores.*

Language manipulation is rampant in the marketplace. Product prices that used to get "raised" are now *adjusted.* When the term "rebate" became tainted, auto dealers began offering *incentives* to their customers. IKEA calls out-of-stock merchandise *temporarily oversold,* including furniture with a synthetic veneer they call *birch effect.* This is on par with calling products that have no butter in them *buttery,* and naming ones without any cream *crème* or *krem.* As with menu writers, copywriters rely on such pseudospeak for the simple reason that it works. Fancy, euphemistic descriptions help sell merchandise.

In ethnic restaurants, "authentic" is the word of the hour, though never in a restaurant that's genuinely authentic (i.e., one that caters to customers from the country whose cuisine is being served). In the recurring pattern of a euphemism meaning the opposite of what it euphemizes, "authentic" is far more likely to indicate food dumbed down and cooled off for the popular palate (Mexican, Thai, etc.). When fused with "style," the authenticity gets diluted even further. A stall at Cincinnati's Findlay Market sells "authentic-style" tamales. This verbiage is the source of much euphemistic mischief. Think *Southern-style* (fried chicken), *restaurant-style* (tortilla chips), *Oktoberfest-style* (beer), *homemade-style* (lots of things).

The government sometimes colludes in this verbal hocus-pocus. The U.S. Department of Agriculture allows frozen chicken to be called *hard-chilled.* With its approval, a certain amount of *mechanically separated meat,* or *MSM*—a slurry of marginal meat such as tendons, bone marrow, and a permitted amount of bone bits ("calcium")—can be included in hot dogs. So can a certain amount of *variety meats.*

Those who favor sterilizing perishable products with radiation have long bemoaned the unfortunate term "irradiation" used to describe that process. This word brings to mind a green-glowing T-bone steak that could lead to bone rot and hair loss among those who eat it. When approving irradiation in 1985, the Department of Health and Human Services gave it a new name: *picowave.* This was coined by the head of a company that manufactured irradiators. In order to catch on, however, euphemisms must have some clear relationship to what they're describing. This one didn't. A subsequent euphemism, *cold pasteurization* wasn't much better, though the Department of Health and Human Services still allows food irradiators to use that term on their products' labels.

We pay a price for the increasing manipulation of language on behalf of commerce. When our leading purveyor of coffee calls its smallest cup a *tall,* our grip on reality loosens a bit. It enters an alternate euphemistic universe when Spirit Airlines installs stationary seats on its airplanes and calls them *pre-reclined.* Questions of propriety also come into play when euphemisms enter the deception zone this way. A hospital that calls a bag of ice *thermal therapy* and a box of tissues a *disposable mucus-recovery system* can obfuscate billing and boost its bottom line. (One charged fifteen dollars for the former, eleven dollars for the latter.) Terms such as *free, complimentary,* and *courtesy* are little more than euphemisms for "part of the price." When buying tickets to a baseball game recently, I was charged a *convenience fee* of four dollars. Whose convenience?

This is the latest twist in commercial euphemization: disguising price hikes as "fees." That practice has become both ubiquitous and insidious. Banks collect stiff *courtesy overdraft-protection* fees for bounced checks. Apparently, bankers are unusually courteous people. When my son's bank calls him to pitch credit-card offers, they say it's a *courtesy call.*

What this really is, of course, is manipulation of customers through creative use of euphemisms. Surcharges with euphemistic names are commonplace. According to *Consumer Reports,* Americans as a group pay $216 billion a year for surcharges over and above the stated price of products or services. In its polling, the magazine has found that having to pay these fees tops the list of Americans' everyday complaints, well ahead of tailgaters and dog doo. No wonder. What really sticks in customers' craws is the shiftiness and indecipherability of names given such surcharges. When a federal tax on Internet service was repealed, some providers began charging a *regulatory-cost recovery fee* in the same amount. Exactly what that fee covered was never made clear. Then there's the *merchant-function charge,* which, according to one utility that includes this on its bills, "reflects certain costs associated with procuring and storing natural gas and electricity, as well as costs incurred by the company related to credit and collections activities and uncollectible accounts."

Car rental companies are particularly deft at loading up their invoices with hidden charges that have incomprehensibly euphemistic names. A list collected by consumer activist Bob Sullivan includes fees for *highway use, peak season, concession recovery, vehicle license recoupment, facility usage, consolidated facility charges, refueling, stadium surcharge, frequent flier miles,* and *tire and battery recovery.* Sullivan posts examples of such "sneaky fees" on his Red Tape Chronicles website. He calls them "anti-coupons." Sullivan estimates that the average American consumer spends nearly a thousand dollars a year on hidden charges with foggy names, ones few consumers challenge because they can't even figure out what they're for (which is exactly the intent).

TERMINOLOGICAL INEXACTITUDES

Early in his political career, Winston Churchill warned fellow members of Parliament about the risk of *terminological inexactitudes.* In time, Churchill's phrase became a popular euphemism for "a lie." Several decades later, Britain's Cabinet Secretary Sir Robert Armstrong created an uproar by admitting that he'd been "economical with the truth" when testifying in a court case.

Even when straying from the path of honesty, we wouldn't want to say we've become more dishonest. Certainly, we don't want to admit to telling lies. "Lied is a rough phrase:" wrote Robert Browning, "say he fell from the truth."

Men in particular avoid giving other men an opportunity to say "You callin' me a liar?" Once those fatal words are spoken, it's hard for dialogue to continue without fists being thrown, or worse. Members of the Canadian parliament can shout "Lies!" during debate, but saying "Liar!" is grounds for suspension. According to the *Oxford English Dictionary,* the term "liar" is "normally a violent expression of moral reprobation, which in polite conversation tends to be avoided."

No wonder there's such a great demand for euphemisms in this area, and so many to choose from. Rather than accept lying as a fact of life, we manipulate notions of truth. We *massage* the truth; we *sweeten it;* we tell *the truth improved.* In the course of writing *The Dance of Deception,* Harriet Lerner asked women friends what lies they'd told recently. This question was generally greeted with silence. When Lerner asked the same friends for examples of "pretending," they had no problem complying. "I pretended to be out when my friend called," said one without hesitation.

(continued)

All manner of creative phrase-making has been devoted to explaining why lies are something else altogether. Instead, those who tell them *misspeak*. They make *bad choices* or *exercise poor judgment*. Swindler-broker Bernard Madoff, whose multiple lies lost billions of dollars for clients who'd trusted him with their investments, later apologized for his "error of judgment."

As an inspiration for euphemisms, lying rivals copulation and defecation. Those discussing their own departures from honesty can be remarkably inventive. *I buffed up the truth a bit. I engaged in a little impression management. You could say I suffer from fictitious disorder syndrome.*

In addition to golden oldies such as *humbug* and *credibility gap*, consider these synonyms for lies, lying, and liars:

lie (verb): *alter, buff, burnish, dissemble, dissimulate, embroider, equivocate, exaggerate, fabricate, fictionalize, inflate, mislead, misrepresent, misstate, prevaricate, puff, reframe, shade, spin, stonewall, trim, whitewash*

lie (noun): *alternative reality, categorical inaccuracy, counterfactual statement, equivocation, evasion, fabrication, fact-based statement, factually flexible fiction, hyperbole, improved reality, misstatement, plausibly true statement, untruth*

liar: [someone who is] *creative, disingenuous, imaginative, less than honest, a man of two truths, a serial exaggerator, a trimmer, truth-challenged*

Another way to euphemistically refer to liars is to say they're "in denial" (as was often said of Richard Nixon). This concept is borrowed from psychotherapy, of course, as are a lot of euphemisms for dishonesty. Sexologists William Masters and Virginia Johnson once said that patients who lied "altered their verbal response patterns." One of my favorite euphemisms for "liar" was coined by a psychiatrist who called a client "someone for whom truth is temporarily unavailable."

Workplace

A friend I'll call Angie has worked in management at a Fortune 500 company for more than three decades. Her workplace, she tells me, is rife with euphemisms. They include: *not value-added* (a waste of time), *let's take this off-line* (when a meeting becomes contentious), *budget challenge* (budget cut), *new news* (to rationalize a mistaken analysis or forecast), *improvement opportunity* (performance weakness), and *three-rated* (a poor performer).

According to Angie, mastering these and other euphemisms is crucial for new hires. "Those who don't learn to do this quickly do not progress far," she says. This is true in general, at workplaces of any size. In the TV series *Mad Men,* an ad executive fires his secretary for, among other things, saying she "covered" for him when he was away from his desk for reasons unknown. "You don't *cover,*" he tells her. "You *manage expectations.*"

The more complex working environments have grown, the more essential euphemisms have become for discourse there. In some workplaces, an employee warned not to *dip your pen in the company ink* must discern that this refers to having sex with a coworker. When dealing with contracts, it helps to know the difference between a *big-boy clause* (whose signer affirms awareness of risk) and a *bad-boy guarantee* (cosigning a risky borrower's loan). Should the scope of a project expand due to added elements, this expansion is called *scope creep* by some. Those working on projects that shrink due to budget cuts are forced to engage in *value engineering*.

The cubicles that their inhabitants call "cubes" were renamed *designated work areas* by one organization that wanted to upgrade its image. Those working there quickly defeated this purpose by acronymizing them as *DWAs*. Creating acronyms is a popular office pastime, especially among those who work in information technology. *PICNIC* is a euphemism used by tech support personnel that means "problem in chair, not in computer." *PEBKAC* means pretty much the same thing: "problem exists between keyboard and chair." This type of problem is called *Code 18* by other tech supporters (because its source is 18 inches from the computer monitor, in the user's head).

A friend of mine who has spent decades toiling in Silicon Valley companies once e-mailed me that he'd just been "onboarded and provisioned" in a new job. What did that mean? *Provisioned,* Jack explained, meant being provided with a building pass, computer, network access, desk, and directions to the mens' room. All the essentials. *Onboarding* referred to orientation of recent hires like him. ("Onboarding session for all new employees at three this afternoon.") At a company where Jack once worked, he and his fellow cube mates showed up for work one Monday to find their cubicles six inches smaller than they were on Friday. They'd been *reconfigured.* That became his coworkers' sardonic euphemism for any degraded work space: *it was reconfigured.* At this company, workers given no specific assignment because they were about to be fired were *on the beach.* ("Wendy's been on the beach for a few weeks.") Those under disciplinary action or review were *in the penalty box.* ("Dave sure got himself in the penalty box when he lost the Figley account.")

Being familiar with workplace euphemisms is essential not only for workers but also for work seekers. Knowing in advance what type of job you're applying for can save a lot of headaches down the road. In help-wanted ads, a *fast-paced work environment* might be one that's understaffed and filled with frantic, stressed-out employees. Applicants solicited to handle *data processing and customer relations* will probably be typing and answering the phone. When explicitly gender-based ads were banned in England, euphemistic terms such as *attractive* replaced "woman" among employers who preferred female employees for certain positions (e.g., "Company president seeks attractive, efficient secretary").

Some on-the-job euphemisms are relatively common and not that hard to decipher. *An ambitious timeline* is usually a wildly unrealistic deadline. A *rough order of magnitude* refers to what used to be called a "back of envelope calculation" (aka a guess). In many offices *SWAG*, an acronym for "silly wild ass guess," refers to the same thing. In more than one workplace, unproductive employees are said to be working on *the Penske file* (after a *Seinfeld* episode in which George Costanza spends days at a new job fiddling around with "the Penske file"). Then there's the dreaded *learning experience*. "When we describe a project as a 'learning experience,'" says one corporate trainer, "we mean 'disaster.' You can use tone of voice and emphasis on syllables to convey exactly how much of a disaster it was. Example: 'How did your project turn out?' 'Oh, it was a learning experience.'"

Other euphemisms are more setting specific. A task beneath one's pay grade is called *toast and water* at a company whose owner sometimes asks department heads to fetch these items from a nearby café. In another, *forest killer* refers to someone who generates more paper than product. *Installing Publisher* (a software program) is euphemistic for "wasting time" among employees of a high-tech firm. A related abbreviation, *ETW,* is short for an "external time waster," a gabby coworker who distracts you from your work. In one office, absent employees are said to be *DTH.* This technically means "down the hall" but actually means "I have no idea where this person is."

"Nowhere in our language is there so much misplaced inventiveness and ludicrous contrivance as in workplace euphemisms," British word maven Nigel Rees told a reporter. These euphemisms serve all the usual purposes — politeness, evasion, obfuscation, deception, deflection — and others unique to any setting where a group of people develop their own lingo over time. They incorporate insider talk, reference to shared experience, and, least appreciated of all, fun. Arch-euphemisms are tedium busters. When we murmur, "Wouldn't you say Tammy's a bit three-rated?" with a cocked eyebrow and elicit a knowing nod and "Yeah, I'd say she has lots of improvement opportunities," our office-specific euphemisms become cool team builders.

Euphemism-rich working environments are a relatively modern phenomenon. They reflect the growth of white-collar workforces where men and women are colleagues who need to watch what they say. Among the mostly male workforces on farms and in factories, mines, and other settings where manual labor took place, circumlocutions were seldom necessary. One study of loggers in the mid-1920s found them using slangy terms such as *bull of the woods* for "foreman," *ink-slinger* for "clerk," and *pimp-stick* for "cigarette" (at a time when they were considered effete by blue-collar workers). One logger unhappy with another might threaten to *knock his ears down, pat him on the lip,* or *shove his nose down to his navel.* This would never pass muster in an office, of course. As growing numbers of us work in genteel, politics-ridden settings, the need to master euphemisms has exploded.

Most workplaces are filled with indirect ways to describe dicey employees. Overly picky staff members can be called *fastidious* or *detail oriented.* Such employees may show a *high level of professionalism.* They are *hardworking* and *conscientious* (if not particularly productive). It takes a keen awareness of nuance to realize that positive-sounding descriptives can be negative or positive depending on the context and who's doing the describing.

An obsessive-compulsive employee's lazy counterpart might be called *laid back.* Unimaginative plodders are *diligent.* Ineffectual employees who don't offend anyone have *good people skills.* Ones too timorous to make waves are *team players. Good micromanagers* can't see the forest for the trees.

The natural home of such euphemisms is in letters of reference. Since those who write them can be legally liable for what they say, an ability to decipher reference-letter euphemisms is crucial for those who read them in *human resources* or *human capital management* (aka personnel departments). Does *enthusiastic* mean over-the-top manic? Is *conscientious* a tip-off that this person lacks imagination? Is a *self-starter* an obnoxious individual who works alone because he can't get along with anyone? Only the letter writer knows for sure.

You're Furloughed!

A few months after he was *onboarded* by his new employer, Jack wrote to tell me he'd been *RIFFED*. This term, Jack explained, was based on *RIF*, an acronym for "reduction in force." In other words, he'd been fired.

Discharging employees is one of the leading occasions for euphemistic discourse in the workplace. No one is fired, of course, or sacked, though they might be *furloughed* (or, more likely, *placed on indefinite furlough*). Discharged employees were part of a *staff reduction*, a *recalibration of personnel*, or a *redeployment of resources*. Alternatively, they might be *deaccessioned*, *decommissioned*, *dehired*, *discontinued*, *outplaced*, *separated*, *terminated*, *unassigned*, *made redundant*, or, in the latest circumlocution, *decruited*. Employees at a big bank in New York talk of being *excessed*. ("Jake got excessed last week due to a re-org.") Counterparts in a Silicon Valley company worry about being *surplussed*. The voicemail of a dismissed computer company executive there told callers he'd been *uninstalled*.

"We don't fire anyone anymore (except for illegal activity)," e-mails my friend Angie. "When we want to get rid of people, we start with those who have the lowest ratings and 'offer them a package,'" meaning a financial incentive to leave the company. *Offer a package*, in other words, is basically a euphemism for "lay off."

The bigger the layoff, the milder the euphemisms. An economist at Morgan Stanley first called the mass discharging of workers *downsizing*. This is only one of many useful verbal evasions available when lots of employees are let go. For public consumption, *workforce adjustments* are made *to curtail redundancies*. Jobs get eliminated due to a *skill-mix adjustment*.

We didn't fire all those people. We simply *restructured* our organization. *Rationalized* it. You know what I'm saying? We *re-engineered.* If you catch my drift. *Streamlined* the operation. We *reconfigured our resources to align them better with emerging market conditions.*

Putting bland labels on brutal acts this way is a key source of workplace frustration and fury. It's as if an executioner took to calling beheadings a form of weight reduction. If ever euphemisms help us speak about the unspeakable it's here.

Euphemisms are no less prevalent on the receiving end, among those who leave jobs under pressure to *pursue other opportunities* or to *spend more time with my family.* A *New York Times* article about such verbal feints traced this one back to at least 1956 when the president of the Federal Reserve Bank of New York said he was leaving to find work that would allow him to spend more time with his family. As *Times* reporter Katie Hafner pointed out, many who subsequently offered this explanation for why they left jobs soon found demanding new ones that took them away from their families again. Some won't use such euphemistic language, however. When Carly Fiorina was dismissed as CEO of Hewlett Packard in 2005, she refused to say she'd decided to move on or that she wanted to spend more time with her family, as board members suggested. Instead Fiorina announced that she'd been fired. According to court documents examined by Hafner, another HP executive said he was leaving to protest deceptive information-gathering at the computer company. "Don't you dare say I resigned to spend more time with my children," this executive warned as he departed.

Job Descriptions

My first job out of college was as a special assistant to the publisher of a newspaper. What made this job so special was never entirely clear. Eventually, I left that position to become a freelance writer only to discover that—like "consultant" or "model"—this job title is perceived by many as a euphemism for "unemployed." Today, of course, I'm no longer a writer. Now, I'm a *content provider.*

Americans are particularly partial to fancy job titles. A direct linguistic line can be drawn from America's physicians to its morticians, beauticians, and estheticians (who specialize in cosmetic skin care). Such puffed-up titles are part and parcel of what historian Daniel Boorstin has called the "booster talk" of exuberant New World palaver. Cut loose from more circumscribed job descriptions in countries they left behind, Americans felt free to concoct their own more grandiose versions. Today this is known as "uptitling." The guy who services my photocopier is a *field engineer.* A roofer in my area has recast himself as a *home enhancement specialist.* A man I know in Indianapolis recently got his sub made by a *sandwich artist.* And don't forget *baristas.*

Fiddling with titles provides a great opportunity to create new euphemisms, especially ones meant to glorify mundane jobs. Did I say "jobs"? I meant to say *positions.* Some up-to-date companies have even done away with *positions* in favor of *roles* or *assignments* for their employees. The *human capital department* of a grocery chain in Canada has a mandate to "design, develop and enhance and execute talent acquisitions strategies that facilitate and support a high performance culture." In a nutshell: they try to hire good people.

Walmart pioneered the modern era of title inflation after deciding that it would no longer employ salesmen or saleswomen, only *sales associates*. Other euphemistic titles followed elsewhere: *purchase advisers, product specialists, sales consultants, customer service representatives, service providers*, or simply *team members*. IKEA calls them all *coworkers*.

This is part of a trend dating back decades in which — with no change in their job descriptions — "waiters" became *servers*, and "stewardesses" were retitled *flight attendants*. "Typists" became *secretaries*, then *administrative assistants* (*admins* in some settings). *Secretaries' Day* was renamed *Administrative Assistants' Day*, then *Administrative Professionals' Day*. "Janitors" were redubbed *custodians*, then *maintenance workers*. At a hospital recently, I heard "I need Environmental Services to clean up a spill" over the intercom.

After American prisons became *correctional institutions*, prison guards were renamed *correctional officers*. "Watchmen" became *security guards*. "Bodyguards" are now *personnel protection specialists*; "housekeepers," *domestic workers*. "Dogcatchers" were promoted to *animal control specialists* in the United States, *canine control officers* in the United Kingdom. There, yesterday's "dustmen" have been upgraded to today's *refuse collectors*, "bookies" to *turf accountants*, and "rat catchers" to *rodent officers*. Nigel Rees considers such verbal promotions a misguided effort to buff up the image of jobholders who aren't particularly interested in having their image buffed.

During the past century, "engineer" — a designation that first appeared in the 1850 census — was grafted on to all manner of humdrum pursuits to give them added cachet (most notably *sanitary engineer* for "garbage man"). Needless to say, this trend did not make actual engineers happy. For a time the

Engineering News-Record devoted a weekly column to record-ing outrages such as *vision engineer* (optician), *wrapping engi-neer* (gift wrappers), *box engineer* (packing specialists), *fumigating engineer* (exterminator), and *household engineer* (housewife). Before World War II, the National Society of Professional Engineers waged an unsuccessful campaign to have the engi-neers who ran train locomotives redubbed *enginemen*.

"Technician" is our era's answer to "engineer." The one-time "mechanic" who works on my car is now an *automotive technician*. A local beauty salon no longer employs "manicur-ists." They do, however, have *nail technicians*. One year the American Dialect Society gave its "Most Euphemistic" award to the job title *scooping technician*, for someone whose work involves cleaning up dog poop.

The name used for those who sell real estate underwent its own transformation a century ago. This was at their own behest. In 1915 Minneapolis real estate agent Charles Chad-bourn grew annoyed by the media's reference to a "real estate man" who exploited widows. Didn't members of his vocation deserve a more dignified title? *Real estate* itself was fine, a term that originated with royal grants of land. But *man* or *agent* lacked distinction. The suffix *-or,* Chadbourn thought, sug-gested a doer, someone who acts (executor, administrator, etc.). By combining the two, Chadbourn came up with *realtor*. His energetic efforts to get colleagues and the public to accept this new designation bore lasting fruit.

When it comes to creating and purveying euphemistic modifiers, realtors stand alone. Perhaps the power of positive euphemizing is something they teach in realty school. Real estate agents don't sell small houses but do list *charmers* that are *snug, intimate, cute, cozy,* or, in England, *bijou.* If inexpensive, such modest dwellings are *starter homes.* Disheveled houses have *character.* They show *great potential.* If small to boot, they are *quaint.* Larger down-at-the-heels homes are *gracious* or *elegant.* Or *classic.* Or *colonial.* A *rustic* or *historic* house probably needs work. *Handyman specials* need lots of work (*TLC* in realtorspeak). They are *ideal for modernization.* When all else fails, any ramshackle house can be called *welcoming.*

Realtors are not alone in developing their own euphemistic vocabulary, of course. Every occupational group does. How could it be otherwise? As our sense of community declines and work has become more central in our lives, the vocational groups we belong to have grown in importance as tribes. Like any tribe worthy of the name, these groups develop an insider nomenclature heavy with euphemisms. As my young son noticed while commuting to day care with his mother, when the train they were on didn't move for an extended period of time, conductors would announce that this was an *unscheduled stop.* ("Maybe there's a derailment up the line," he'd say to his mother.)

Like coworkers, members of professional groups have their own euphemistic terminology. Among circus clowns, *too much spaghetti* describes a gag that's limp and unfocused. Unicyclists don't fall off their vehicle but now and again do have *unplanned dismounts.* Museum directors would never be avaricious enough to "sell" a work of art but do sometimes *deaccession* them. Among museum curators, *tombstones* refers to the block of copy that includes title, date, creator, and so on, next to items on display.

Like museum employees and circus clowns, police officers have a vocabulary all their own. One who grips you tightly by your shoulder and wrist has you in what members of this profession call an *escort hold*. If you resist, that officer can, in police lingo, upgrade to *joint manipulation,* a *counterjoint* hold that involves bending the wrist toward the elbow. Ideally, this results in *pain compliance*.

If these euphemisms sound like warrior words, that's no coincidence. There is much overlap between the nomenclature of police officers and that of soldiers. As with any other vocational group, members of the military rely on a rarefied argot rich in euphemisms, many of which were born on the battlefield.

9

Words of War

Until late in the Civil War, William Tecumseh Sherman was regarded as a loose cannon, unfit for high command. One reason this Union general wasn't given significant commands was that he was so outspoken. Sherman made little effort to mince words when discussing his occupation. He compared war to a monster that "demands its victims." Sherman referred to "the piles of dead and wounded and maimed" and said that "Those who die by the bullet are lucky compared to those poor fathers and wives and children who see their all taken and themselves left to perish, or linger out their few years in ruined poverty." Although he may never have said "War is hell," Sherman did say "War is cruelty. There is no use trying to reform it; the crueler it is, the sooner it will be over." About war he concluded, "Its glory is all moonshine."

Sherman was way off message. In his time, military officers were supposed to extol honor, valor, and heroism. As late as 1898, when Teddy Roosevelt charged up San Juan Hill (more of a plain, actually) during the Spanish-American War, it was still possible for Secretary of State John Hay to call Roosevelt's act part of "a splendid little war."

This approach to armed conflict did not survive the First World War. The carnage of extended trench warfare was in no way splendid, valiant, or glorious. Midway through this conflict, Britain's prime minister, David Lloyd George, observed that if noncombatants knew how horrible war really was, if it were ever depicted accurately, they'd insist it come to an end. But, he added, this would never happen. Warring parties have too much invested in surrounding the harsh realities of combat with clouds of verbal fog. That fog grew especially thick between 1914 and 1918.

The Great War

When Austria's Archduke Franz Ferdinand was assassinated in Sarajevo in 1914, the British consul cabled London that Ferdinand had been killed "by means of an explosive nature."

This elliptical language proved to be a harbinger. The four-year war that followed Ferdinand's assassination was so barbaric that a genteel vocabulary was conjured to obscure what was actually going on. If ever horrific events demanded bland words, it was during the Great War. The mass slaughter taking place on its battlefields and in its trenches simply could not be depicted in ordinary, clear language. Verbal camouflage was called for and supplied. Engagements with the enemy that resulted in lots of casualties were called *sharp* or *brisk* by Allied spokesmen. During a period when seven thousand British soldiers were killed or wounded daily, Britain's general staff referred to the "wastage" of their forces. After French soldiers mutinied in 1917, their officers characterized the revolt as an act of "collective indiscipline." British authorities at first told parents of executed soldiers that their sons' fate was due to "acts prejudicial to military discipline" (desertion, usually). Even this circumlocution was considered a bit too candid, though, so from 1916 on, such parents were informed that their executed child had "died of wounds."

In the trenches, British soldiers drew on their renowned capacity for understatement. The bloodshed around them was "'darned unpleasant,' they wrote home, "'Rather nasty,' or, if very bad, simply 'damnable.'" The ambiguous term *mop up,* for killing or capturing lingering enemy soldiers after a successful operation, became common during World War I. The machine guns both sides used to mow each other down were called *sewing machines* by Allied soldiers because their chatter resembled that of Singer's appliance. Pilots perfecting the new arts of aerial warfare called "bomb dropping" *laying eggs.* And so it went.

When discussing such terminology in *The Great War and Modern Memory,* Paul Fussell suggests that World War I gave birth not only to the modern euphemisms of war but also to euphemistic public discourse in general. "It would be going too far to trace the impulse behind all modern official euphemism to the Great War alone," Fussell concedes. "And yet there is a sense in which public euphemism as the special rhetorical sound of life in the latter third of the twentieth century can be said to originate in the years 1914 to 1918. It was perhaps the first time in history that official policy produced events so shocking, bizarre, and stomach-turning that the events had to be tidied up for presentation to a highly literate mass population."

The wars that followed were at least as shocking, brutal,

and stomach turning. No less than during the Great War, evasive language was needed to hide their horrors. World War II, Korea, Vietnam, and both wars in Iraq produced their own euphemisms and plenty of them. Any sophisticated modern warrior realizes that proper choice of evasive words is an essential part of a coordinated military strategy. A crucial entry in any military man's vita is demonstrated mastery of the euphemisms of war.

Fogging War

When British soldiers were being beaten back by Erwin Rommel's forces in northern Africa, Winston Churchill received a communiqué from the front lines saying, "Our forces are now engaged in a fluid action." What they were doing, of course, was retreating. This military action is rarely called by that word, however, at least for public consumption. Instead, modern military forces leaving the field of battle under duress *fall back, shorten the line, disengage,* or *withdraw.* An orderly retreat is a *coordinated withdrawal.* A disorderly one—a rout—is an *uncoordinated withdrawal.* Outright defeat is a *defensive victory,* an *adjustment of the front,* a *strategic movement to the rear,* or, in sardonic soldierspeak, an *advance to the rear.* At one time, the American military brass toyed with calling the exit of those who had infiltrated enemy territory *exfiltration,* but it was a nonstarter.

Try to imagine William Tecumseh Sherman referring to the *exfiltration* of his troops. Sherman would never make it in today's military environment where *the fog of war* refers as much to the way it's depicted as to the way it's fought. Every modern war has generated its own euphemistic way of describing soldiers who break down during combat. In World War I, this condition was called *shell shock* because it was thought to result from shell-generated shock waves traumatizing the nervous system. During the next world war and subsequent fighting in Korea, combat-induced trauma was more euphemistically labeled *battle fatigue* or *combat fatigue*. ("They call it combat fatigue," one of its victims told a reporter during the Korean War. "Combat fatigue, hell, I cracked up.") Soldiers suffering from this condition in Vietnam were said to have had an *acute environmental reaction*. Vietnam also gave birth to the related *post-traumatic stress disorder*, or *PTSD*, a label that persisted through both wars in Iraq. Vagueness escalated as syllables multiplied, and we went from a stark, descriptive phrase to one that was blandly bureaucratic.

The word "war" itself has proved a bit too stark for military euphemizers who today are more likely to refer to *armed conflict, military operations*, or even *special action*. The latter was a phrase often used by Nazis to describe their genocidal activities during World War II. Following that war, Soviet leaders who met to discuss the development of chemical and biological weapons said their meetings were about *special problems*. "Special" is a word much beloved by obfuscating soldiers. If someone in a military uniform ever tells you you've been singled out for *special treatment*, head for the hills.

Since it suits even militaristic regimes to say they're only defending their populace, yesterday's "armies" are today's *defense forces*. After World War II, the United States changed the name of its Department of War to the Department of Defense (DOD). In 1964, the British followed suit and renamed their War Office the Ministry of Defense.

If Lyndon Johnson had had his way, America's invasion of

Vietnam the following year would have been called an *incursion*. Richard Nixon used the same word to describe our subsequent clandestine invasion of Cambodia. The war in Southeast Asia, according to war correspondent Michael Herr, "spawned a jargon of such delicate locutions that it's often impossible to know even remotely the thing being described." That's the whole point, of course. Such language has the effect of soothing rather than arousing, of promoting a sense of apathy more than one of alarm. It is verbal Prozac. "You always write it's bombing, bombing, bombing," complained an American officer during the Vietnam war. "It's not bombing. It's air support."

In the modern military lexicon, "bombs" have become *explosive devices*. Cluster bombs that disperse their lethal force among human beings in a broad vicinity are *area-denial weapons*. Airplanes that drop them are *force packages*. Nuclear weapons capable of killing millions and devastating the earth are *strategic devices*. The radiation they give off is measured in *strontium units* (following a failed Pentagon effort to call them *sunshine units*).

The greater our capacity to destroy the planet and its inhabitants, the more demand there is for euphemistically bland words to distract us from this reality. During Ronald Reagan's presidency, he was less affected by discussions about mass nuclear destruction, with all its talk of *throw weights* and *kill ratios,* than by a TV movie of the week called *The Day After* that graphically depicted the devastation following such a conflict. After he watched this horrifying film, Reagan got serious about forging an agreement with the Soviet Union to ban nuclear weapons.

Reagan's awakening would not have surprised George Orwell. In his classic essay "Politics and the English Language," Orwell pointed out that a key purpose of euphemistic expressions is to provide words for horrific events that make it hard to visualize them. Thus, the bombing of villages, routing of their residents, machine-gunning of livestock, and burning of homes is called *pacification*. Sending the now-homeless residents elsewhere is a mere *transfer of population*. Those displaced from their homes who were once known as "refugees," then "displaced persons," in the contemporary military lexicon have become *ambient noncombatant personnel*.

In too many cases, such people are reviled ethnic minorities. This raises the ever-sensitive question of how the majority deals with an undesired minority in the midst of conflict. Certainly, one wouldn't want to "expel," "intern," or "kill" them. But perhaps they could be *transferred* to another country. Alternatively, an inconvenient minority might be sent to *relocation centers*, as Japanese Americans were during World War II. (Until the implications became clear, such centers were called concentration camps by Franklin Roosevelt and others.) At an extreme, minority groups could be *cleansed*, as happened in the Balkans and Rwanda during the 1990s and in Darfur after that. When public discourse involves such terms, neither speaker nor listener is burdened by having to picture what's actually being done. Those directly engaged certainly can, but the words used by military officers, government officials, and members of the media protect folks back home from the brutal realities they depict.

Shielding civilians from the specifics of combat and desensitizing them to war's horror are the paramount goals of warrior euphemisms. But such language also serves an important internal purpose. As in any profession, the evasive speech of military officers—including the commander in chief—is an important bureaucratic CYA ("cover your ass") tool. When the barracks of troops Ronald Reagan sent to Lebanon in 1983 were bombed, the president ordered them to withdraw. Reagan said this constituted "redeployment of the marines from Beirut airport to their ships offshore." This depiction of our departure from Lebanon was successful enough that *redeploy* was used by the *New York Times* to describe what departing U.S. Marines had done. British troops, on the other hand, had *pulled out* of Beirut. Or so said the *Times*.

After U.S. troops landed in Grenada in 1983, Reagan reprimanded reporters for calling this act an invasion. He wanted them to call it a *rescue mission*. (The Pentagon preferred *a predawn vertical insertion*.) With his show-business background, Reagan was unusually deft at this type of verbal buck and wing. At the president's behest, his administration renamed the multiwarhead MX missile—capable of destroying multiple major cities and tens, if not hundreds, of millions of civilians—*Peacekeeper*.

The ubiquitous euphemizing of war talk places an added burden on veterans. It's not grunts who speak in euphemisms but officers, spokespersons, reporters, and folks back home who adopt the verbal gruel they're fed. The savagery soldiers witnessed, and took part in, is depicted by military officials and bureaucrats in soporific terms that deny the experience of those involved in combat. One reason vets have so much trouble discussing war with civilians is that the two groups speak different languages.

WHAT'S *FNG* MEAN?

When John Kennedy was accused of calling John Diefenbaker an SOB, he told his friend Ben Bradlee that he didn't actually think the Canadian prime minister was a son of a bitch. He thought Diefenbaker was a prick. Bradlee made no apologies for the president's potty mouth, saying that combat veterans like them were steeped in the notoriously profane lexicon of soldiers. "There is nothing inherently vulgar in the legendary soldier's description of a broken-down Jeep," said Bradlee. "'The fucking fucker's fucked.' Surely, there is no more succinct, or even graceful, four-word description of that particular state of affairs."

A curious inversion in language taboos occurs on the battlefield. There, profanity is the norm, "fucking" being used so routinely as an intensifier that its absence indicates gravity. Thus, if a sergeant says, "Get in fucking formation," things can't be too serious. But if he barks, "Get in formation!" they must be.

What to do back home, though? On the one hand, veterans brought back their propensity to cuss. On the other, they knew they couldn't use the language they'd used in barracks in their parents' parlors. The result was verbal schizophrenia. After World War II, Britons liked to tell of a veteran who was charged with assaulting his wife's lover. He defended himself by explaining, "I come home after three fucking years in fucking Africa, and what do I fucking-well find? My wife in bed, engaging in illicit cohabitation with a male!"

In *The Naked and the Dead,* Norman Mailer's 1948 novel based on his combat experience, Mailer was forced to euphemize the GI's constant use of "fuck" as *fug.* (After being introduced to the young novelist at a party, Dorothy Parker said, "So you're the man who can't spell 'fuck.'") Transitioning from combat profanity to civilized discourse took practice

(continued)

and still does. Ex-soldiers learned to tell civilians that *SNAFU* was short for "situation normal, all fouled up." Viet vets did not admit to just anyone that *FNG* stood for "fucking new guy." Or that the *I & I* they enjoyed on their *R & R* was "intoxication and intercourse." GIs called the vehicle they used to clean latrines an *SST,* "super sonic transport" to you; "shit-sucking truck" to them.

Light 'Em Up and *Buy the Farm*

Each war generates new euphemisms for risking death and losing that gamble. American soldiers entering combat during the Civil War said they were *going to see the elephant.* Today, they might say they're being *put in harm's way.* In a more valiant age, soldiers who actually died *made the ultimate sacrifice.* They *laid down their life.* For centuries, those killed on the battlefield *fell. Fallen in battle* is a longtime euphemism for dying during combat, but its conversion into *the fallen* first occurred during World War I when a euphemistic noun was needed to refer to the masses of dead soldiers.

As the carnage of war increased, along with the cynicism of those fighting, euphemisms for combat deaths underwent a change of flavor. Doughboys in World War I adapted an American Indian expression to say that casualties had *gone west.* Alternatively, they *bought it.* In Vietnam, casualties *bought the farm.* (Various explanations for this euphemism include the fact that owners of farm fields where mid-twentieth century jet pilots crashed were compensated by the government. Since the amount farmers received could be enough to pay off a mortgage, pilots who died when their planes went down were said to have "bought the farm.") The most barren euphemism of all is *KIA*, "killed in action." To the Pentagon, soldiers who were KIA became *combat ineffective.*

Job one of soldiers is killing other soldiers, of course, and trying to avoid being killed. Training recruits to kill is harder than getting them to risk death. Some never learn and persist in shooting their guns over, around, or beneath their targets. This reticence could explain why *Roget's Thesaurus* has more synonyms for killing than for dying. Among soldiers, such synonyms are heavy with bland and slangy terms that describe what they're up to. They don't kill other people so much as *off, ice, burn, dust, dispatch, eliminate, liquidate, nullify, take out, blow away, do in, finish off, whack, wax, waste, grease, smoke,* or *zap* them. The verb "liquidate" could refer to unloading excess merchandise or to killing someone (or many someones). This makes it an ideal euphemism: ambiguous, multipurpose, context specific. "Neutralize" is another such term. Describing how they'd dealt with several Somali pirates who had seized a French yacht, a French government representative said their forces "neutralized them."

In modern militaryspeak, to *attrit* enemy forces involves killing as many of them as possible (think attrition). *Degrade* means the same thing. During the first Iraq war, a *Boston Globe* cartoonist created a "Gulf War Word Quiz." This included a list of words in one column—*pounding positions, softening up, collateral damage, saturation strikes, carpet bombing*—that were to be matched with their actual meaning in a second column. That column had a single word: "killing."

"I prefer not to say we are killing other people," an American artillery captain said during the Gulf War. "I prefer to say we are 'servicing the target.'" When using drones to do this during the second war in Iraq, members of the military said these unmanned aircraft made it easier to *dynamically address* enemy forces. In the midst of that war, two American gunships confronted what they took to be a group of insurgents on the ground. After radioing headquarters for permission to shoot them, crew members were told, "You are free to engage" and "Just open 'em up." On a leaked video of this exchange, one crew member can be heard saying, "Light 'em all up." Seconds later, another reports, "All right. We just engaged eight individuals."

A classic modern euphemism for killing is *terminate with extreme prejudice*. This one came from America's Central Intelligence Agency. Members of the CIA display a certain mordant wit in this area, as when they called a group formed to determine eligible targets for assassination the Health Alteration Committee. Extralegal killings such as these were sometimes called *executive actions*. Members of the Nixon administration once considered eliminating Panamanian General Manuel Noriega through *total and complete immobilization*. In spookspeak, such covert lethal activity is called *wet work*.

CD and BOB

In modern bombing, a distinction is made between *hard* targets (buildings) and *soft* ones (human beings). Bombardment in advance of a ground operation involves *softening up* soldiers and civilians alike. Civilians are not usually targeted, of course, but often get hit by bombs that miss their mark due to *navigation misdirections*. These wayward bombs are called *incontinent ordnance*.

Civilians killed by mistake in Vietnam were sometimes

referred to as *regrettable by-products.* More commonly, these victims were regarded as *collateral damage,* a euphemism that first appeared in the American military lexicon during this war and remains in use today (sometimes shortened to *CD*). Gulf War veteran Timothy McVeigh characterized the hundreds of innocents killed by his bombing of the federal building in Oklahoma City—including children at a day-care center—as "collateral damage." An Air Force publication defines "collateral damage" as "unintentional damage or incidental damage affecting facilities, equipment, or personnel occurring as a result of military actions directed against targeted enemy forces or facilities. Such damage can occur to friendly, neutral, and even enemy forces." Since military officers assume that collateral damage is inevitable in any large-scale operation, they sometimes talk of conducting *fast CD,* a computer-aided assessment of possible unintended effects.

Over time "collateral damage" has lost its blandly euphemistic flavor as it's become clear what this phrase actually refers to: killing innocents. The same thing is true of *friendly fire,* a term shortened from phrases such as "friendly artillery fire," for the accidental killing of fellow soldiers. ("Friendly" is longtime soldierspeak for one's own forces and ordnance.) Other ways of describing the same event include *fratricide, nonbattle casualties,* and *amicicide,* a term coined in 1982 by U.S. Army Lieutenant Colonel Charles Shrader for the accidental killing of fellow troops. Even though Colonel Shrader's term met two criteria for successful euphemisms—being multisyllabic and neo-Latinate—it didn't catch on.

Blue on blue is another euphemism used when soldiers accidentally fire on their own. This originated either with American police slang for one blue-uniformed officer inadvertently shooting at another one, or because British officers designated the locations of their forces in blue on maps. Take your pick.

To Baghdad and Beyond

When U.S. troops invaded Iraq in 2003, President George W. Bush echoed Lyndon Johnson by calling this act an *incursion* or an *intervention.* American personnel there included what used to be known as "mercenaries" or "paramilitary forces" but now were called *civilian contractors* employed by *security firms* (such as Blackwater).

After three detainees being held at Guantanamo Bay hanged themselves, the camp's commander said it was an act of *asymmetric warfare,* a tony synonym for unconventional warfare that became popular during both Iraq wars. Among other things, this euphemistic phrase—first recorded in 1991—allowed American and British spokespeople to avoid referring to an insurgency. In *Unspeak,* author Steven Poole called "asymmetric warfare" a "term employed by the US military for fighting people who don't line up properly to be shot."

When George W. Bush proposed sending thousands of additional troops to Iraq in 2006, during a Senate Foreign Relations Committee hearing, Senator Chuck Hagel (R-NE) referred to the "escalation" of our presence there. Secretary of State Condoleezza Rice responded, "I would call it, Senator, an augmentation." National Public Radio at first called this augmentation an "influx," but that term didn't catch on. Like most media outlets, NPR eventually adopted the Bush administration's preferred term—*surge*—making the massive influx of fresh American troops into Iraq sound like a sports drink.

(From 1996 until 2002, Coca-Cola sold a drink by that name.) *Surge* actually euphemized the more controversial but accurate term "counterinsurgency."

Censorship in both Iraq wars was characterized as *security review,* one in which censored material underwent *redaction.* This word was easy to confuse with *rendition,* which referred to the forcible transport of suspected terrorists to countries where they could be freely tortured. The fact that few people knew what such terms referred to made them perfect euphemisms.

Put to the Question

To maintain the pretense that Americans don't torture *detainees* (i.e., prisoners), members of the Bush administration called such tactics *robust* or *enhanced interrogation.* A CIA report given to members of the Congressional Appropriations Committee was titled "Member Briefings on Enhanced Interrogation Techniques (EITs)." American interrogators used what they called *aggressive* or *coercive* or *special* or *professional interrogation techniques* when conducting *interrogation in depth,* especially during the *increased pressure phase.* President Bush characterized such techniques as *an alternative set of procedures.* These procedures included: shackling hands above the head of a standing prisoner for extended periods (called a *stress position* or a *safety position*), repeated slamming against a wall (*walling*), and confinement in a small, covered coffinlike box (complete with bugs for one bug-phobic prisoner). This approach came under the broad heading of *sensory deprivation. Sensory overload* referred to blasting music at prisoners for hours on end. *Food deprivation, sleep management* (deprivation), and *environmental manipulation* (extremely cold or hot in-cell temperatures) rounded out the alternative procedures. Even though American interrogators denied inflicting pain, they did admit to *applying pressure.*

Somewhere, Tomás de Torquemada is smiling. Torquemada would easily have recognized this approach to interrogating suspects, both the methods and the way of depicting them. Although he may have had Jewish ancestors, as Spain's Grand Inquisitor, this Dominican friar subjected Spanish Jews who wouldn't renounce their faith to unspeakable torture. That wasn't how he looked at it, of course. Even the most sadistic torturer is unlikely to say of his occupation, "I hurt people." To Torquemada and his henchmen, they were merely having suspected heretics *put to the question.* "Inquisition" simply meant "inquiring." The Grand Inquisitor thought such inquiries should be done "with all possible severity and vigor."

One way Spain's inquisitors encouraged suspects to admit heresy was by inserting a piece of linen in the prisoner's throat, then gradually soaking it with water until the victim felt as though he were drowning. This procedure was called *toca,* literally "touch" (also the name of the piece of cloth being moistened). During succeeding centuries, similar techniques were used by other interrogators who gave this practice names of their own. U.S. soldiers who used a version of *toca* when suppressing an insurgency in the Philippines more than a century ago called it *water cure.* American interrogators who employed a similar method when encouraging suspected terrorists to divulge information after 9/11 dubbed this technique *water application.* Since it was first used early this century, *waterboarding* has been the preferred euphemism for what the Red Cross more accurately describes as "water suffocation." That is exactly what all of these methods actually do: simulate a sense of drowning in the person being interrogated.

"Euphemism has been the leading quality of American discussions of the war in Iraq," concluded Yale professor David Bromwich. Bromwich believes this results from "a euphemistic contract between the executive branch and many journalists." At least one journalist agreed. Early in the war, Keith Woods suggested that members of his profession were too inclined to adopt the foggy jargon used by members of the military because doing so made them sound in the know. Woods proposed avoiding the use of loaded words such as "smart bombs" and "surgical strikes" in favor of more neutral terms like "computer-guided bombs."

With all of its technological upgrades, modern warfare places new burdens on soldiers to soften the hard facts of what they are up to. Mass media conveys the results to the home front. As a result, the type of euphemistic discourse relied on by military men and women doesn't just characterize the way they communicate but the way we all do. Soldiers have shown us how it's done. The fogged words of modern war both illustrate and accelerate our increasing dependence on euphemisms in public discourse. In this discourse, the old standbys of evasive talk about bodies, their secretions, and sex take a backseat to euphemizing of a much different sort.

10

Brave New Words

THE STARR REPORT about Bill Clinton's relationship with Monica Lewinsky didn't mince words. Though rather prudish himself, special prosecutor Kenneth Starr felt little need to euphemize when reporting salacious details of the president's sexual encounters with his White House intern. "According to Ms. Lewinsky," Starr's 1998 report told a rapt public, "she and the President kissed. She unbuttoned her jacket; either she unhooked her bra or he lifted her bra up; and he touched her breasts with his hands and mouth." And so on. You get the picture.

Because we're so much less euphemistic than we used to be about sex and the body parts involved, it's natural to assume that we've drastically reduced our use of euphemisms altogether. Nothing could be further from the truth. All we've done is shift our targets and revise our words. The supply is constant. Only the topics change, and the form.

As we've seen throughout this book, euphemisms speak to concerns of their time. This is as true today as it was when the Victorians considered legs too titillating to be mentioned by name. Things concern us that didn't concern them, however. Just as we find many of our ancestors' euphemisms amusing, some that we use would have made them giggle. "It is easy to laugh at the prudery of former generations," wrote Peter Fryer in *Mrs. Grundy: Studies in English Prudery*, "it is far from easy to detect our own."

Imagine your great-grandparents visiting Montgomery Woods in northern California. At its entrance a sign warns that "State Parks staff will be intermittently conducting feral pig depredation. . . . Depredation may involve hunting and live-capture enclosures for humane dispatch." In other words, a lot of wild pigs are going to die. This message reflects a modern squeamishness about killing animals or at least about referring to this act directly. When the federal government gassed seven million chickens to try to curb a flu outbreak in Pennsylvania, they said they'd "depopulated" the flocks. *Cull* is another euphemism for killing animals, sometimes done as part of a *population management* program. So are *euthanize* and *harvest*. Hunters themselves have picked up on the latter. An Idaho resident licensed to shoot wolves said he hoped to "harvest" such an animal at least once in his lifetime. Try to picture a colonial Pilgrim saying he was going out to harvest a wild turkey for dinner.

The words we use and those we avoid illustrate what we care about most deeply. Euphemisms are the press secretary of values. But values change, taking euphemisms with them. Our euphemizing ancestors devoted a lot of effort and ingenuity to creating stand-ins for blasphemous terms, as well as vague allusions to the body and its functions. We have other things on our minds.

Although contemporary euphemisms have been noted

throughout this book, this chapter focuses on what makes modern verbal evasions unique: how they differ from those in the past, and, especially, what today's euphemisms tell us about who we are, what bugs us, and why. Some concerns are perennial, though in many cases the rationales for being concerned about them have changed. Even though crude expressions may be heard in public more often today than a century ago, they remain euphemism-eligible for new reasons. Such references are now considered more insensitive than profane, and even a form of harassment. Thus, if a man today were to call a coworker a bitch, he'd be in more trouble for the misogyny of his insult than for its vulgarity. When White House chief of staff Rahm Emanuel said a group of liberal activists were "fucking retarded," he was roundly condemned for dropping an R-bomb that way.

Name and Frame

The changes in which words we use freely and which ones we avoid reflect a broader semantic shift. Especially when it comes to public discourse, modern euphemisms have points to make. Those points are frying bigger fish than merely hiding the body or avoiding swear words. Euphemisms have become an integral part of political and social agendas. Politicians of every stripe compete to portray their positions in the most benign language available. Liberals no longer "spend" money on government programs but do *invest* it. Conservatives have reintroduced the clearly named "trickle-down" approach to economics with a more vaguely labeled *supply-side* version. Conservative and liberal politicians alike call their own negative advertisements *contrast ads*. Those used by opponents are dubbed *attack ads*. (This suggests an adage: Your euphemism obfuscates; mine clarifies.)

Politicians continue to muddy our linguistic waters this way for the simple reason that it works. Words matter. As political figures like to say, "Name it and frame it." A survey conducted by the National Opinion Research Center at the University of Chicago found that 24 percent of those polled opposed spending more money on "welfare," but 68 percent favored greater *assistance for the poor. National defense* was more popular than "the military," and *assistance to other countries* sounded better to far more than "foreign aid" did.

Based on his testing of word associations in focus groups, political consultant Frank Luntz recommended that Republican candidates refer to *opportunity scholarships* for students instead of "vouchers," and *exploring for energy* rather than "drilling for oil." In a 2003 memo, Luntz advised White House staffers that "The terminology in the upcoming environmental debate needs refinement. While *global warming* has catastrophic connotations attached to it, *climate change* suggests a more controllable and less emotional challenge." Since then, *climate change* has become the preferred terminology not just among Republicans but among the press and the public as well.

In recent decades, conservative Republicans have worked aggressively, creatively, and effectively to ensure that we debate the issues on their terms. Tax cuts become *tax relief.* Changes in legal codes are *tort reform.* George W. Bush's proposed easing of environmental regulations was called the Clean Air Act. Bush touted increased logging in national forests as the fire-preventing Healthy Forest Initiative. These are calculated ploys to call something what it isn't. William Lutz, who's spent decades collecting examples of such "doublespeak" in several books on this subject, calls it "language that only appears to communicate." Not coincidentally, our ability to deal with the topics involved is degraded. Rather than debate real issues on actual terms, we discuss them with words that divert our attention from what's really being considered. That's the whole idea. "Verbicide" is what linguist Geoffrey Hughes calls this process.

Democrats are no less inclined than Republicans to frame their positions euphemistically. Bill Clinton called his opportunistic three-pronged political strategy *triangulation*. (Not a great choice of word, actually; it suggests "strangulation.") As part of this strategy, Clinton backed a bill allowing banks to merge with investment firms that was titled the Financial Modernization Act. During the financial crisis that resulted in part from this modernization, Barack Obama's Treasury Department called its proposed plan to buy toxic assets from banks a Legacy Securities Program.

As soon as they entered the White House, members of Obama's administration began polling the efficacy of certain terms before using them. Thus, the program of financial assistance that most called a "stimulus plan" they called an *economic recovery plan* (prompting representative Barney Frank [D-MA] to caution that "Most people would rather be stimulated than recover"). What members of the Bush administration called a "war on terror," their Democratic successors termed an *overseas contingency operation*. Attacks by terrorists became *man-caused disasters*. With the euphemistic shoe now on the other foot, former Bush speechwriter David Frum charged that a "National Euphemism Initiative" had been launched by the new administration.

In general, conservatives have been better at semantic

hocus-pocus than liberals, particularly when it comes to the taxes they swear never to raise. Ever since the distinguished Athenian leader Solon called taxes "contributions" more than twenty-five hundred years ago, the T-word has sparked a lot of impressive verbal tap-dancing. Some modern counterparts of Solon have called it *revenue enhancement*. *Assessments* is another alternative, or *levies*. But no synonym for taxes has proved more functional than *fees*. To take a single example, vehemently anti-tax governor Tim Pawlenty (R-MN) imposed all manner of "fees" on Minnesotans, including a seventy-five-cents-a-pack *health impact fee* on cigarettes. Not to be outdone, liberal linguist George Lakoff suggested *membership fees* as a way for Democrats to refer to taxes without naming them.

Lakoff calls this *reframing*, itself a bit of a euphemism for fooling around with terminology. He's been instrumental in pushing Democrats to take a leaf from the Republican playbook and choose their words more carefully. Pointing out that "climate change" could evoke images of palm trees and warm breezes rather than of hurricanes and floods, Lakoff suggests *climate crisis* as a more apt alternative. Words such as these don't just communicate; they take stands. Liberals who refer to an *underserved community* are not only using a euphemism but making a statement. Conservatives who talk of minerals being *extracted* from the ground (not "mined"), and trees being *harvested* (not "logged"), are doing the same thing. Those who substitute *genital cutting* or *genital mutilation* for the act long known as "female circumcision" denounce this practice with their choice of words. Others, such as University of Chicago anthropologist Fuambai Ahmadu, defend it with their own terminology. After she voluntarily had her clitoris removed in her ancestral home of Sierra Leone, Dr. Ahmadu called the procedure an *excision*. At a forum on female circumcision the anthropologist said, "I am *not* 'mutilated.'" Calling this "the M-word," Ahmadu contended that those who referred to the ritual removal of young women's clitorises this way were insulting her ancestors' culture as much as if they used the N-word to describe their race.

ETHIOPIANS IN THE FUEL SUPPLY

When Britain competed with Holland for dominance on land and at sea, disparaging references to Dutchmen were ubiquitous. Many of these terms migrated to the New World. Not just *Dutch courage,* for bravado fueled by alcohol, or a *Dutch treat* in which both parties share the cost, but a *Dutch concert* for a drunken ruckus and *do the Dutch,* which at one time referred to committing suicide. In chilly England, the hot-water bottles so often taken to bed were *Dutch wives.* Diaphragms used for birth control were *Dutch caps.*

We reveal our stereotypes and biases when requisitioning the names of nationality groups this way. A onetime euphemism for farting was *talking German.* A *Turkish ally* was one considered unreliable. Desertion from military service used to be called *taking French leave.*

The French have been particularly vulnerable to having their good name applied to sexual practices considered deviant, by English speakers, anyway. At the benign end is tongue-to-tongue *French kissing.* Oral sex was considered a *French* practice. (GIs in France called baguettes *cocksucker bread.*) Pictures considered pornographic were *French prints* or *postcards.* Condoms were *French letters, French devices,* or *French safes.* The French themselves called this form of birth control *capotes Anglaises* ("English overcoats"). On the eve of World War I, however, they began calling condoms *capotes Allemandes* ("German overcoats").

On the continent, *English* was long an integral part of euphemisms for sadomasochistic sexual activity. *English guidance* alluded to sadism. *English education* involved lots of flogging. Pederasty has historically been called a *Greek* predilection, anal intercourse *Italian*. During a French court proceeding, Benvenuto Cellini was accused of having sex with his mistress in *the Italian manner*.

The names we use for minority groups, and those they use for themselves, can be at the mercy of headlines. Following 9/11, some Middle Eastern restaurants began to call their cuisine *Mediterranean*, as did some Americans of Arab descent, in the same way that my mother's ancestors who migrated to America from Romania a century ago said they were *European*. Ironically, *Arabs* was sometimes used as a euphemism for Jews at that time. Alternatively, in a misguided attempt to be respectful, some called them *Hebrews*. Thus, *Hebrew holidays, Hebrew businessmen, Hebrew comedians*, even *Hebrew rabbis*.

Before the Civil War, American residents of African origin were commonly called *blacks*. After that war ended and slavery was abolished, this gave way to the softer term *colored* among those who didn't want to give offense, then to the more genteel *Negro*. Black soldiers who fought Indians on the frontier were known as *brunettes*. (A cavalry squadron commanded by Major Guy Henry was called "Henry's Brunettes.") Other long-lost alternatives include *ebony, dusky, chocolate, coffee, café au lait, sepia*, and *bronze*. *Nonwhite* was a nonstarter. *Moor, Abyssinian,* and *Ethiopian* were sometimes used for anyone of African descent. In *My Little Chickadee*, W. C. Fields satirized the demeaning catchphrase *nigger in the woodpile* when he said, "Hmm. There's an Ethiopian in the fuel supply."

No Offense

An increasingly multicultural world has euphemism issues unheard of in years past. Our ancestors felt far less need for today's types of verbal nicety because (1) their world was more homogeneous than ours, and, (2) minding each others' sensitivities wasn't considered a high priority. Today it is.

The more diverse our societies become, the greater is our demand for words that refer to each other's ethnic heritage without giving offense. This isn't always easy. According to one poll, American immigrants from Spanish- and Portuguese-speaking countries are evenly divided on whether they'd rather be called Hispanic or Latino. Although in Canada descendants of residents who predated European settlers are called *first nation* or *aboriginal peoples,* south of the Canadian border *Native American* is the preferred term for those who were once known as "Indians." Many Native Americans prefer *Indians.* Among U.S. citizens of African descent, *black, African American,* and *of color* are all quasi-euphemistic terms that have been used, discarded, then revived once more as better than the alternatives.

Within reason, paying attention to ethnic sensitivities is a matter of common courtesy. Few would disagree that we're better off dispensing with the expression *Jew down. Indian giver* and *Mexican standoff* are phrases best left in our past. Adamant anti-euphemizers who think we should always call a spade a spade are unlikely to do so when talking with a black man. But when the quest for offensive words that need to be avoided goes further afield, absurdities abound. At one time students at the University of California at Santa Cruz were discouraged from using phrases such as "a chink in one's armor" or "a nip in the air," for fear of inadvertently offending Asian students.

A long list of words that textbook writers have been advised to avoid includes *niggardly;* instead, *frugal* or *cheap* are recommended. The list was compiled by education historian Diane Ravitch after extensive research on ways in which words used in textbooks are dictated by contemporary concerns advocated by interest groups. In *The Language Police,* Ravitch devotes twelve pages to recording terms banned by publishers of such textbooks and the state agencies that choose them. Entries—with objections to their use and suggested replacements—include *able-bodied* (offensive; replace with *person who is non-disabled*), *tribe* (ethnocentric; replace with *ethnic group* or *nation* or *people*), *brotherhood* (sexist; replace with *amity, unity, community*), and *fairy* (suggests homosexuality; replace with *elf*).

As this list illustrates, sensitivity to marginalized members of society lies at the heart of a multitude of brave new euphemistic words. Some of this language overhaul represents progress. I'd much rather live in a society concerned enough about those at the margins to euphemize their status than one obsessed with creating euphemisms for body parts and functions. At the same time, when this process gets out of hand, as it so often does, awfully fishy euphemisms can ensue. Some of the most egregious overlap with educator jargon.

Jargon as Euphemism

At an extreme, students don't "fail" any longer. According to a group of British teachers, they simply experience *deferred success*. Those who have trouble learning have been gradually promoted from "stupid" to *dumb* to *slow* to *special* to *exceptional*. Or, simply, *underachieving*. A Nevada school board decreed that failing students should henceforth be characterized as *emerging*, middling students as *developing*, and those with top grades as *extending*. I have no idea what they're talking about.

This sensibility was mocked in an episode of *The Wire* in which a retired policeman working for the Baltimore school district vividly characterized better behaved students as "stoop kids" and their more obstreperous classmates as "corner kids." "I don't like those terms," says an education professor studying Baltimore students. "Can't we say 'acclimated' and 'unacclimated'?" This terminology grew out of the actual experience of *Wire* consultant Ed Burns, a retired detective who later taught at a Baltimore school where classes were divided between *acclimated* and *unacclimated* students.

Kids themselves aren't fooled by such verbal pirouettes, of course. If ever euphemisms get contaminated quickly, it is on the playground. After *retarded* became a polite euphemism for "idiot," "moron," or "imbecile" just over a century ago, it was abbreviated by kids and turned into an insult: "You retard!" The clinical term "spastic" became *spaz* as a playground taunt. When "learning disabled" begat *LD*, the taunt "LD!" reverberated among finger-pointing children. Even the smaller buses used to transport special ed students became fodder for invective ("He's one of the *short-bus* kids.").

Today's schoolchildren also don't hesitate to throw "free lunch!" at classmates whose families can't afford to pay for their midday meal. In bureaucratic jargon, these students come from *food-insecure households*. According to a Canadian newspaper account, such children live "in low-income circumstances." Alternatively they could be considered *under-privileged* or *deprived* or *economically disadvantaged.* "You must not use the word 'poor,'" admonished Winston Churchill sardonically shortly after World War II. "They are described as 'the lower income group.'"

This is typical of the modern euphemizing process: We replace a clear, vigorous word such as "poor" with ones that are vague and mealy mouthed. According to a jest that once made the rounds (one apparently based on a Jules Feiffer cartoon), a member of the lower income group observed, "I used to think I was poor before I went to the welfare office. Then I learned I wasn't 'poor,' I was 'needy.' Then it became self-defeating to think I was needy, so they said I was 'culturally deprived.' Then 'deprived' became a bad word, and I was 'underprivileged.' Shortly afterward, instead of 'underprivileged,' I was told to think of myself as 'disadvantaged.' I am still poor, but my vocabulary has improved."

As this soliloquy illustrates, well-intentioned euphemizing is not only futile but can patronize those it's meant to help. Nowhere is that more evident than in the terms we've come up with to describe those who have physical and other types of limitations.

Less Abled

Disabled was originally a euphemism for *handicapped,* which began as a polite synonym for "crippled." More recently *disabled* has ceded ground to *differently abled.* How do the beneficiaries feel about such verbal courtesy? Not too good, it turns out.

Peg-legged Bill Veeck insisted that he was crippled, not

disabled or anything else euphemistic. As the plain-spoken baseball executive explained, those like him who were limited physically felt tremendous pressure from without and within to apologize for themselves because they were "handicapped." His dictionary defined handicap as "to place at a disadvantage." The irascible World War II veteran, who'd lost a leg while fighting in the Pacific, in no way felt disadvantaged. Veeck's dictionary defined crippled as "a lame or partly disabled person." That described him to a T. Calling himself a cripple was Bill Veeck's way of not making excuses. He was unabashedly, flamboyantly crippled.

So is author Nancy Mairs. Mairs, who's had multiple sclerosis since her late twenties, rejects "disabled" and "handicapped" to describe her life in a wheelchair. Like Bill Veeck, she calls herself a cripple. "'Cripple' seems to me a clean word, straightforward and precise," Mairs explained in an essay on this topic. "It has an honorable history, having made its first appearance in the Lindisfarne Gospel in the tenth century. As a lover of words, I like the accuracy with which it describes my condition: I have lost the full use of my limbs. 'Disabled,' by contrast, suggests any incapacity, physical or mental. And I certainly don't like 'handicapped,' which implies that I have deliberately been put at a disadvantage, by whom I can't imagine (my God is not a Handicapper General).... Whatever you call me, I remain crippled. But I don't care what you call me, so long as it isn't 'differently abled,' which strikes me as pure verbal garbage designed, by its ability to describe anyone, to describe no one."

Some wheelchair users call themselves "crips" (or at least did before a Los Angeles street gang co-opted that name). This term has a sharp edge that invites blunting. So do most of the words traditionally used for those with physical disabilities. As John Ayto points out in *Wobbly Bits and Other Euphemisms*, words such as "blind," "deaf," "dumb," "lame," and "cripple" are of ancient Anglo-Saxon vintage "and can sound brutally frank to modern ears." That's even truer of words used for those with intellectual limitations: "simpleminded," "feebleminded," "imbecile," "moron," "idiot." Such terms virtually cry out for euphemisms. Hence *mentally challenged, developmentally delayed,* and *learning impaired.*

Seeking polite words as alternatives to rude ones is commendable in principle. Why call someone "stupid" or "moronic" if a more benign term is available? Have we lost anything by condensing "idiot savant" to "savant" alone? Or by forsaking "deaf and dumb"? On the other hand, have we gained anything (other than extra syllables) by calling the deaf (which is what they call themselves) *hearing impaired?* Or the blind *visually impaired?* Relabeling drug addicts as *substance abusers* or saying they have a *chemical dependency* does little to speed their recovery.

At the same time, it is neither possible nor desirable to avoid euphemistic words in every instance. Nancy Mairs says she wouldn't presume to call anyone else in a wheelchair a cripple; only herself. I strive for the most descriptive terms that are neither pejorative nor jargony or patronizing. Even though my sister, Nicky, is quite special, I'd never use that word to describe the multiple physical and neurological problems she's dealt with since birth. Nicky would spot the dodge in an instant.

My own rule of thumb is that when a word demeans (e.g., "mongoloid," "hunchback"), why use it if there's a plausible alternative? At the same time, I try to avoid playing musical chairs with words. The primary purpose of language is to communicate, after all, to be clear, not to score some political point or avoid giving offense. Going too far in the don't-give-offense direction opens the floodgates to censored language and stilted discourse.

Trying to use "correct" euphemisms in every instance is a mug's game. Who's to say what is correct? Furthermore, devoting too much attention to appropriate word choice can create a climate of fear. This is nothing new, of course. Ever since the clergy mandated proper use of euphemisms centuries ago and etiquette experts did the same during the Victorian era, there has always been one group or another telling us which words to use and which ones to avoid. This is no less true today than it was during Queen Victoria's reign. Even if the taboo words and recommended alternatives have changed, their intent hasn't. Nor has their impact. Inhibited speech and thought is the inevitable result of ideologically mandated euphemizing.

The Price of Euphemania

Too much euphemizing fosters an evasive frame of mind, one that tiptoes around issues rather than confronting them. That's the way we often want it, of course. But relying on euphemisms can ring up hidden charges. Some feminists have pointed out how much it costs women to use verbal evasion as a survival strategy. They question whether "telling it slant"— in Emily Dickinson's memorable phrase—is worth what it costs. Canadian linguist Gillian Michell concluded that women who take Dickinson's advice don't just deprive men of information they need to hear; over time they lose the capacity to tell it straight, even to other women. When relied on as a coping mechanism, evasive speech keeps those who depend on it mired in verbal timidity. "We tell it slant," Michell concluded, "at the cost of perpetuating the situation that makes it necessary."

The same thing can be said more broadly about relying on euphemisms. When we use them to avoid facing problems, those problems become harder to solve. In a prescient paper written three decades ago, medical psychologist Fred Frankel warned about the consequences of emptying mental hospitals without having alternative facilities in place. Frankel thought that recasting "mental illness" as *mental health* had helped make this situation possible by easing the sense of severity involved. Patients who were no longer considered mentally ill but were deemed deficient in mental health presumably could be treated more effectively outside of institutions. This euphemistic shift smoothed the transition from mental hospitals to community-based treatment centers. Except those centers seldom materialized, leaving seriously disturbed patients without a roof over their heads, literally. The *community placement* that supposedly followed the closing of mental hospitals proved to be a euphemism for "put out on the street."

Overreliance on euphemisms has consequences. When put to work on behalf of specific agendas, euphemistic discourse doesn't just hinder communication, it clouds thought. The tortured prose in annual reports both conceals problems and promotes the muddled thinking that created those problems in the first place. By contrast, direct speech reflects clear thinking. The Ford Motor Company — whose then-CEO wrote in a 2002 annual report that the previous year's results were "unacceptable" — weathered the subsequent auto industry collapse far better than its mealymouthed competitors. As Bill

Ford explained at the time, "We pursued strategies that were either poorly conceived or poorly timed. The real cause of our poor performance, however, was that we lost track of the things that made us great." This candor lay at the heart of a willingness to face problems squarely that led to Ford's subsequent rebound.

Candor Restoration

The prevalence of euphemistic public discourse in recent years has sparked a reaction. While euphemizers try to blunt the sharpness of our speech, this countermovement seeks to hone its edge. A group of lesbian bikers calls itself Dykes on Bikes. Gay blogger Dan Savage has asked readers to address him as "Hey, faggot." By titling their respective books *Nigger,* Dick Gregory and Randall Kennedy deliberately rubbed our faces in a taboo word, hoping in the process to defang it. Playwright Eve Ensler did the same thing in her *Vagina Monologues.* All followed in the footsteps of taboo-challenging comedians Lenny Bruce, Richard Pryor, and George Carlin, to say nothing of authors such as James Joyce, Henry Miller, and D. H. Lawrence. Lawrence defended his liberal use of lascivious words by saying, "I want men and women to be able to think sex, fully, completely, honestly, and cleanly."

Like the replacement of invasive plants with native vegetation, anti-euphemism activists want to restore candor by reviving abandoned words. These words aren't necessarily profane or even insensitive. Some should never have been discarded in the first place. Two cars colliding was originally called a "crash." Over time "crash" was euphemized to *accident.* That word portrayed this event in less horrific terms and made it harder to visualize. In recent years, however, a move to revert to *car crash* (or *collision*) seeks to keep the horror of this event in the front of our minds.

There are many other instances in which contemporary discourse has dispensed with unfortunate euphemisms from the past. At one time, a father who beat his children was euphemistically called *demanding, a stern disciplinarian,* or *a hard man in his own house.* Today, we're more likely to call such fathers what they are: child abusers.

Of course, candor restoration is not always pursued to improve communication by dispensing with euphemisms. Too often an agenda is involved. Which words you think need to be clarified and which ones euphemized depends on where you stand. When the "estate tax" is recast as a *death tax,* a political statement is being made. Dedicated vegetarians who call "meat" *flesh* and "poultry" *birds* have goals other than clarity.

In an era of data glut and mute buttons, some advertisers have concluded that candor is an effective way to get customers' attention. This is true even in some personal hygiene ads where words such as "diarrhea" and "constipation" have resurfaced, and Always maxi pads sport a cheery message on their adhesive backing that says HAVE A HAPPY PERIOD. In 2010, the TV ad campaign for a colorfully packaged new tampon called U by Kotex featured young women who used the word "vagina" when discussing their periods. Even after "vagina" was euphemized to *down there,* two of the three major TV networks rejected these ads. More candor was possible on the product's website where women were invited to sign a "Declaration of Real Talk," pledging to fight for more open discussion of women's health concerns. "Let's help bring society up to speed on vaginal issues and take back the word 'vagina,'" stated this website. Kotex framed its new approach as a "mission" to change social attitudes toward menstruation. "U by Kotex empowers women and young girls to challenge euphemisms that hide the truth," said a company spokeswoman.

Despite the risk of exploiting candor for commercial and political gain, an apolitical, noncommercial case can be made for avoiding the overuse of euphemisms. First and foremost, doing so fertilizes communication. One reason we delight in hearing children talk is that they speak directly. On the other hand, by euphemizing words he considered vulgar, Noah Webster sapped the King James Bible of its vigor. So did most Bible bowdlerizers. Imagine what would happen to the readability of textbooks that incorporated every entry on Diane Ravitch's list of euphemisms recommended by censors. This list contends that "bookworm" is an offensive word that should be changed to *intellectual*. On the grounds of sexism, "Cassandra" should be replaced with *pessimist,* "Pollyanna" with *optimist,* and "straw man" with *unreal issue*. Wake me when it's over.

At some level we realize that plain speaking encourages the lucid thinking that euphemisms degrade. Yet, we continue to use evasive language even when doing so adds nothing to communication. As we've seen throughout this book, from one era to another, and across all cultures there is a nearly irresistible human need to communicate indirectly. All that differs is the context, the rationale, and the euphemisms themselves. A demand for substitute words is constant and constantly changing. Why should this be? What obvious and not-so-obvious human needs are met by our persistent use of euphemisms?

11

Why We Euphemize

Euphemisms have a bright side and a dark side. On the one hand, they can be a source of evasion, a way to avoid topics that should be confronted and of choosing not to face unpleasant truths. At worst, euphemisms are employed by politicians, bureaucrats, merchants, and others as tools of manipulation. On the other hand, when used judiciously, euphemisms can civilize discourse and be a welcome form of courtesy in rude times. Does anyone want to routinely take part in conversations larded with "shits" and "fucks," let alone hear them constantly in the media? At the very least, that gets tedious. In the right spirit, euphemisms can be creative, verbal fresheners and a great source of fun (as Shakespeare knew better than anyone). They also allow us to allude to private matters in public, mediate gender issues, and identify each other's origins.

The primary social value of euphemisms is that they make it possible to discuss touchy topics while pretending we're talking about something else. Ideally, all parties know exactly what's under consideration and can discuss it obliquely without having to admit what they're up to. "Your place or mine?" is so much more civil an invitation than "Wanna ball?" It also gives the inviter deniability. ("I meant just for a chat.") As French sociologist Pierre Bourdieu put it, euphemisms double our profits when speaking—"the profit of saying and the profit of denying what is said."

To Bourdieu, all communication is more or less euphemized, from the least consequential conversation to the most learned work of scholarship. We constantly monitor what we say, assess how much candor is permissible, then decide what kind of euphemisms to use. Everyone calibrates their speech to suit various audiences. College students who don't use euphemisms when discussing sex or body functions with dorm mates fall back on them among peers whom they don't know. (One amused researcher observed that many respondents who told her the word "fuck" didn't offend them, in e-mails referred to it as "the f-word, "--ck," and "f---.") Even though my wife and I are freely profane with each other, we're less so around our two grown sons, and hardly at all among others. With those outside our family, we're as apt as anyone to call "fucking," *sleeping together;* and "shit," *feces.* Why so? Among other reasons, this is simply to raise the level of conversational comfort, for ourselves as much as for others. Replacing bad words with good ones can make us feel better, inside and out.

Comfort

When we say we're making other people comfortable by using euphemisms, we're just as likely to be comforting ourselves. Evasive words we rely on to protect the sensibilities of others also protect our own. Imagine an exchange in which someone asks, "Where's Jason?" The most direct, accurate response might be, "He's in the can taking a shit." Few of us would say this, however. Instead, we might respond, "He had to excuse himself for a few minutes," or simply, "He'll be back shortly." Do we speak this way primarily to protect the tender ears of our listeners? Or to keep them from thinking that we're the sort of person who uses coarse language (even if we do offstage)?

When we think others can't identify us, we're far more prone to forgo euphemisms. During anonymous interactions, particularly on the Internet, euphemistic discourse drops dramatically. Why bother? A study conducted at Lafayette College found that subjects who thought their identities would be revealed used more euphemisms for unpleasant phenomena, such as urine and feces, than did those who assumed they'd remain anonymous. This suggests that the desire to save one's own face may be an even stronger motivator than the wish to protect other people's feelings. When one's identity isn't known, however, there's no face to save. Speak freely. If others know who's speaking, though, the need to protect one's dignity soars. The euphemisms that ensue create a cloak of privacy.

Privacy

Like slang, euphemisms allow those in the know to discuss private matters openly while keeping other people in the dark. Unlike slang, euphemisms are usually innocuous enough to escape notice. For that reason, they have proved especially useful to members of ostracized groups.

At a time when theirs was "the love that dare not speak its name," homosexuals used euphemisms to communicate in code. According to biographer Gary Schmidgall, Oscar Wilde's plays were filled with euphemistic winks at gay friends, such as these lines from *A Woman of No Importance:* "Women kneel so gracefully; men don't," and "The future belongs to the dandy. It is the exquisites who are going to rule." Since *earnest* was a sometime euphemism for homosexuality in Wilde's days, the very title of his play *The Importance of Being Earnest* may have been a nod to gays and a tweak of straights' noses.

In Wilde's time, "aesthetes" was often applied semi-euphemistically to those of his sexual preference. During the 1930s, some British homosexuals called themselves *musical* or *artistic*. Because they were so often called, and frequently called themselves, *pansies, buttercups,* and *fruit,* some said ironically that they were *horticultural lads.*

Between the world wars, *gay* became a term homosexual men used to discreetly identify each other. "Supposing one met a stranger on a train from Boston to New York and wanted to find out whether he was 'wise' or even homosexual," wrote such a man on the eve of World War II. "One might ask: 'Are there any gay spots in Boston?' And by slight accent put on the word 'gay' the stranger, if wise, would understand that homosexual resorts were meant. The uninitiated stranger would never suspect, inasmuch as 'gay' is also a perfectly normal and natural word to apply to places where one has a good time."

After "gay" lost its utility as a sub-rosa code word, new ones were called for. Since Judy Garland was such a gay icon, *friend of Dorothy*—referring to the role Garland played in *The*

Wizard of Oz—became euphemistic for "homosexual." A gay friend of mine recently took a cruise on which a sign reading FRIENDS OF BILL MEET AT 7 P.M. (referring to Alcoholics Anonymous founder Bill Wilson) was posted side by side with an announcement for a gathering of FRIENDS OF DOROTHY.

Like gays, heterosexual couples commonly develop a euphemistic private language that allows them to communicate in public with no one the wiser. One couple uses "Let's go for a bike ride" as a way of saying, "Let's go smoke some marijuana." "Let's go home and watch some TV" is a second couple's way of saying, "Let's leave and make love." Other couples' code phrases for "Let's make love" include "My ears are popping," "I want some ice cream," and "Wanna do a load of laundry?"

A young unmarried couple who took part in a study of partners' unique idioms said one of the main reasons they'd developed their own sexual euphemisms was so they could mention this topic on the sly when around their parents. Another couple—who'd nicknamed the man's penis "Peter J. Firestone"—were more specific about how they did this. He got a kick out of asking, "Would you like to double-date with Peter tonight?" in the presence of his mother and father, hoping they wouldn't notice his girlfriend's beet-red face. A third couple, who'd nicknamed the man's penis "Winston" (based on the cigarette slogan "Winston tastes good, like a cigarette should"), enjoyed discussing "Winston's good taste" in the presence of friends and family.

As this illustrates, creating euphemisms can be an inventive, good-humored way to safely skirt taboos. There's a world of difference between prudishly insisting on the use of vague words for earthy topics and developing an imaginative vocabulary to say the unsayable.

GREEBLES, TWANGERS, AND DOOEYS

Members of a family in Arizona know that when they're discussing underwear, *bookcase* means "bra." That's because a mortified preteen daughter in this family warned her mother that when they went shopping for her first brassiere, if anyone asked where they were going, the mother was to say, "Out to buy a bookcase."

Every family develops its own euphemisms, ones that have meaning only to them. *Bork* and *scrog* are used as all-purpose expletives in a family that coined them. ("Bork you!" "You're scroggin' kiddin' me!") Another family refers to all body secretions as *goozlies*. Yet a third calls "farts" *boofs* because—when asked if she had a "number two" in her diaper—a toddler in this family responded, "No, Mom, it was just a boof."

Euphemisms like these tend to be event based, referencing shared episodes. Members of one Missouri family call making the best of a bad situation "getting your curtains up." This recalls the year when they hired a part-time minister to paint their rambling old house. He turned out to be better at preaching than painting. As his customers surveyed the damage, their preacher-painter suggested cheerfully, "It'll look better once you get your curtains up."

During a month-long drive across the country, our skinny thirteen-year-old concluded that "refreshing" was a euphemism for jumping into excruciatingly cold bodies of water, and that "scenic" was the word his parents used to describe long, boring stretches of undeveloped land. Ever since then, those words have been our own private euphemisms: *refreshing* for "freezing" and *scenic* for "boring." ("That party sure was scenic.") During an earlier trip, we were stranded for days in central Illinois while waiting for an axle to arrive from Michigan so our car could be repaired. This part was a "Detroit item," we were told. As a result, *Detroit item* became our euphemism for any hard-to-find product. In a similar vein, *seasonal* is what we call a product that's not available, because a nearby dairy always says about ice-cream flavors they're out of or no longer sell, "That one's seasonal." (Rocky Road?)

One reason families develop such personalized references is to have secret words known only to club members. These can be fun to conjure. The inventive mother of novelist David Foster Wallace enjoyed creating words for her children to use: *greebles* for "lint" (particularly the bits that catch between toes), and *twanger* for something whose name escapes your mind. Since John Cheever got so many traffic tickets for driving under the influence (DUI), the author's wife and children took to calling them *dooeys*. When the father of Australian writer Mark Kurzem engaged in a bit too much hyperbole, his wife told him, "You've put the enlarger on again, luv."

Many families invent code words to warn a male that his fly is open: *Burtie* in the case of one Indiana family (because they had a neighbor by that name whose fly was constantly unzipped), or one invented by Catherine Storr's grandson: "You've lost your license." (The boy couldn't say where this came from.) For reasons mislaid in the mists of their collective history, members of another family say *Clara* to warn each other that their slacks are stuck in their buttock cheeks.

Creativity

Those subjected to censorship have historically relied on euphemisms to get their message across in the face of strict limits on the words they're allowed to use. Doing this can spur their imaginations. Mae West said she would never have become such an imaginative purveyor of double entendres if she hadn't been forced to play cat and mouse with the Hays Office. Scriptwriters for contemporary sitcoms find that the need to get around network standards and practices restrictions forces them to be creative. In an episode of *Friends*, one character says of another, whose penis is peeking out of his unusually short shorts, "The man is showing brain!" Writers for *How I Met Your Mother* didn't just replace "bitch" with *grinch* but conjured *reading a magazine* as a euphemism for "in the bathroom pooping." As a gibe at censorship, when the movie *Repo Man* ran on television, its director substituted *melon farmer* for "motherfucker." Others picked up that beat. In the televised version of *Die Hard: With a Vengeance*, Samuel L. Jackson calls another character a "racist melon farmer."

Some TV scriptwriters have created an alternative euphemistic vocabulary altogether to work their way around censors. Writers for *Gossip Girl* have come up with *fustercluck*, *motherchucker*, and *basshole*. When unusually vexed, trolls on *The Tenth Kingdom* said "Suck an elf!" or "Sniff a sandal!" As for taboo sex talk, Fox TV's *House M.D.* included this exchange between Dr. House and a mother who thinks her young daughter may be having epileptic seizures:

House: In actuality, all your little girl is doing . . . is
saying yoo-hoo to the hoo-hoo.

Mother: She's what?

House: Marching the penguin. Ya-yaing the Sister-hood. Finding Nemo.

[...]

Mother: Are you saying she's masturbating?

House: I was trying to be discreet. There's a child in the room.

From the creative tropes of today's scriptwriters to the punning euphemisms of Shakespeare, double entendres of Mae West, and elaborate metaphors employed by authors from Swift to Tolstoy, remarkable creativity can be summoned to make one's point indirectly. At a reading, I once heard a poet use the term *moist underbelly of pleasure*. Better that than "vagina." Creating euphemisms this way demands far more of a writer than resorting to taboo words does. When comedians rely on profanity for laughs, it's not so much their lack of taste that offends as their lack of imagination.

The kind of ingenuity summoned by those who need to euphemize certain words can fertilize languages. Because some Polynesian dialects banned the use of so many terms (including ones even tangentially associated with a sovereign or a sovereign's near relatives), those languages were continually refreshed with new euphemistic words that replaced older taboo ones. As we've seen, English too is filled with words that were originally created to skirt sensitive subjects (e.g., cemetery, halitosis, downsize).

Not just in literature, but in everyday discourse, euphemisms show imagination. After finding so many synonyms for "bull" in use among ill-educated New England farmers half a century ago, linguist H. D. Rowe concluded that such substitute words most likely are more prevalent in the spoken vernacular than in the written one. Rowe cautioned against belittling such "barnyard bowdlerism," writing, "While we can adopt a superior pose and say that it proceeds from the distortions of a diseased mind, we must recognize that there is a certain amount of verbal genius among a people who can invent forty-two circumlocutions in order to avoid uttering the undesired syllable." Noting how many fewer euphemisms were used by better-educated groups he studied, Rowe added, "I have not been able to determine whether this disparity...is caused by some inherent dirtiness of mind in the lesser educated or a dismal lack of verbal ingenuity on the part of the more learned."

Class

The euphemisms we use and those we spurn are important class markers. Many words considered crude by proper speakers have historically been used freely by members of the lower classes. (Which is one reason to avoid them, of course, to create distance from the foul-mouthed masses.) Apparently, the closer one is to the grass roots, the earthier one's language becomes. In English, earthy words tend to be Anglo-Saxon in origin, those favored by genteel speakers more Latinized.

Word choice reveals social status as much as accents do. This was a key idea expounded by Nancy Mitford in a celebrated distinction she made between "U" (upper-class) and "non-U" speech—referring to those whom Americans might call "highbrow" and "lowbrow." Drawing on the work of linguist Alan Ross, Mitford wrote in her 1956 book *Noblesse Oblige,* "one U-speaker recognizes another U-speaker almost as soon as he opens his mouth." At that time *dentures* were worn by the upper classes, *false teeth* by the lower. *Lavatory* was the preferred upper-class euphemism for England's smallest rooms, *the WC* more common among members of the working class. *Lavatory-paper* was U; *toilet-paper,* non-U (which, as Russell Lynes pointed out in his introduction to the American edition of Mitford's book, made all Americans non-U).

Those who aspire to rise from a lower to a higher class regard euphemisms as a ladder to help them climb the status cliff. From their perspective, constant euphemizing is an essential part of the upwardly mobile package. *Pygmalion's* Professor Higgins, after all, was sure that refining Eliza Doolittle's "kerbstone English" was her ticket to a better class. The attempt to emulate U-talk by slavish use of euphemisms is self-defeating, however. U's themselves speak as they please. I still recall being startled when a doyenne from an old Boston family, whom I'd never met, casually dropped the word "fart" into a telephone conversation. Even as the lower classes use terms considered vulgar and the middle classes studiously avoid them, members of the upper classes feel free to roam about, picking and choosing which words suit them as a part of their birthright. Those whom non-U's called *wealthy,* U's themselves called *rich.* Patients whom non-U's euphemistically called *ill,* U's said were *sick.* They used the good Old English term *mad* for those whom non-U's more politely called *mental.*

As these examples suggest, euphemistic nods are not always upward. The rich can be remarkably plainspoken.

That's what makes insistent euphemizing a futile form of status seeking. When it comes to euphemistic speaking, the distinction between U and non-U is too crude. Historically, members of the middle classes have been most prone to rely on euphemisms, those in the upper and lower classes most likely to eschew them.

In a discussion of euphemisms for lavatories, lexicographer James McDonald writes that "Australians, like the British upper and lower classes, have traditionally taken a positive pleasure in discussing lavatorial matters. Hence the free use of terms such as *crap house, shit house,* and *thunder box.*" McDonald believes that middle-class Britons are most prone to using euphemisms such as *whatsit, you know, powder room,* or *cloakroom* when saying where it is they've excused themselves to go. Alternatively, "I'm going to the euphemism."

Due to their variegated class structure, Americans even more than the English listen closely for subtle clues about who stands where. "Class" itself is a word seldom heard in a society that's supposed to be egalitarian. Since Americans like to imagine that one person is as good as another, class divisions are hard for them to discuss openly. It's the elephant in their demographic living room. Euphemisms are a capital way to allude to distinctions of class without using that ugly term. Members of America's *upper classes* wouldn't dream of using this phrase to describe themselves but don't hesitate to talk of *our kind.* Americans wince at references to the *lower class* or *working class* but freely talk about *blue-collar* workers who carry *lunch buckets* and go by the collective nickname *Joe Six-pack.* A more contemporary way to sort out class differences is by marketplace presence: *Walmart shoppers, Volvo drivers, Starbucks denizens,* etc.

Demographic is a modern way to refer indirectly to class. ("Which demographic would you say she belongs to?") *ZIP code* is related. What used to be called a *good* or *bad neighborhood,* or the *right* or *wrong side of the tracks* today is just as likely to be referenced by ZIP code. The Internet buzzes with inquiries such as "Is [75201] a good ZIP code to live in? Is it safe and in a good area?" and "Is 90048 a good ZIP code to raise a family in?" (Answer: "It's a sensational ZIP code....Prohibitive prices keep out the riffraff.") *Riffraff.* What might that refer to? Residents of *inner cities,* perhaps.

Code

Inner city is not just a geographical concept but a term that refers to *the place where blacks live.* Or, one might say, *urban* settings. *Urban* began as a mere synonym for "city," then referred to black ghettos, and recently has become an allusion to African Americans themselves. The literary genre of novels called *urban fiction* is written by black authors for black readers. A satellite radio channel devoted to rhythm-and-blues music sung primarily by black singers is labeled "Urban."

When it comes to ethnicity and race, euphemisms reach new heights of subtlety. The ubiquitous concept of *cultural fit* that corporations rely on when looking for new hires can mask all manner of bias. In football, calling a quarterback "athletic" can be a way of saying he is African American without saying so directly. Casting ethnic minorities in roles usually filled by white actors is considered *nontraditional casting.* When *plantation* is part of the name given to southern housing developments, the implication is "Blacks might not feel comfortable here."

A former resident of Detroit once told me that this city used to be a good one until "they ruined it." On another occasion, I listened to a resident of Allentown, Pennsylvania, struggle to convey to me how *a certain element* was degrading that city's downtown neighborhoods. In a recent twist, some racially prejudiced Americans have taken to calling blacks *Canadians* so they can discuss their feelings about them in public without fear of reproach. ("The Canadians are taking over!") During a visit to Canada itself, I noticed how freely Albertans use *Muslims* as an all-purpose euphemism for immigrants from the Middle East and South Asia, who presumably include Hindus, Buddhists, and Christians.

When euphemisms for ethnic groups enter our conversations, the intent seldom has anything to do with courtesy and sensitivity. Such euphemisms routinely double as code words that allow those of ill will to express their bigotry out loud. Long after the fact, Harvard Law School professor Alexander Bickel recalled how a white-shoe law firm refused to hire him because of his *antecedents* (i.e., his parents were Jewish immigrants). Memoirist Jane Juska remembered her father's warning as she was about to leave for college: "There will be loud people in your classes who talk all the time and are pushy." Juska's response was to date a Jewish classmate.

In politics, euphemism as code abounds. Some call this *dog whistle* discourse; audible only to the cognoscenti. Ethnicity is not the only topic alluded to. During the 2008 presidential campaign, John McCain's aides accused Barack Obama's campaign of age-baiting their seventy-three-year-old candidate by calling him *confused*. Obama's camp in turn wanted to know exactly what a McCain backer was getting at when he called the Illinois senator "John Kerry with a tan." During the same campaign, conservative senator Saxby Chambliss (R-GA) warned supporters of his re-election that "the other folks are voting," leaving little doubt about what color those other folks were in a year when an African American candidate for president was bringing black voters to the polls in unprecedented numbers. As president, Barack Obama said he wanted to appoint a Supreme Court justice who had "empathy," a term many took as code for "a woman."

Gender

In the not-too-distant past, knowing when to call a breast a *bosom*, a leg a *limb*, and realizing who *sweat*, who *perspired*, and who merely *glowed* was central to talking like a lady. Blunt, often profane talk was considered a sign of male virility, while an indirect, highly euphemized manner of speech was associated with femininity. As Robin Lakoff concluded in her 1975 book *Language and Women's Place*, "women are the experts at euphemism."

When their pursuit of status became more focused on salary and power, however, women began to spurn reliance on euphemisms. The table turned. Blunt speech became a way to demonstrate what one wasn't: not dainty, not suburban, not my mother. Someone who talked straight, not slant. Straight talk signified a woman who could hold her own in the rough-and-tumble worlds of business, politics, sports, and military service. A woman who was willing to forgo euphemisms to speak plainly and profanely demonstrated that she was one of the guys. During Columbia University's campus uprising in 1968, a psychologist who taught there observed that coeds were far more likely to curse at police officers than men were.

Among themselves, post-Victorian women have not always been dainty speakers. The talk during a girls' night out can be no less direct and profane than that used by men playing poker. Which words women—or men, for that matter—know and are willing to use is not the issue. *Where* one is willing to speak plainly and where euphemistically is what's at issue, especially when men and women are speaking to each other. But even here the rules have changed. Words like "boobs," "bitch," and "bullshit" have become more acceptable in mixed company in a way that would have horrified our grandparents. No euphemisms necessary. Such candid talk is not always appropriate, however, though for different reasons than in the past. Nowadays it isn't the vulgarity of such words that offends so much as the presumed familiarity. ("Do you know me well enough to refer to my 'boobs'?") When men converse with women, the offensiveness of noneuphemistic talk itself isn't as off-putting as the intimacy such talk implies.

Where two or more men are gathered, overuse of euphemisms is generally considered effete. Yet, when women are present, even the most foulmouthed men will usually resort to euphemisms as a matter of courtesy. Implied permission to skip evasive words and go straight to plain talk may be seen as a sign of closeness. For a woman to respond to or even acknowledge a sexual reference by a man can signal availability. Candid language, in turn, can be a probe, a way men determine just how sexually responsive a newly-met woman might be. A friend of mine who hitchhiked across the United States with another young woman told me that truckers who picked them up would routinely test them with an obscene word here, an off-color comment there. If the driver got no response, "then he treated us like we were his sisters."

Of course, speaking with guarded tongues is hardly a woman's art alone. Men have their own taste for oblique language. One study of cell phone chatting found that women who engaged in this practice called it what it is: *gossip*. Men did not. "We don't like to call it gossip," admitted one, "because it sounds trivial—as though you have nothing better to do." What did men call their cell chatting? *Keeping in touch. Exchanging information.*

In the end, it's all verbal kabuki. Anyone who gives more than cursory thought to euphemizing realizes its ultimate futility. For one thing, the more intently we use euphemisms, the faster they become tainted. Because they become obsolete so quickly, euphemisms can date those who use them and flag them as prissy. Finally, euphemisms too often defeat their own purpose. Substitute words routinely produce a quick mental translation to the word for which they've substituted. After translating them, one must reflect on the topic being avoided, and speculate about the euphemizer's motives. (Why did Amy talk about *getting to know* Jason last night when everyone knows they were upstairs boinking? I didn't think Eric was so uptight that he had to say he was going outside to *tinkle*.)

The risks of using euphemisms are not difficult to surmise. So why do we continue to use so many? The obvious reasons aren't always the real ones. Our motives for relying on substitute words can be complicated and contradictory. We often use them when a more direct term would have done just as well: for the sake of appearances, to save face, or for the sheer hell of it. Or who knows why? A felt need to speak euphemistically taps motivations that aren't always rational or conscious. The fact that human beings have relied on evasive speech for so long and in so many different forms suggests that there might be an innate need to express ourselves indirectly.

The Euphemizing Instinct

When taking notes for an essay about my mother's death, I found I could only do so by writing "dth," much like an observant Jew writing "G-d." This wasn't a conscious choice. Writing the letters d-e-a-t-h was simply something my fingers wouldn't do. That alone hardly suggests a hardwired need to euphemize, but other evidence does. Is it entirely voluntary when a soldier says he *offed* or *dispatched* or *neutralized* an enemy soldier rather than saying he killed him? Or when those who lived in close proximity to bears chose to call them *honey-eaters*?

It's well established that humans have a gene called FOXP2 that allows us to speak. We also know that different parts of our brains manage speech differently. Those who lose their ability to use complex language after suffering damage to the parts of the brain that control conscious thought processes often retain an ability to curse that's rooted in the more primitive limbic region of their brains. Some linguists believe that swearing is only a distant cousin to speaking per se, more an ejaculation than a serious attempt to communicate. That could explain why the capacity to use bad words often outlives the loss of an ability to use good ones. Following a stroke, say, some patients who are incapable of saying, "How are you?" can still exclaim, "Damn!" or "Shit!" Although "shit" was among the few words one stroke victim could utter, when given a piece of paper with that word written on it and asked to read what he saw, the man could not. Evidence such as this suggests that cursing may be a form of protolanguage that has more in common with a dog's bark than, say, Plato's *Republic*. In some cases, swearing is more of a reflex than a deliberate choice of words, including euphemistic alternatives. No one who hits his thumb with a hammer exclaims "Intercourse!" or "Excrement!"

Metaphorically speaking, swearing is part of our hardwired ROM ("read only") memory, while euphemizing is controlled by newer, more flexible RAM ("random access") circuits found in the cerebral cortex. Evasive speech apparently originates in the newer parts of our brain where complex thought originates. While words that we utter spontaneously when provoked are more likely to emerge from the uncensored limbic brain, given an opportunity to ruminate we turn to the cortex and choose from among its vast supply of euphemisms. Since the brain and a capacity to speak have evolved jointly, it may even be that creating euphemisms contributed to our ability to think. If this is true, then euphemistic speech and the brain fit each other like a lock and key.

"Euphemism is such a pervasive human phenomenon," noted University of Chicago linguist Joseph Williams, "so deeply woven into virtually every known culture, that one is tempted to claim that every human has been pre-programmed to find ways to talk around tabooed subjects." Euphemistic words for topics such as bears and flatulence are among our oldest and most universal. Medical researcher Valerie Curtis thinks that a need for euphemisms to refer to body secretions and other toxic effluvia could be one of the earliest linguistic imperatives felt by human beings. The same thing might be true of euphemisms for sexual activity, a topic that is typically taboo because of its potential for disrupting the social order (among other things).

In the process of concocting substitute words for such subjects, early humans undoubtedly realized how much fun this
could be. One might even argue that the need to come up with
euphemisms for terms considered taboo is our most ancient
source of verbal creativity. After all, it's far more difficult to
say what one doesn't mean than what one does. An ability to
do so—to create euphemisms and use them effectively—
demonstrates a high order of intellectual sophistication.

If we accept the pure logic of natural selection, a capacity
to euphemize may have arisen and stuck around because of
the adaptive advantage it gave human beings who were good
at it. From this perspective, those who best demonstrated an
ability to express themselves euphemistically gained an edge
in the evolutionary sweepstakes. We are their heirs.

Acknowledgments

For his exacting and helpful reading of this book's manuscript, my brother Gene deserves special thanks. So does Rosalie Maggio, for her solid feedback on the manuscript. My brother Steve and sister, Nicky, gave me ongoing support on this book as they did on my others. As ever, my sons David and Scott gave me invaluable assistance along the way. Librarians at the Greene County Library were their usual helpful selves on this project, as were those at Antioch University's Olive Kettering Library, especially Ritch Kerns, Sandy Coulter, and Scott Sanders. I would also like to thank Sol Steinmetz, for steering me toward this project, and Helena Santini, for helping launch it.

For help with specific aspects of this book, my thanks to Andi Adkins, Larry Ballen, Joseph Barbato, Nancy Lowe Clapp, Gay Courter, Joycie Singer D'Aprile, John Dickinson, Paul Dickson, Bob Fogarty, Gene Forsythe, Leonard Roy Frank, Louis Goldman, Brad Hadfield, Lou and Jonellen Heckler, Jill Hershorin, Virgil Hervey, Holly Hudson, Richard Langworth, Linda Lesher, Priscilla Long, Rosalie Minkin, Patrick O'Connor, Philomene Offen, Kathryn Olney, Bill

Phillips, Nindy Silvie, David Smith, Jane Tomlin, and Mary Tom Watts.

My agent, Colleen Mohyde, gave me her usual valuable guidance, support, and reading of the manuscript. My editor, Tracy Behar, was helpful beyond the call with her painstaking reading and rereading of the manuscript, as was her assistant Christina Rodriguez. I didn't realize that this type of careful, thoughtful line editing was still done and am grateful for it. Marie Salter's meticulous copyediting made this a better book. Every writer should have the kind of backing that Little, Brown's crack marketing and publicity teams — Heather Fain, Marlena Bittner, Amanda Tobier, Brittany Boughter, and Brianne Beers — have given *Euphemania*. Thanks also to Amanda Brown, associate director of domestic subsidiary rights.

Most of all, I would like to thank my wife, Muriel, whose help with research, manuscript review, and overall good counsel improved the quality of this book (to say the least). Every writer needs a wise counselor, and Muriel is mine.

Any book such as this draws on the work of others. The principal works that I consulted follow. Detailed notes on sources for specific discussions in this book can be found in the "Euphemania" section of my website: www.ralphkeyes .com.

Bibliography

Abel, Ernest L. *Dictionary of Alcohol use and Abuse: Slang, Terms and Terminology.* Westport, CT: Greenwood, 1985.

Adams, J. N. *The Latin Sexual Vocabulary.* Baltimore: Johns Hopkins University Press, 1982.

Allan, Keith, and Kate Burridge. *Euphemism and Dysphemism: Language Used as Shield and Weapon.* New York: Oxford University Press, 1991.

———. *Forbidden Words.* Cambridge: Cambridge University Press, 2006.

Aman, Reinhold, ed. *The Best of Maledicta: The International Journal of Verbal Aggression.* Philadelphia: Running Press, 1987.

———, ed. *Opus Maledictorum: A Book of Bad Words.* New York: Marlowe, 1996.

Ames, Nathaniel. *A Mariner's Sketches.* Providence, RI: Cory, Marshall, and Hammond, 1830.

Anderson, Robert Charles. *The Great Migration Begins: Immigrants to New England, 1620–33,* vol. 1. Boston: New England Historic Genealogical Society, 1995.

Anthony, Rey. *The Housewife's Handbook on Selective Promiscuity.* New York: Documentary, 1962.

Aries, Philippe. *Western Attitudes Toward Death: From the Middle Ages to the Present.* Translated by Patricia M. Ranum. Baltimore: Johns Hopkins University Press, 1974.

Armstrong, David. "Silence and Truth in Death and Dying." *Social Science and Medicine* 24 (1987): 651–57.

Aucoin, James L., and Jill. R. Haynes. "Downsizing, Rightsizing, and Other Euphemisms: The Questionable Ethics of Some Corporate Communications." Paper presented to Association for Education in

Journalism and Mass Education Conference, Baltimore, MD, August 1998.

Austen, Jane. *Emma*. 1816. London: Dent, 1906.

Ayto, John. *Wobbly Bits and Other Euphemisms*. London: A & C Black, 2007.

Bache, Richard Meade. *Vulgarisms and Other Errors of Speech*. Philadelphia: Claxton, Remsen, and Haffelfinger, 1869.

Baird, Jonathan. "The Funeral Industry in Boston." In *Death: Current Perspectives*, edited by Edwin S. Shneidman. Palo Alto, CA: Mayfield, 1976.

Beer, Patricia. "Elizabeth Bennett's Fine Eyes." In *Fair of Speech: The Uses of Euphemism*, edited by D. J. Enright, 108–21. Oxford: Oxford University Press, 1985.

Beeton, Mrs. Isabella. *The Book of Household Management*. London: Beeton, 1861.

Bell, Robert A., and Jonathan G. Healey. "Idiomatic Communication and Interpersonal Solidarity in Friends' Relational Cultures." *Human Communication Research* 18 (1992): 307–35.

Bertram, Anne, ed. *NTC's Dictionary of Euphemisms: The Most Practical Guide to Unraveling Euphemisms*. Chicago: NTC, 1998.

Black, David. *The Plague Years: A Chronicle of AIDS*. New York: Simon & Schuster, 1986.

Blackledge, Catherine. *The Story of V: A Natural History of Female Sexuality*. London: Weidenfeldt & Nicholson, 2004.

Bloch, Ivan. *Sexual Life in England Past and Present*. 1908. Translated by William H. Forstern. London: Francis Aldor, 1938.

———. *The Sexual Life of Our Time and Its Relations to Modern Civilization*. 1908. Translated by M. Eden Paul. New York: Allied, 1928.

Bloomfield, Leonard. *Language*. New York: Holt, 1933.

Boase, T. S. R. "King Death: Mortality, Judgment and Remembrance." In *The Flowering of the Middle Ages*, edited by Joan Evans. New York: McGraw-Hill, 1966.

Bolinger, Dwight. *Language: The Loaded Weapon*. London: Longman, 1980.

Bourdieu, Pierre. *Language and Symbolic Power*. Cambridge, MA: Harvard University Press, 1991.

Bradlee, Benjamin C. *Conversations with Kennedy*. New York: Pocket, 1976.

Brain, James Lewton. *The Last Taboo: Sex and the Fear of Death*. Garden City, NY: Anchor Doubleday, 1979.

Brasch, R. *How Did Sex Begin?* Sydney: Angus & Robertson/Collins, 1995.

Bromwich, David. "Euphemism and American Violence." *New York Review of Books*, April 3, 2008, 28–30.

Brophy, John, and Eric Partridge, eds. *Songs and Slang of the British Soldier, 1914–1918*. London: Scholartis, 1930.

Brown, Ivon. *A Word in Your Ear and Just Another Word*. New York: Dutton, 1945.

Brown, Penelope, and Stephen C. Levinson. *Politeness: Some Universals in Language Usage*. Cambridge: Cambridge University Press, 1987.

Brumberg, Joan Jacobs. *The Body Project: An Intimate History of American Girls*. New York: Random House, 1997.

Bryson, Bill. *The Mother Tongue: English and How It Got That Way*. New York: Morrow, 1990.

Buckingham, J. S. *The Slave States of America*, vol. 2. London: Fisher, 1842.

Burchfield, R. W. *The English Language*. Oxford: Oxford University Press, 1985.

———. "An Outline History of Euphemisms in English." In *Fair of Speech: The Uses of Euphemism*, edited by D. J. Enright, 13–31. Oxford: Oxford University Press, 1985.

———. *Unlocking the English Language*. New York: Hill and Wang, 1991.

Byrd, William. *The London Diary (1717–1721) and Other Writings*. Edited by Louis B. Wright and Marion Tinling. New York: Oxford University Press, 1958.

———. *The Secret Diary of William Byrd of Westover, 1709–1712*. Edited by Louis B. Wright and Marion Tinling. Richmond, VA: Dietz, 1941.

The Cambridge History of the English Language, vols. 1, 4, 6. Cambridge: Cambridge University Press, 1992.

Cameron, Deborah, and Don Kulick. *Language and Sexuality*. Cambridge: Cambridge University Press, 2003.

Carver, Craig M. *A History of English in Its Own Words*. New York: Harper-Collins, 1991.

Chaucer, Geoffrey. *The Canterbury Tales*. Edited by Jill Mann. London: Penguin, 2005.

Chauncey, George. *Gay New York*. New York: Basic, 1994.

Cheever, Susan. *Desire: Where Sex Meets Addiction*. New York: Simon & Schuster, 2008.

Cicero. *The Letters of Cicero*, vol. 3. Translated by Evelyn S. Shuckburgh. London: George Bell, 1900.

Clapin, Sylvia. *A New Dictionary of Americanisms: Being a Glossary of Words Supposed to Be Peculiar to the United States and the Dominion of Canada*. New York: Louis Weiss, 1902.

Clyne, Michael. "The Role of Linguistics in Peace and Conflict." *Australian Review of Applied Linguistics* 10 (1987): 76–97.

Cochran, Robert. *Vance Randolph: An Ozark Life*. Urbana: University of Illinois Press, 1985.

Cohen, W. A., and R. Johnson. *Filth, Dirt, Disgust, and Modern Life*. Minneapolis: University of Minnesota Press, 2005.

Coleman, Hywell, and Lynne Cameron, eds. *Change and Language*. Clevedon, UK: British Association for Applied Linguistics, 1996.

Cook, Guy. *Language Play, Language Learning*. Oxford: Oxford University Press, 2000.

Cook, Guy, and Tony Walter. "Rewritten Rites: Language and Social Relations in Traditional and Contemporary Funerals." *Discourse & Society* 16 (2005): 365–91.

Corbett, Jenny. *Bad-mouthing: The Language of Special Needs*. London: Palmer, 1996.

Cordesman, Anthony. *The Iraq War: Strategy, Tactics, and Military Lessons*. Westport, CT: Praeger/Greenwood, 2003.

Cornog, Martha. "Naming Sexual Body Parts: Preliminary Patterns and Implications." *Journal of Sex Research* 22 (1986): 393–98.

———. "Tom, Dick and Hairy: Notes on Genital Pet Names." In *Opus Maledictorum: A Book of Bad Words*, edited by Reinhold Aman. New York: Marlowe, 1996.

Coughlin, Anne M. "Representing the Forbidden." *California Law Review* 90 (December 2002): 2143–83.

Crawford, Allison. "Born Still: Euphemism and the Double-Taboo of Women's Bodies and Death," 2008. http://www.chass.utoronto .ca/~cpercy/courses/6362-CrawfordAllison.htm (accessed January 2, 2009).

Crespo Fernandez, Eliecer. "The Language of Death: Euphemism and Conceptual Metaphorization in Victorian Obituaries." *SKY Journal of Linguistics* 19 (2006): 101–30.

Crisp, Quentin. *Manners from Heaven: A Divine Guide to Good Behavior*. New York: Perennial/Harper & Row, 1986.

Crystal, David. *The Cambridge Encyclopedia of the English Language*. Cambridge: Cambridge University Press, 1995.

Cunnington, C. Willett, and Phillis Cunnington. *The History of Underclothes*. London: Michael Joseph, 1951.

Curtis, Valerie A. "Dirt, Disgust and Disease: A Natural History of Hygiene." *Journal of Epidemiological Community Health* 61 (2007): 660–64.

Dawidowicz, Lucy. *The War Against the Jews 1933–1945*. New York: Holt, Rinehart, and Winston, 1975.

Dawson, Jim. *Who Cut the Cheese? A Cultural History of the Fart.* Berkeley, CA: Ten Speed Press, 1999.

Deetz, James. *In Small Things Forgotten: The Archeology of Early American Life.* Garden City, NY: Anchor Doubleday, 1977.

Degner, Robert L. "Should You Market Chevon, Cabrito or Goat Meat?" 1991. http://www.agmarketing.ifas.ufl.edu/pubs/1990s/GOAT.pdf (accessed November 11, 2009).

Degner, Robert L., and C. T. Jordan Lin, "Marketing Goat Meat: An Evaluation of Consumer Perceptions and Preferences," 1993. http://www.agmarketing.ifas.ufl.edu/pubs/1990s/Marketing%20Goat%Meat%20An%20Evaluation.pdf (accessed April 16, 2010).

Dent, Susie. *Fanboys and Overdogs: The Language Report.* Oxford: Oxford University Press, 2005.

de Vere, M. Schele. *Americanisms: The English of the New World.* New York: Scribner, 1872.

Dickson, Paul. *Drunk: The Definitive Drinker's Dictionary.* Hoboken, NJ: Melville, 2009.

———. *Family Words,* Reading, MA: Addison-Wesley, 1988.

———. *Slang: The Topical Dictionary of Americanisms.* New York: Walker, 2006.

———. *War Slang: American Fighting Words and Phrases from the Civil War to the Gulf War.* New York: Pocket / Simon & Schuster, 1994.

Dohan, Mary Helen. *Our Own Words.* New York: Knopf, 1974.

Douglas, Mary. *Purity and Danger: An Analysis of Concepts of Pollution and Taboo.* London: Routledge & Kegan Paul, 1966.

Draper, Robert. *Dead Certain: The Presidency of George W. Bush.* New York: Free Press, 2007.

Drury, John. *Rare and Well Done: Some Historical Notes on Meats and Meatmen.* Chicago: Quadrangle, 1966.

Dunbar, Robin. *Grooming, Gossip, and the Evolution of Language.* Cambridge, MA: Harvard University Press, 1996.

Eble, Connie. *Slang and Sociability: In-Group Language Among College Students.* Chapel Hill: Univeristy of North Carolina Press, 1996.

Elting, John R., Dan Cragg, and Ernest L. Deal. *A Dictionary of Soldier Talk.* New York: Scribner's, 1984.

Enright, D. J., ed. *Fair of Speech: The Uses of Euphemism.* Oxford: Oxford University Press, 1985.

Enright, Dominique. *In Other Words: The Meanings and Memoirs of Euphemisms.* London: Michael O'Mara Books, 2005.

Ensler, Eve. *The Vagina Monologues.* New York: Villard, 1998.

Epstein, Joseph. "Sex and Euphemism." In *Fair of Speech: The Uses of Euphemism,* edited by D. J. Enright, 56–71. Oxford: Oxford University Press, 1985.

Evans, Joan, ed. *The Flowering of the Middle Ages.* New York: McGraw-Hill, 1966.

Farb, Peter. *Word Play: What Happens When People Talk.* New York: Knopf, 1974.

Farmer, John S., ed. *Americanisms Old and New: A Dictionary of Words, Phrases and Colloquialisms.* London: Thomas Poulter & Sons, 1889.

Farmer, John S., and W. E. Henley. *Slang and Its Analogues,* vols. 1–7, 1890–1904. Reprint, New York: Arno, 1970.

Faust, Drew Gilpin. *The Republic of Suffering: Death and the Civil War.* New York: Knopf, 2008.

Ferrier, Susan. *Memoir and Correspondence of Susan Ferrier, 1782–1854.* Edited by John A. Doyle. London: John Murray, 1898.

Fischer, David Hackett. *Albion's Seed.* New York: Oxford University Press, 1989.

Flexner, Stuart Berg. *I Hear America Talking: An Illustrated History of American Words and Phrases.* New York: Touchstone/Simon & Schuster, 1979.

———. *Listening to America: An Illustrated History of Words and Phrases from Our Lively and Splendid Past.* New York: Simon & Schuster, 1982.

Foucault, Michel. *The History of Sexuality,* vol. 1. New York: Vintage, 1990.

Frankel, Fred. "What's in a Name? The 'Mental Health' Euphemism and the Consequences of Denial." *Hospital & Community Psychiatry* 26 (1975): 104–6.

Fraser, Edward, and John Gibbons. *Soldier and Sailor Words and Phrases.* London: Routledge, 1925.

Frazer, James. *Aftermath: A Supplement to The Golden Bough.* New York: Macmillan, 1937.

———. *The Golden Bough: A Study in Magic and Religion,* vol. 1. 1890. New York: Macmillan, 1951.

Friedman, Lawrence M. *History of American Law.* New York: Touchstone/Simon & Schuster, 1973.

Friedrich, Otto. "Of Words that Ravage, Pillage, Spoil." *Time,* January 9, 1984, 76.

Frost, J. William. *The Quaker Family in Colonial America.* New York: St. Martin's Press, 1973.

Fryer, Peter. *Mrs. Grundy: Studies in English Prudery.* New York: London House & Maxwell, 1964.

Fussell, Paul. *Class: A Guide Through the American Status System.* New York: Summit, 1983.

———. *The Great War and Modern Memory.* New York: Oxford University Press, 1975.

Garces-Foley, Kathleen, and Justin S. Holcomb. "Contemporary American Funerals: Personalizing Tradition." In *Death and Religion in a Changing World*, edited by Kathleen Garces-Foley, 207–27. Armonk, NY: Sharpe, 2006.

Gardner, Gerald. *The Censorship Papers: Movie Censorship Letters from the Hays Office, 1934 to 1968.* New York: Dodd, Mead, 1987.

Gay, Peter. *The Bourgeois Experience: Victoria to Freud*, vol. 1, *Education of the Senses.* New York: Oxford University Press, 1984.

———. *The Bourgeois Experience: Victoria to Freud*, vol. 2, *The Tender Passion.* New York: Oxford University Press, 1986.

———. *The Bourgeois Experience: Victoria to Freud*, vol. 3, *The Cultivation of Hatred.* New York: Norton, 1993.

Geher, Glenn, and Geoffrey Miller, eds. *Mating Intelligence: Sex, Relationships, and the Mind's Reproductive System.* New York: Erlbaum, 2008.

Gladney, George Albert. "Euphemistic Text Affects Attitudes, Behavior." *Newspaper Research Journal* (Winter 2005): 1–9.

Gogarty, Oliver St. John. *William Butler Yeats: A Memoir.* Dublin: Dolmen, 1963.

Goldberg, Michelle. *The Means of Reproduction: Sex, Power, and the Future of the World.* New York: Penguin, 2009.

Goldman, Louis. "The Logic of Euphemisms and the Language of Education." *Educational Theory* 26 (1976): 182–87.

Goodmane, W. F. *Seven Years in America.* London: R. Jones, 1845.

Gorer, Geoffrey. *Death, Grief and Mourning in Contemporary Britain.* London: Cresset, 1965.

Goshgarian, Gary, ed. *Exploring Language.* New York: Longman, 1998.

Grahn, Judy. *Another Mother Tongue: Gay Words, Gay Worlds.* Boston: Beacon Press, 1984.

Graves, Robert. *Lars Porsena: Or the Future of Swearing.* London: Kegan Paul, 1927.

Gray, Richard A. "The Art of Speaking Fair: A Bibliographical Study of Euphemism and Dysphemism." *Reference Services Review* 20 (1992): 33–46, 76.

Green, Harvey. *The Light of the Home: An Intimate View of the Lives of Women in Victorian America.* New York: Pantheon, 1983.

Greenough, James Bradstreet, and George Lyman Kittredge. *Words and Their Ways in English Speech.* 1901. New York: Macmillan, 1930.

Griffin, Jasper. "Euphemisms in Greece and Rome." In *Fair of Speech: The Uses of Euphemism,* edited by D. J. Enright, 32–43. Oxford: Oxford University Press, 1985.

Groneman, Carol. *Nymphomania: A History.* New York: Norton, 2000.

Grose, Francis. *A Classical Dictionary of the Vulgar Tongue.* 1785. Edited by Eric Partridge. New York: Barnes & Noble, 1963.

Gross, John. "Intimations of Mortality." In *Fair of Speech: The Uses of Euphemism,* edited by D. J. Enright, 203–220. Oxford: Oxford University Press, 1985.

Gustaffson, Sofie. *The Language of Death and Dying: A Corpus Study of the Use of Euphemisms in British and American English.* Växjö, Sweden: Växjö University Press, 2007.

Haliburton, Thomas. *The Clockmaker; or the Sayings and Doings of Samuel Slick of Slickville,* vol. 2. London: Richard Bentley, 1843.

Harmetz, Aljean. *On the Road to Tara.* New York: Abrams, 1996.

Harrell, Robert A., and Gary S. Firestein. *The Effective Scutboy.* New York: Arco, 1983.

Harris, Marvin. *Good to Eat: Riddles of Food and Culture.* New York: Simon & Schuster, 1985.

Harvey, Keith, and Celia Shalom, eds. *Language and Desire: Encoding Sex, Romance and Intimacy.* New York: Routledge, 1997.

Hawthorne, Nathaniel. *The American Notebooks.* Edited by Randall Stewart. New Haven, CT: Yale University Press, 1932.

———. *Our Old Home and English Note-Books,* vol. 1. 1863. Boston: Houghton Mifflin, 1912.

Hays, Will H. *The Memoirs of Will H. Hays.* Garden City, NY: Doubleday, 1955.

Healey, Tim. "A New Erotic Vocabulary." *Maledicta* 4 (1980): 181–201.

Hendrickson, Robert, ed. *The Facts on File Encyclopedia of Word and Phrase Origins.* New York: Checkmark/Facts on File, 2004.

Hey, David. *Family Names and Family History.* London: Hambledon and London, 2000.

Hills, E. C. "Exclamations in American English." *Dialect Notes* 5 (1924): 253–84.

Hitchings, Henry. *Defining the World: The Extraordinary Story of Dr. Johnson's Dictionary.* New York: Picador, 2006.

Hoffman, David E. *The Dead Hand: The Untold Story of the Cold War Arms Race and Its Dangerous Legacy.* New York: Doubleday, 2009.

Holder, R. W. *How Not to Say What You Mean: A Dictionary of Euphemisms.* Oxford: Oxford University Press, 2007.

Hopper, Robert, Mark L. Knapp, and Lorel Scott. "Couples' Personal Idioms: Exploring Intimate Talk." *Journal of Communication* 31 (1981): 23–33.

Houghton, Walter E. *The Victorian Frame of Mind, 1830–1870.* New Haven, CT: Wellesley / Yale University Press, 1957.

Howard, Philip. *The State of the Language: English Observed.* New York: Penguin, 1986.

Hudson, Kenneth. *The Jargon of the Professions.* London: Macmillan, 1978.

Hughes, Geoffrey. *Swearing: A Social History of Foul Language, Oaths and Profanity in English.* London: Penguin, 1998.

———. *Words in Time: A Social History of the English Vocabulary.* Oxford: Basil Blackwell, 1988.

Hughes, Robert. *The Culture of Complaint.* New York: Oxford University Press, 1993.

Hume, Janice. *Obituaries in American Culture.* Jackson: University Press of Mississippi, 2000.

Jay, Timothy. *Cursing in America.* Philadelphia: John Benjamins, 1992.

———. *Why We Curse.* Philadelphia: John Benjamins, 2000.

Jesperson, Otto. *Growth and Structure of the English Language.* 1905. London: Blackwell, 1967.

Johnson, Diane. "Doctor Talk." In *Exploring Language,* edited by Gary Goshgarian. New York: Longman, 1998.

Johnson, Diane, and John F. Murray. "Do Doctors Mean What They Say?" In *Fair of Speech: The Uses of Euphemism,* edited by D. J. Enright, 151–58. Oxford: Oxford University Press, 1985.

Juska, Jane. *Round-Heeled Woman: My Late-Life Adventures in Sex and Romance.* New York: Windsor, 2003.

Kafka, Franz. *Letters to Friends, Family, and Editors.* Translated by Richard and Clara Winston. New York: Schocken, 1977.

Kamen, Henry. *The Spanish Inquisition.* New York: Mentor, 1968.

Keesing, Nancy. *Lily on the Dustbin: Slang of Australian Women and Families.* Ringwood, Australia: Penguin, 1982.

Kenneally, Christine. *The First Word: The Search for the Origins of Language.* New York: Viking, 2007.

Kennedy, Randall. *Nigger.* New York: Pantheon, 2002.

Kiernan, Pauline. *Filthy Shakespeare: Shakespeare's Most Outrageous Sexual Puns.* New York: Gotham, 2007.

Kinney, Katherine. *Friendly Fire: American Images of the Vietnam War.* New York: Oxford University Press, 2000.

Kira, Alexander. *The Bathroom*. New York: Viking, 1976.

Knecht, G. Bruce. *Hooked: Pirates, Poaching and the Perfect Fish*. Emmaus, PA: Rodale, 2006.

Knight, Robert M. *The Craft of Clarity: A Journalistic Approach to Good Writing*. Ames: Iowa State University Press, 2003.

Knightley, Philip. *The First Casualty: The War Correspondent as Hero and Myth-Maker from the Crimea to Kosovo*. Baltimore: Johns Hopkins University Press, 2004.

Krutch, Joseph Wood. *If You Don't Mind My Saying So*. New York: Sloane, 1964.

Kübler-Ross, Elizabeth. *On Death and Dying*. New York: Collier, 1970.

Laderman, Gary. *Rest in Peace: A Cultural History of Death and the Funeral Home in Twentieth-Century America*. New York: Oxford University Press, 2003.

———. *The Sacred Remains: American Attitudes Toward Death, 1799–1883*. New Haven, CT: Yale University Press, 1996.

Lakoff, George *Don't Think of an Elephant: Know Your Values and Frame the Debate*. White River Junction, VT: Chelsea Green, 2004.

———. *Metaphors We Live By*. Chicago: University of Chicago Press, 1980.

Lakoff, Robin. *Language and Women's Place*. New York: Harper & Row, 1975.

Langworth, Richard, ed. *Churchill by Himself: The Definitive Collection of Quotations*. New York: Public Affairs, 2008.

Laporte, Dominique. *History of Shit*. 1978. Translated by Nadia Bernabid and Rodolphe el-Khoury. Cambridge, MA: MIT Press, 1993.

Leff, Leonard, and Jerold L. Simmons. *The Dame in the Kimono*. Lexington: University Press of Kentucky, 2001.

Lehman, David. "From Euphemism to Bloody Lies." *American Enterprise* (May 1999): 51.

Leider, Emily Wortis. *Becoming Mae West*. New York: DaCapo, 2000.

Lewis, Jeremy. "In the Office." In *Fair of Speech: The Uses of Euphemism*, edited by D. J. Enright, 92–107. Oxford: Oxford University Press, 1985.

Lifton, Robert Jay. *The Nazi Doctors: Medical Killing and the Psychology of Genocide*. New York: Basic, 1986.

Lighter, J. E., ed. *Random House Dictionary of American Slang*, vols. 1–2. New York: Random House, 1994.

Linfoot-Ham, Kerry. "The Linguistics of Euphemism: A Diachronic Study of Euphemism Formation." *Journal of Language and Linguistics* 4 (2005): 227–58.

Liszka, James Jakób. "Euphemism as Transvaluation." *Language and Style* 23 (1990): 409–24.

Livia, Anna, and Kira Hall. *Queerly Phrased: Language, Gender, and Sexuality.* New York: Oxford University Press, 1997.

Luntz, Frank. *Words That Work: It's Not What You Say, It's What People Hear.* New York: Hyperion, 2007.

Lutz, William. *Doublespeak Defined, Cut Through the Bull**** and Get the Point!* New York: HarperResource, 1999.

MacDougald, Duncan, "Language and Sex." In *The Encyclopedia of Sexual Behavior,* vol. 2, edited by Albert Ellis and Albert Abarbanel, 585–98. New York: Hawthorn, 1961.

Maines, Rachel P. *The Technology of Orgasm: "Hysteria," the Vibrator, and Women's Sexual Satisfaction.* Baltimore: Johns Hopkins University Press, 1999.

Mairs, Nancy. "On Being a Cripple." In *Exploring Language,* edited by Gary Goshgarian, 355–56. New York: Longman, 1998.

Maranda, Pierre, ed. *Mythology: Selected Readings.* Baltimore: Penguin, 1972.

Marckwardt, Albert H. *American English,* 2nd ed. Revised by J. L. Dillard. New York: Oxford University Press, 1980.

Markham, Gervase. *The English Housewife.* 1615. Kingston, ON: McGill-Queen's University Press, 1986.

Marryatt, Frederick. *A Diary in America, With Remarks on Its Institutions.* 1839. New York: Knopf, 1962.

———. *Peter Simple.* 1833. New York: Dutton, 1907.

Marsh, J. *Word Crimes: Blasphemy, Culture, and Literature in Nineteenth-Century England.* Chicago: University of Chicago Press, 1998.

Martin, III, Robert F. "Celluloid Morality: Will Hays' Rhetoric in Defense of the Movies, 1922–1930." Ph.D. diss., University of Indiana, 1974.

Mathews, Mitford M., ed. *A Dictionary of Americanisms: On Historical Principles,* vols. 1–2. Chicago: University of Chicago Press, 1951.

McArthur, Roshan. "Taboo Words in Print." *English Today* 12 (1996): 50–58.

McDonald, James. *A Dictionary of Obscenity, Taboo and Euphemism.* London: Warner, 1994.

McGlone, Matthew S., Gary Beck, and Abigail Pfiester. "Contamination and Camouflage in Euphemisms." *Communication Monographs* 73 (2006): 261–82.

McHenry, F. A. "A Note on Homosexuality, Crime and the Newspapers." *Journal of Psychopathology* 2 (1941): 533–48.

McKnight, George H. *English Words and Their Background.* New York: Appleton, 1930.

McQuain, Jeffrey. *Power Language: Getting the Most Out of Your Words.* Boston: Houghton Mifflin, 1996.

Mencken, H. L. *The American Language*. New York: Knopf, 1936.

Meredith, Mamie. "Inexpressibles, Unmentionables, Unwhisperables, and Other Verbal Delicacies of Mid-Nineteenth Century Americans." *American Speech* 5 (1930): 285–87.

Merrill, James M. *William Tecumseh Sherman*. New York: Rand McNally, 1971.

Michell, Gillian. "Women and Lying." In *Hypatia Reborn: Essays in Feminist Philosophy*, edited by Azizah Y. Al-Hibri and Margaret A. Simons, 175–91. Bloomington: Indiana University Press, 1990.

Miller, W. I. *The Anatomy of Disgust*. Cambridge, MA: Harvard University Press, 1997.

Millwood-Hargrave, Andrea. *Delete Expletives?* London: Advertising Standards Authority, British Broadcasting Corporation, Broadcasting Standards Commission, Independent Television Commission, 2000.

Mitford, Jessica. *The American Way of Death*. New York: Simon & Schuster, 1963.

Mitford, Nancy. *Noblesse Oblige: An Enquiry into the Identifiable Characteristics of the English Aristocracy*. New York: Harper & Brothers, 1956.

Moley, Raymond. *The Hays Office*. Indianapolis: Bobbs-Merrill, 1945.

Montagu, Ashley. *The Anatomy of Swearing*. New York: Collier, 1973.

Montaigne, Michel de. "On the Power of the Imagination." In *The Complete Essays*. Translated by M. A. Screech. London: Penguin, 1993.

Moreau de St. Méry, M. L. E. *Moreau de St. Méry's American Journey (1793–1798)*. Edited and translated by Kenneth Roberts and Anna M. Roberts. Garden City, NY: Doubleday, 1947.

Morelock, Catherine Nichole. "Personal Idiom Use and Affect Regulation in Romantic Relationships," Ph.D. diss., Texas Tech University, 2005.

Morrow, Honoré Willsie. *The Father of Little Women*. Boston: Little, Brown, 1927.

Mullen, Peter. "The Religious Speak-Easy." In *Fair of Speech: The Uses of Euphemism*, edited by D. J. Enright, 159–73. Oxford: Oxford University Press, 1985.

Müller, Herta. *The Land of Green Plums*. Evanston, IL: Northwestern University Press, 1998.

Müller, Max. *Lectures on the Science of Language*, vol. 2. 1861. London: Routledge/Thoemmes, 1994.

Murphy, Cullen. "The E Word." *Atlantic Monthly*, September 1996, 16, 18.

Murphy, Peter F. *Studs, Tools, and the Family Jewels: Metaphors Men Live By*. Madison: University of Wisconsin Press, 2001.

Neaman, Judith S., and Carole G. Silver. *Kind Words: A Thesaurus of Euphemisms*. New York: Avon, 1991.

Nunberg, Geoffrey. *Talking Right: How Conservatives Turned Liberalism into a Tax-Raising, Latte-Drinking, Sushi-Eating, Volvo-Driving,* New York Times–Reading, Body-Piercing, Hollywood-Loving, Left-Wing Freak Show. New York: Public Affairs, 2006.

———. *The Way We Talk Now: Commentaries on Language and Culture.* Boston: Houghton Mifflin, 2001.

O'Brien, Darcy. *W. R. Rodgers.* Lewisburg, PA: Bucknell, 1979.

Offill, Jenny, and Elissa Schappell, eds. *Money Changes Everything: Twenty-Two Writers Tackle the Last Taboo with Tales of Sudden Windfalls, Staggering Debts, and Other Surprising Turns of Fortune.* New York: Doubleday, 2007.

Oliver, Paul. *Screening the Blues: Aspects of the Blues Tradition.* New York: Da Capo / Plenum, 1968.

Orwell, George. "Politics and the English Language." In *The Orwell Reader: Fiction, Essays, and Reportage by George Orwell,* 355–66. San Diego: Harvest / HBJ, 1956.

Paros, Lawrence. *The Erotic Tongue: A Sexual Lexicon.* New York: Holt, 1984.

Partridge, Eric. *A Dictionary of Slang and Unconventional English.* New York: Macmillan, 1961.

———. *Origins: A Short Etymological Dictionary of Modern English.* New York: Macmillan, 1958.

———. *Shakespeare's Bawdy.* London: Routledge, 1968.

———. *Words, Words, Words.* Freeport, NY: Books for Libraries Press, 1970.

Patterson, James T. *The Dread Disease: Cancer and Modern American Culture.* Cambridge, MA: Harvard University Press, 1987.

Pei, Mario. *Double Speak in America.* New York: Hawthorn, 1973.

———. *The Story of Language.* Philadelphia: Lippincott, 1965.

———. *Words in Sheep's Clothing: How People Manipulate Opinion by Distorting Word Meanings.* New York: Hawthorn, 1969.

Perrin, Noel. *Dr. Bowdler's Legacy: A History of Expurgated Books.* New York: Atheneum, 1992.

Pickett, Joseph. *Word Histories and Mysteries.* Boston: Houghton Mifflin, 2004.

Pinker, Steven. *The Stuff of Thought: Language as a Window into Human Nature.* New York: Penguin, 2007.

Poole, Steven. *Unspeak: How Words Become Weapons, How Weapons Become a Message, and How That Message Becomes Reality.* New York: Grove, 2006.

Postman, Neil. "Euphemism." In *Language Awareness,* edited by Paul Escholz, Alfred Rosa, and Virginia Clark, 343–47. New York: St. Martin's Press, 1986.

Pound, Louise. "American Euphemisms for Dying, Death and Burial." *American Speech* 11 (1936): 195–202.

Pudney, John. *The Smallest Room*. New York: Hastings House, 1955.

Pyles, Thomas. *The Origins and Development of the English Language*. New York: Harcourt, Brace & World, 1964.

Pyles, Thomas, and John Algeo. *English: An Introduction to Language*. New York: Harcourt, Brace & World, 1970.

Quinion, Michael. *Ballyhoo, Buckaroo, and Spuds: Ingenious Tales of Words and Their Origins*. Washington, DC: Smithsonian, 2004.

Rait, Robert S. *Life in the Medieval University*. Cambridge: Cambridge University Press, 1912.

Randolph, Vance. *Blow the Candle Out: "Unprintable" Ozark Folksongs and Folklore*, vol. 2. Fayetteville: University of Arkansas Press, 1992.

———. *The Ozarks: An American Survival of Primitive Society*. New York: Vanguard, 1931.

———. *Roll Me in Your Arms: "Unprintable" Ozark Folksongs and Folklore*, vol. 1. Fayetteville: University of Arkansas Press, 1992.

———. "Verbal Modesty in the Ozarks." *Dialect Notes* 6 (1928): 57–64.

Randolph, Vance, and George P. Wilson. *Down in the Holler: A Gallery of Ozark Folk Speech*. Norman: University of Oklahoma Press, 1953.

Ravitch, Diane. *The Language Police: How Pressure Groups Restrict What Students Learn*. New York: Knopf, 2003.

Rawson, Hugh. *Rawson's Dictionary of Euphemisms and Other Doubletalk*. New York: Crown, 1995.

Read, Allen Walker. "Noah Webster as a Euphemist." *Dialect Notes* 6 (1984): 385–91.

———. "An Obscenity Symbol." *American Speech* 9 (1934): 264–78.

Regan, Geoffrey. *Back Fire: The Tragic Story of Friendly Fire*. London: Robson, 1995.

Rejali, Darius. *Torture and Democracy*. Princeton, NJ: Princeton University Press, 2007.

Reynolds, Reginald. *Cleanliness and Godliness*. Garden City, NY: Doubleday, 1946.

Rothstein, William. *American Physicians in the Nineteenth Century*. Baltimore: Johns Hopkins University Press, 1972.

Rowe, H. D. "New England Terms for 'Bull': Some Aspects of Barnyard Bowdlerism." *American Speech* 32 (1957): 110–16.

Rusbridger, Alan. *A Concise History of the Sexual Manual*. London: Faber and Faber, 1986.

Ruskin, John. "Fiction, Fair and Foul." *The Works of John Ruskin*, vol. 34. Edited by E. T. Cook and Alexander Wedderburn. London: George Allen, 1908.

Sabbath, Dan, and Mandel Hall. *End Product: The First Taboo.* New York: Urizen, 1997.

Safire, William. *Coming to Terms.* New York: Doubleday, 1991.

———. *No Uncertain Terms.* New York: Simon & Schuster, 2003.

———. *The Right Word in the Right Place at the Right Time.* New York: Simon & Schuster, 2004.

———. *What's the Good Word?* New York: Times Books, 1982.

———. *William Safire on Language.* New York: Times Books, 1980.

———. *You Could Look It Up.* New York: Times Books, 1988.

Sanders, Janet S. "Male and Female Vocabularies for Communicating with a Sexual Partner." *Journal of Sex Education and Therapy* 4 (1978): 15–18.

Sanders, Janet S., and William L. Robinson, "Talking and Not Talking About Sex: Male and Female Vocabularies." *Journal of Communication* 29 (1979): 22–30.

Savan, Leslie. *The Sponsored Life: Ads, TV and American Culture.* Philadelphia: Temple University Press, 1994.

Schmidgall, Gary. *The Stranger Wilde: Interpreting Oscar.* New York: Dutton, 1994.

Schulz, Muriel R. "The Semantic Derogation of Woman." In *Language and Sex: Difference and Dominance,* edited by Barrie Thorne and Nancy Henley, 64–75. Rowley, MA: Newbury, 1975.

Sexton, James. "The Semantics of Death and Dying: Metaphor and Reality." *Et cetera* 54 (1997): 333–45.

Sheidlower, Jesse, ed. *The F Word.* New York: Random House, 1999.

Shipley, Joseph T. *In Praise of English: The Growth and Use of Language.* New York: Times Books, 1977.

Shrader, Charles R. *Amicicide: The Problem of Friendly Fire in Modern War.* Fort Leavenworth, KS: Combat Studies Institute, 1982.

Simon, André L. *A Concise Encyclopedia of Gastronomy.* 1952. New York: Overlook, 1981.

Smith, Bradley. *The American Way of Sex: An Informal Illustrated History.* La Jolla, CA: Gemini Smith, 1978.

Smith, Ken. *Junk English.* New York: Blast, 2001.

Sontag, Susan. *Illness as Metaphor.* New York: Farrar, Straus and Giroux, 1978.

Spears, Richard A. *Forbidden American English: A Serious Compilation of Taboo American English.* Lincolnwood, IL: Passport Books, 1994.

———. *Slang and Euphemism: A dictionary of oaths, curses, insults, ethnic slurs, sexual slang and metaphor, drug talk, college lingo, and related matter.* Middle Village, NY: Jonathan David, 2001.

Stein, Howard F. *Euphemism, Spin, and the Crisis in Organizational Life.* Westport, CT: Quorum, 1998.

Steinmetz, Sol. *Semantic Antics: How and Why Words Change Meaning.* New York: Random House, 2008.

———. *There's a Word for It: The Explosion of the American Language Since 1900.* New York: Harmony, 2010.

Steinmetz, Sol, and Barbara Ann Kipfer. *The Life of Language: The Fascinating Ways Words Are Born, Live, and Die.* New York: Random House, 2006.

Stephens, Meic. *A Dictionary of Literary Quotations.* London: Routledge, 1990.

Stephenson, John S. *Death, Grief and Mourning.* New York: Free Press, 1985.

Stevens, James. "Logger Talk." *American Speech* 1 (1925): 135–40.

Storr, Catherine. "Euphemisms and Children." In *Fair of Speech: The Uses of Euphemism,* edited by D. J. Enright, 79–91. Oxford: Oxford University Press, 1985.

Sullivan, Bob. *Gotcha Capitalism.* New York: Ballantine, 2007.

Tannahill, Reay. *Food in History.* New York: Stein and Day, 1973.

Tate, Jordan. *The Contemporary Dictionary of Sexual Euphemisms.* New York: St. Martin's Press, 2007.

Thompson, Henry. *Food and Feeding.* London: Frederick Warne, 1899.

Time-Life. *Variety Meats.* Alexandria, VA: Time-Life, 1982.

Tocqueville, Alexis de. *Democracy in America.* 1835. Edited by Richard D. Heffner. New York: Mentor, 1956.

Trollope, Frances. *Domestic Manners and the Americans.* 1832. Edited by Donald Smalley. New York: Vintage, 1960.

Van Lancker, D., and J. L. Cummings, "Expletives: Neurolinguistic and Neurobehavioral Perspectives on Swearing." *Brain Research Reviews* 31 (1999): 83–104.

Veeck, Bill, with Ed Linn. *Veeck as in Wreck: The Autobiography of Bill Veeck.* New York: Putnam, 1962.

Vehling, Joseph Dommers, trans. *Apicius: Cookery and Dining in Imperial Rome.* Chicago: Walter Hill, 1936.

Velica, Carmen. *War Casualties, Friendly Fire, Intervention, and Other Treacherous Words.* Galati, Romania: Galati University Press, 2004.

Wansink, Brian. *Marketing Nutrition.* Urbana: University of Illinois Press, 2005.

————. *Mindless Eating: Why We Eat More Than We Think.* New York: Bantam, 2006.

Warren, Beatrice. "What Euphemisms Tell Us About the Interpretation of Words." *Studia Linguistica* 46 (1992): 128–72.

Weekley, Ernest. *The Romance of Words.* London: John Murray, 1917.

Weston, Elizabeth Dudley. "[fʌk]: The Ultimate Four-Letter Word." *UC Davis: Prized Writing.* http://prizedwriting.ucdavis.edu/past/2004-2005/flk-the-ultimate-four-letter-word (accessed May 3, 2010).

White, Richard Grant. *Words and Their Uses, Past and Present: A Study of the English Language.* New York: Sheldon, 1876.

Willard, Francis E. *Glimpses of Fifty Years: The Autobiography of an American Woman.* Chicago: H. J. Smith, 1889.

Williams, Joseph M. *Origins of the English Language: A Social and Linguistic History.* New York: Free Press, 1975.

Woods, Keith M. "Take Back the Language." *Poynteronline,* March 20, 2003. http://www.poynter.org/content/content_view.asp?id=25910&sid=2 (accessed December 23, 2008).

Zwicky, Ann D., and Arnold M. Zwicky. "America's National Dish: The Style of Restaurant Menus." *American Speech* 56 (1981): 83–92.

Websites

About.com: http://urbanlegends.about.com/
Filmsite: http://www.filmsite.org/
The Huffington Post: http://www.huffingtonpost.com/
The Internet Movie Data Base (IMDB): http://www.imdb.com/
Investopedia: http://www.investopedia.com/
Merriam-Webster Online: http://www.merriam-webster.com
Online Etymology Dictionary: http://www.etymonline.com
Online Parallel Bible: http://bible.cc/
Oxford English Dictionary Online (OED): http://dictionary.oed.com
The Phrase Finder: http://www.phrases.org.uk/meanings/index.html
Questia: http://www.questia.com/Index.jsp
Schott's Vocab: http://schott.blogs.nytimes.com/
Snopes: http://www.snopes.com/
TVTropes: http://tvtropes.org/pmwiki/pmwiki.php/Main/HomePage
Urban Dictionary: http://www.urbandictionary.com
Wikipedia: http://www.wikipedia.org/
Word Spy: http://www.wordspy.com/
World Wide Words: http://www.worldwidewords.org

Index

Index

Index

Index

Index

Index

Index

About the Author

Ralph Keyes is the author of fifteen books, including the best-selling *Is There Life After High School?* which was made into a Broadway musical that is still produced in the United States and abroad; *Chancing It*, a *New York Times* Notable Book; and *The Courage to Write*, which has been in print continuously for fifteen years. A graduate of Antioch College, Keyes did graduate work at the London School of Economics and Political Science, then was assistant to the publisher of Long Island's *Newsday* from 1968 to 1970. Following a decade spent as a fellow of the Center for Studies of the Person in La Jolla, California, Keyes worked as a freelance writer and lecturer in the Philadelphia area. He has been featured in *People* magazine, on *Oprah*, the *Today show*, the *Tonight Show*, *ABC World News Tonight*, *20/20*, *Fresh Air*, *All Things Considered*, *Talk of the Nation*, *On the Media*, and the *Bob Edwards Show*. Keyes has written for publications ranging from *GQ* to *Good Housekeeping*. An article he coauthored for the *Harvard Business Review* won its prestigious McKinsey Award for best article of the year. Keyes lives in Yellow Springs, Ohio, with his wife, Muriel, where he writes, lectures, and is a trustee of the Antioch Writers' Workshop.